SOVIETICA

PUBLICATIONS OF THE INSTITUTE OF EAST-EUROPEAN STUDIES

UNIVERSITY OF FRIBOURG / SWITZERLAND

Edited by

J. M. BOCHEŃSKI

PHILOSOPHY IN THE SOVIET UNION

A SURVEY OF THE MID-SIXTIES

PHILOSOPHY
IN THE SOVIET UNION

A SURVEY OF THE MID-SIXTIES

Compiled and edited by

ERVIN LASZLO

D. REIDEL PUBLISHING COMPANY / DORDRECHT-HOLLAND

FREDERICK A. PRAEGER, INC., PUBLISHERS

NEW YORK · WASHINGTON

Published in the United States of America in 1967
by FREDERICK A. PRAEGER, INC., PUBLISHERS
111 Fourth Avenue, New York, N.Y. 10003

This book is Number 195 in the series
Praeger Publications in Russian History and World Communism

Library of Congress Catalog Card Number: 67–26137

Printed in The Netherlands by D. Reidel, Dordrecht

FOREWORD

Soviet philosophy can no longer be ignored by any serious student of contemporary thought. It is the work of academic philosophers who, on the whole, are neither more nor less competent than their colleagues in the free world. They have, however, inherited a reputation for the dogmatic repetition of superannuated doctrines. This reputation, engendered by poor work under political pressure, was justified until about the mid-fifties. However, in the mid-sixties, when declining pressures make for the toleration of a wider scale of qualified opinion, it is no longer that. The present survey of Soviet thought in the mid-sixties, comprising papers by Western specialists in its major domains, gives an up-to-date account of an impressive field of philosophical endeavor which, awakened from dogmatic slumbers, rapidly gains in interest and encourages hopes of becoming a valuable component in the vast complex of contemporary philosophy.

The studies on Soviet logic and atheism have originally appeared in a special issue of *Inquiry* (Vol. 9,1) devoted to philosophy in Eastern Europe and edited by the present writer on behalf of Professor Arne Naess. The other papers of this volume are reprinted from *Studies in Soviet Thought,* the only Western philosophical review entirely dedicated to systematic studies in this field. The necessary permissions by editors and publishers have been granted and are gratefully acknowledged.

ERVIN LASZLO

V

CONTENTS

CONTENTS

PART TWO / STUDIES ON THE RELATION OF WESTERN AND SOVIET THOUGHT

J. M. BOCHEŃSKI

WHY STUDIES IN SOVIET PHILOSOPHY? *

While other departments of Sovietology – above all historiography, but also law, political economy, political science and sociology – are constantly developing, little attention is being paid in the non-Communist world to the study of Soviet *philosophy*. There must be at present something like 12,000 teaching philosophers outside the Soviet Bloc, and probably more: but there are certainly no more than a few dozen among them who manifest any degree of academic knowledge of Soviet thought. At the Universities we do not know of a single regular chair entirely dedicated to the study of Soviet philosophy. In the great American and European centers of Soviet Studies there are only very few competent philosopher-Sovietologists. Some centers have, it is true, a Marxologist: but Marxology is not the same as Sovietology. When we read American or European philosophical magazines, we find only an exceptional paper or a review concerning Soviet doctrines. At the philosophical congresses, if no philosophers from Communist countries are present, nobody even cares to mention the subject.

The result is that, while Soviet philosophers are ever better informed about the philosophy abroad, the great majority of non-Communist philosophers do not have even the slightest notion about the work of their Soviet colleagues. Few of them, indeed, even care to read a synthetic presentation of the subject, such as offered in the books of Acton, Wetter or the undersigned.

When this fact is brought to the attention of non-Communist philosophers, they usually state that there are two reasons for not studying Soviet philosophy: first, they say that it is sheer nonsense; second, that it is irrelevant for any purpose. The study of nonsensical texts which do not have even a practical relevance, is obviously useless. And this is why, it is often concluded, Soviet philosophy need not be studied by non-Communists.

We disagree with this conclusion. We believe that the study of Soviet philosophy is useful and even necessary, for both theoretical and practical

1

purposes. And we do so because of two premises which are contradictorily opposed to the premises assumed by the philosophers quoted above. Namely, we think that:

(i) not all Soviet philosophy is nonsense; on the contrary, much of it is philosophically interesting;

(ii) Soviet philosophy is not irrelevant; it is an important factor in the phenomenon of Communism, which, as everybody will agree, is important, both theoretically and practically.

I

Much in Soviet philosophy is not lacking in interest for the philosopher. There was a time when the contrary could be rightly asserted; namely the time between the anti-Deborin decree of 1931[1] and the speech of Ždanov of 1947. During that time, especially after 1938 (when the *Short Course of the History of CPSU (b)* with the chapter by Stalin was published), what Soviet philosophers produced looked far more like quotatology (to quote professor Baskin, a Soviet philosopher himself) than philosophy.[2] But, since 1947 and especially since 1950 (Stalin's pronouncements on language) the situation has at least partly changed.[3] There is now in the Soviet Union a steadily growing body of respectable thought. There are lively discussions between Soviet philosophers; problems are worked out which are not only their own esoteric problems, but are common to all philosophers. A number of Soviet philosophers have shown a degree of mental independence and of courage worthy of thinkers and the number of their publications which are relevant to philosophers in general is increasing.

Of course, "the smoke of the cult of personality" of which a Bulgarian philosopher wrote recently[4] is still present and, perhaps the *majority* of Soviet philosophers could not be called 'philosophers' in any acceptable meaning of the word, at least as used in the non-Communist world. But Soviet writers on philosophy certainly number more than 2000; and in that great mass there is a minority – estimated at more than one hundred – who "wish to use reason", to quote Whitehead. Moreover, many among them are teaching in the great centers of Moscow, Leningrad and Tiflis.

To this one may object that even those relatively few are dogmatically bound by their Communist faith. But this should not be considered as a

2

serious objection. Nobody maintains that, e.g., Hindu thought is worthless, in spite of the fact that in the great majority of cases it is linked with a religious faith.[5] Secondly, Communist faith is often formulated in terms so vague[6] that as long as one is not bound to keep to the quotations but is allowed to interpret, a very broad spectrum of possibilities is offered to the thinker.

Here is a sketchy picture of what has been already achieved in Soviet philosophy:

Logic: a growing recognition of mathematical logic as *the* formal logic of our times[7] (in that respect the Soviet Union is ahead of Western Europe); much good work in strictly formal logic[8], some valuable studies on particular problems of philosophy of logic – like that of contradictions[9], of multi-valued logic and others.[10]

Ontology: a strenuous effort has been made in order to find some order in the classification of the categories[11] and similar topics[12] (in that respect the Soviet Union is ahead of the United States).

Philosophy of Science: the Soviet Union is one of the few countries where the collaboration between physicists and philosophers is really flourishing and where intense discussions are being held on the basic problems on the border between philosophy and physics.[13] Moreover, it is, as far as is known, the only country in the world where (a) the State itself organizes and promotes the collaboration between physicists and philosophers and (b) all students of philosophy have to have three semesters of natural sciences. One great discussion took place around the theory of relativity[14]; another on realism in microphysics[15]; we may also mention those on quantum mechanics, cybernetics and cosmogony.

Cosmology: in this dogmatically bound field, there is at least one interesting doctrine to be mentioned: namely the appearance in Soviet philosophy of a theory of emergence, which is not always linked with naïve optimistic evolutionism.[16]

Psychology: here, since 1950[17] the situation seems less favorable – from the philosophical point of view – than it was before. Still, there is a number of studies on the psycho-physical problem which are worth reading by anybody interested in the subject.[18]

Social philosophy: little progress up to now; and yet, at least the problem of the relation of philosophy to sociology has been stated and one may expect some developments.[19]

3

Axiology: the field has been recently discovered[20] and everything indicates that it will be cultivated.[21]

History of Philosophy: the general level of the Soviet writings was not brilliant up to now.[22] However, there are some scientific books on single authors (Aristotle[23], Kant[24], Hegel[25], and others[26]), which seem to be growing in number. Moreover even the rather unfortunate and large *History of Philosophy*[27] presents at least one interesting feature: it offers a panorama of history not centered upon Europe.

It is true that nothing transcendental has been achieved; even in the fields where Soviet philosophy is most developed – like in logic – we do not find epoch-making ideas. But in several fields – above all perhaps in philosophy of science – good work is sometimes being done. In any case, some problems which are also problems for other philosophers are discussed. Moreover, if we are not very much mistaken, there is every chance that Soviet philosophy will rapidly improve. The number of younger workers and their ardor is such that only a major catastrophe could stop this progress.

That is why we say that Soviet philosophy is relevant to philosophy *tout court.* Whoever is interested in philosophical problems has an interest in what is being done on such problems in the Soviet Union. Often, it is true, he may be disappointed; but often again he might find in the thoughts of his Soviet colleagues things useful for his own work.

II

Soviet philosophy is an important factor in Communism. In the non-Communist countries there is a wide-spread theory that ideology has lost its influence on the practice of Communism, especially in the Soviet Union. Moreover, it is sometimes claimed that academic philosophy is distinct from ideology so that, even if the latter had any real importance, it would not follow that philosophy does.

But both contentions are unwarranted. As to the first, specialists are talking today not of de-ideologization, but of a re-ideologization in the Soviet Union and elsewhere. There has seldom been so much stress laid on ideology, both in the official declarations of the Parties and their leaders, and in the practice of supporting the study of Marxism-Leninism. What is often said about power-policy of the Soviet leaders, does not

4

contradict this fact: for power-politics is prescribed by ideology itself. Nor do phenomena of *embourgeoisement* noticed here and there in the Soviet Union contradict the thesis. It may be that they reflect a certain trend in the Soviet population; but the question is not what the populations wish: we are concerned with the will of the Party leaders. Also, if we consider phenomena which are most akin to Communism – namely the great religions – we see, that such *embourgeoisement* did not prevent, e.g., Buddhism or Christianity from remaining great powers during thousands of years. What right has one in face of such facts to proclaim that Communism lost its ideological basis in less than fifty years?

Moreover, the above-mentioned theory is mostly motivated by a sort of extrapolation of the writers' own scepticism about doctrines, and especially about ideologies – which, of course, is not legitimate. It must be remembered that the Russians have always been far more addicted to generalizations and dogmatic formulas than Westerners – and that this attitude found a counterpart in the Marxian doctrines. There is no justification at all for the contention that all that has been radically changed in a few years. And if it has not, then ideology remains an important factor in Soviet, and consequently, in Communist reality.

As to the distinction between ideology and philosophy, there is perhaps some justification for it. There certainly are in the Soviet Union some philosophers who work in fields rather remote from ideology. There may even be some – certainly very few – who have liberated themselves from the dogma and are working without taking into consideration any ideological assumption. Also, a distinction must be drawn between academic writings and those textbooks like *Osnovy Marksizma-Leninizma*, which are destined for the masses of students. There certainly is a difference of level between them.

But still, philosophy is, on the whole, far more strictly linked with ideology in the Soviet Union than in any non-Communist country. On one side, the prevailing majority of Soviet philosophers assume the basic doctrines of Diamat and of Histomat, i.e. ideological premisses. On the other side, even the popular products, such as the said *Osnovy*, are written by men who work in the same institutions as the more academic workers and do not escape their influence. In spite of the disastrous level of, say, *Osnovy Marksistskoj Filosofii*, it is easy to show that purely academic discussion influenced its content. But these *Osnovy* have been distributed in more than one million copies. Every university student, every technician, every future manager and politician has to learn out of them. Through them academic philosophy has a real influence on the masses.

We do not wish to exaggerate. We do not claim that philosophers are ruling the Soviet Union. Certainly politicians, or even great physicists and top managers are more influential than even the leading philosophers. Nevertheless, philosophy is, in the Soviet Union, a more important factor than philosophy in any non-Communist country. And that is why Soviet philosophy is relevant, quite apart from its interest for philosophers, both theoretically and practically. Theoretically, because its study shows what trends exist in the intellectually leading circles of that empire, and so help to understand the Soviet phenomenon in its totality. Practically, because that understanding has today a paramount importance for the survival of the free countries.

III

The attitude of non-Communist philosophers towards Soviet philosophy. We may ask ourselves, why does the majority of non-Communist philosophers preserve the above-mentioned attitude of indifference toward the Soviet efforts? Why are there so few serious studies in Soviet philosophy in Europe and in the United States?

There seem to be several reasons for it. The first and certainly most important one is simply the lack of knowledge. This is not entirely the fault of the non-Communist philosophers: what they have as sources of information are either publications by Western Communists or systematic works produced by one or the other Sovietologist-philosopher. Now the first kind of writings is usually presented in a way apt to discourage any philosopher who happens to read them. For one thing they rarely offer the best of the Soviet production; usually it is rather the worst of it. Then, even if some good piece of work is translated, it is presented in a context which appears to the philosophical reader to be intolerably political and dogmatic. As to the systematic works, by the very fact that they are systematic they are late; moreover, they mostly concentrate on the essentials, which are dogmatic; they seldom give information about work on special problems, i.e. on that which is of greatest interest in Soviet thought. So the great majority of Western philosophers is either not informed at all, or, what is worse, misinformed about Soviet philosophy. They mostly take it to be just another form of political propaganda without any interest for them.

But there seem to be other reasons for such indifference. There are a number of philosophers – unfortunately, as it seems, equally large on both sides of the Iron Curtain – who are, so to say, completely cloistered in their own views. Whatever does not completely fit into their own conceptual scheme, they evaluate as worthless. To quote two outstanding other instances of this attitude, whatever is done by phenomenologists is said to be sheer nonsense by some members of the analytical school; and, conversely, whatever is produced by the latter is declared to be irrelevant and pre-philosophical by some of the former. Now Soviet philosophy moves, as a whole, inside a very different frame of reference and supposes quite different basic assumptions than most schools flourishing now in the non-Communist world. E.g. practically all Soviet philosophers are frankly metaphysicians (in the non-Soviet meaning of the word); they are also thorough-going epistemological realists. Once this is observed by some philosophers, they declare, of course, they are not interested, exactly as they would do with other schools in the West.

However, one may disagree with that sort of sectarianism. Humanity has now, *grosso modo,* three major types of philosophy; the phenomenological, the analytic and the Soviet. Contemporary philosophy is not only what pleases *Herr Professor* in a given university, but all these together, right or wrong. Moreover, in all three camps there are thinking men who work, perhaps with other methods, perhaps with unequal success, but still do work toward the solution of identical or similar problems; what has been said above about philosophy of logic sufficiently shows this, we believe. Therefore, it does not seem either prudent or reasonable to close ones eyes to what is going on beyond the walls of one's own group. And once this is admitted, the study of Soviet philosophy appears to be very useful indeed.

Finally, there is perhaps still a third reason. Soviet philosophers usually accuse the bulk of non-Communist thinkers of being party-philosophers, indeed, lackeys and defenders of the bourgeoisie. This is, certainly as far as the enormous majority of philosophers is concerned, not only untrue, but even ludicrously untrue. Yet, something of what the Soviet writers say may be true, in as far as the attitude toward our subject is concerned.

7

One sometimes has the feeling that many among our philosophers are more or less consciously persuaded that Soviet philosophy, being Communist, cannot be an interesting philosophy. In other terms, they *are*, in one sense, party-men: they do not consider Soviet philosophy for its own value, but decide *a priori*, that being the philosophy of a party alien to their own, it must be wrong. In that respect, at least, they seem to have taken over something of the worst they found in their Soviet colleagues.

But this is certainly not the right attitude for a philosopher. If there is anything on which all free thinkers agree, it is certainly that they should make every effort to look at things as they are, not as it is useful to any party or human group. That is why such a prejudice, which seems to be present in many cases, must be said to be regrettable and one hopes that it shall be overcome.

University of Fribourg,
Inst. of East-European Studies

REFERENCES

* Originally published in *Studies in Soviet Thought* III,1 (March 1963).
[1] On the period before 1931 (concerning logic) cf. V. I. Čerkesov: *Materialističeskaja dialektika kak logika i teorija poznanija* (The Materialist Dialectic as Logic and Epistemology). Moskva, Izd. MGU, 1962. p. 12 f. (cf. *SST* II (1962) 321 f. and 3 (1963) 74); D. Joravsky: *Soviet Marxism and Natural Science* (1917–1932). London. 1961. (cf. *SST* 2 (1962) 142–148).
[2] It seems that at the beginning there was some philosophical life, especially in philosophy of physics and in history of philosophy; later on the situation became far worse, culminating in the 'quotatology' here referred to.
[3] For a description of the 1947 to 1958 development cf. J. M. Bocheński: *Einführung in die sowjetische Philosophie der Gegenwart* (Introduction to Contemporary Soviet Philosophy). (*Aus Politik und Zeitgeschichte* B 45/59. Bonn. 1959; reprinted in part in *Der sowjetrussische dialektische Materialismus* (Soviet-Russian Dialectical Materialism)). 3. Aufl. Bern-München. 1960. A bibliography on this period is being published by the Fribourg Institute: *Bibliographie der sowjetischen Philosophie* (Bibliography of Soviet Philosophy). (Sovietica) D. Reidel, Dordrecht, I and II, 1959, III, 1962; IV, 1963; cf. T. J. Blakeley: 'A Bibliography of Soviet Philosophy'. *SST* I (1961) 12–15.
[4] D. Spasov, in *Ruch Filozoficzny* 21, 1962, 2, 136; cf. *SST* II (1962) 327.
[5] Similarity between religions and Communism should not be overstressed. The basic difference is that while adherents of the great religions openly admit that their doctrine is not science but faith, Communists proclaim that their ideology is 'scientific'. This is why the logical situation of a Communist is by far worse than that of a believer of a great religion. However, the sociological implications are to a large extent similar and the argument remains valid in spite of these basic differences.

[6] Cf. D. D. Comey: 'Marxist-Leninist Ideology and Soviet Policy'. In *SST* II (1962) 301–320.

[7] On mathematical logic in the Soviet Union, cf. S. A. Janovskaja: 'Matematičeskaja logika i osnovnaja matematika' (Mathematical Logic and Basic Mathematics). In: *Matematika v SSSR za sorok let* (Mathematics in the USSR in 40 Years). I. Moskva. 1959. pp. 13–120; G. Küng: 'Mathematical Logic in the Soviet Union (1917–1947 and 1947–1957)'. *SST* I (1961) 39–43. On the general situation in logic: H. Dahm: 'Renaissance der formalen Logik' (The Renaissance of Formal Logic), *Ost-Probleme* 8 (1957), 254–267; J. M. Bocheński,: 'Soviet Logic', *SST* I (1961) 29–38; D. D. Comey: 'Two Recent Soviet Conferences on Logic', *SST* II (1962) 21–36.

[8] Cf. A. A. Zinov'ev: 'O rabote seminara po logike v Institute Filosofii' (On the work of the Logic Seminar of the IF). In *VF* 1958, 12, 167–172, reviewed by D. D. Comey and G. L. Kline in *The Journal of Symbolic Logic* 24 (1959) 232–233. See also the bibliography cited in note 5 (Janovskaja, Küng) and, among the more recent works published by the Philosophical Institute: *Logičeskie issledovanija* (Logical Investigations). Moskva, Izd. AN, 1959; and *Primenenie logiki v nauke i texnike* (The Application of Logic in Science and Technology). Moskva, Izd. AN, 1960.

[9] G. A. Volkov: 'Konferencija po voprosam protivorečij' (Conference on Contradiction). *VF* 1958, 12, 163–173; and, above all, N. Lobkowicz: *Das Widerspruchsprinzip in der neueren sowjetischen Philosophie* (The Principle of Contradiction in Contemporary Soviet Philosophy). (Sovietica), D. Reidel, Dordrecht, 1959, which contains a German translation of some otherwise not available relevant texts and a general introduction to the field.

[10] Zinov'ev, A. A.: *Filosofskie problemy mnogoznačnoj logiki* (Philosophic Problems of Many-Valued Logic). Moskva, Izd. AN, 1960; and the review by L. H. Hackstaff and J. M. Bocheński in *SST* II (1962) 37–48.

[11] M. M. Rozental', G. M. Štraks: *Kategorii materialističeskoj dialektiki* (The Categories of the Materialist Dialectic). Moskva, 1956; V. P. Tugarinov: *Sootnošenie kategorij dialektičeskogo materializma* (The Interrelation of the Categories of Dialectical Materialism). Leningrad, 1956. For bibliography and a general report of the discussions see H. Fleischer: 'On Categories in Soviet Philosophy'. *SST* I (1961) 65–77.

[12] Cf. H. Dahm: 'Soviet Philosophy's Conception of "Basic Laws", "Order" and "Principles"'. *SST* I (1961) 52–63; H. Fleischer: 'The Materiality of Matter'. *SST* II (1962) 12–20.

[13] S. Müller-Markus: 'Bibliography of Philosophical Articles in *Uspexi fizičeskix nauk*'. *SST* II (1962) 255–260, and 'Die Organisation der sowjetischen Philosophie der Physik seit Dezember 1960' (The Organization of Soviet Philosophy of Physics Since December 1960). *SST* II (1962) 49–63.

[14] S. Müller-Markus: *Einstein und die Sowjetphilosophie I.* (Sovietica), D. Reidel, Dordrecht, 1960. Cf. 'Einstein and Soviet Philosophy'. *SST* I (1961) 78–87.

[15] A first discussion on the subject was started by the important articles of M. A. Markov: 'O prirode fizičeskogo znanija' (On the Nature of Physical Knowledge), *VF* 1947, 2, 140–176 (cf. the index of *Bibliographie der sowjetischen Philosophie I* under 'Markov, M. A.' p. 68b). Other discussions are continuing now. S. Müller-Markus is preparing an ample report on them. See also his article in *SST* III,1, and C. Olgin: 'Science and Philosophy in the USSR'. *Bulletin, Institute for the Study of the USSR*, 1960, 12, 5–19.

[16] S. T. Meljuxin: *O dialektike razvitija neorganičeskoj prirody* (On the Dialectic of the Development of Anorganic Nature). Moskva. 1960. Cf. V. V. Kazjutinskij: 'O

napravlenii razvitija kosmičeskix ob"ektov'. *FN* 1961, 4, 87–94 (German translation: *Ost-Probleme* 14, 1962, 2–8).

[17] *Naučnaja sessija, posvjasčennaja problemam fiziologičeskogo učenija akademika I. P. Pavlova* (Session on Problems of I. P. Pavlov's Physiology). Moskva. 1950.

[18] Bauer, R. A.: *The New Man in Soviet Psychology*, Cambridge, 1952; review by D. D. Comey of *Recent Soviet Psychology* (ed. by Neil O'Connor) in *SST* II (1962) 251–253.

[19] Cf. V. P. Rožin: *Vvedenie v marksistskuju sociologiju* (Introduction to Marxist Sociology). Leningrad, Izd. LGU, 1962.

[20] Cf. V. P. Tugarinov: *O cennostjax žizni i kul'tury* (On the Values of Life and Culture). Leningrad, Izd. LGU, 1960.

[21] As far as ethics are concerned, see the introduction to R. T. De George: 'A Bibliography of Soviet Ethics', *SST* III,1, 83.

[22] The subject is studied – for the first time as it seems – by K. G. Ballestrem in an article in *SST* III,2.

[23] Axmanov, A. S.: *Logičeskoe učenie Aristotelja* (The Logical Doctrine of Aristotle). Moskva. 1954. Two other books appeared before 1947. The *Bibliographie* also lists seven articles for 1947–1958.

[24] Not less than six books on Kant are known to have been published since 1937. Bibliography in Ballestrem (note 22).

[25] Since 1956 six books were published on Hegel. Eleven articles on Hegel were published in the *VF* 1947–1958 (cf. *Bibliographie I*, p. 93a).

[26] Cf. G. L. Kline: *Spinoza in Soviet Philosophy*. New York–London. 1952.

[27] *Istorija filosofii*. Moskva. Izd. AN. I and II, 1957; III and IV, 1959; V, 1960.

EDITORIAL NOTE

Also see the studies and their references published in the present volume. They have originally appeared shortly *after* Professor Bocheński's paper but bear out his views in full. It is in consequence that the latter remains the best general introduction to the subject.

PART ONE

SYSTEMATIC STUDIES IN CURRENT SOVIET THOUGHT

HELMUT FLEISCHER

THE ACTING SUBJECT IN HISTORICAL MATERIALISM*

A problem which in the traditional formulas of Marxist-Leninist theory of society has been masked rather than solved is becoming increasingly acute today: it is the question as to how firmly we, as thinking, willing and acting subjects, find ourselves integrated into some order of the world as something which Jaspers described as *'Umgreifendes, das nicht wir sind'* (encompassing, that is not we). The problem is also how firmly this 'being integrated' is into a definite order of social evolution, how far it means submission and to what extent it permits us to assert ourselves and our wants.

In its Soviet version, Marxist philosophy has become a system of thought wherein man is conceived as a radically subordinated being. He is, also in his social and historical existence, at the mercy of 'objective laws' and is subjected to an 'objective process' – where 'objective' means precisely independent of the subject, its thought and will. As concerns the legislation of the 'course of the world', the subject assumes an outright eccentric position, although otherwise Marxism-Leninism as a theory of revolutionary action is far from any contemplative and quietistic *laissez-aller*. But the point is that human practice for Marxism seems to be only a secondary executive function, as it appears from the fact that it understands human freedom as 'insight into necessity'. Freedom seems to be reduced to some kind of obedience. Also in several other of its aspects, the historical materialist theory shows a subordinative treatment of man. We shall see how thoroughly consolidated this position still is even in some of the most recent writings of Soviet philosophers.

The problem with which Soviet philosophy is faced has its roots in the fact that in the Marxist tradition the opposite motive of a Prometheic human self-consciousness also has a right of its own, and that this right has found its defenders who wish to bring to it further recognition. Thus, the Polish Marxist philosopher Adam Schaff is pleading most insistently for the return to an 'anthropocentric' philosophizing that starts with, and receives its directives from, the life-activity and self-affirmation of

13

human individuals, their striving for happiness. Therewith he poses a counterinstance to the opinion prevailing in Soviet philosophy that the central aim of philosophy is to codify the most universal laws of reality. Schaff calls the latter the 'Ionian line' against which he supports the 'Socratic line' of a philosophy within the horizon of human-social existence (as it was the original point of view in Marxism).[1] In the Soviet sphere, this divergence of approaches has not become thus explicit, but in the course of a further intensification of anthropologico-axiological reflection it may be expected that there too, new considerations will become imperative. In the following we wish to identify some of the traditional positions which Soviet philosophy will then have to supersede.

MAN AS PRODUCT

Whenever they want to present a fundamental definition of the essence of man, Soviet theoreticians resort to that formula which Marx has given in his theses on Feuerbach: the human essence is the 'ensemble of social relations'. It is not customary among them to dwell on the categorial problems of this formula, nor to reduce it to a common denominator with the other anthropological statements of the early and the later Marx. Rather, their interpretation leads directly to a proposition which Marx in these same theses questioned insistently: that man is the product of his social environment, of the material conditions of his life. As V. P. Tugarinov remarks in his study *Person and Society*, the most usual procedure in Soviet philosophical literature is the attempt to demonstrate the determining and dominant influence of society and its structure on the subject, while considering the subject as the product of society, the total ensemble of social relations.[2]

The statements on the essence of man in M. I. Petrosjan's book on humanism are conceived entirely in this sense. The author describes the transformation that the idea of the 'formative rôle of the social milieu in regard to the person' has undergone in Marxism: above all, Marxism does not confine itself to the political organization and spiritual constitution of society, but discloses the economic, the 'material relations of production' as the 'foundation of society', without ignoring other relations (political, ideological, national etc.). As to man, who underlies continuous historical change, the following statement is made: "He is the

14

product of his epoch, of the social milieu (in the Marxist understanding of the word). His thoughts, his feelings and his behavior are determined by this milieu."[3]

Some qualifications follow: the determination of a man by the class position of his parents is not to be understood as a strict law but only as a tendencial rule[4], furthermore the significance of hereditary individual capacities should not be overlooked.[5] Finally, the activity of the person himself is also to be taken into account: "Notwithstanding their determining function, social conditions themselves are submitted to the transforming power of man. Man transforms nature and social conditions, and he reshapes his own nature by this process." He thus plays the rôle of the active subject in the process of his 'self-transformation'. Marx described this as the 'coincidence of changing circumstances and of human activity or self-alteration'.[6]

It is doubtful whether a well-balanced conception is arrived at in such terms. Certainly, nobody contests today that every man receives infinitely much from society before being able to add something new.[7] But in order to characterize the kind of activity involved here, categories different from those of the Soviets must be applied. Marx formulated the first commandment concisely: "Above all it must be avoided to fixate 'society' as an abstraction contrary to the individual."[8]

The Soviet social theory is abundant with precisely such 'fixations', while the logical analysis of the socio-anthropological categories leaves much to be desired. When 'society' shapes and 'produces' the individual, this means primarily that other individuals do so. It is not by chance that Marx so often prefers to speak about 'the individuals' instead of the abstracted 'fixation' "society".[9] Further, it will be required to define more precisely the notion of 'social conditions' (or 'relations'), e.g. to distinguish explicitly such instances of it as the material objectivations of previous human activity (the 'products' in the proper sense), the modes of human behavior and institutional regulations. Finally – and this is the most important point – it is imperative to clarify the character, impulse and direction of that very activity wherein subjects engage in relation to objects and to each other. By means of the statement 'men are products of other men', no progress is achieved towards an understanding of the essential content, the specific quality of human existence and activity. Consequently it is necessary to acknowledge the spontaneity of

15

the associated and interacting subjects and to interpret it in terms of their needs, interests, hopes and fears, finality, and axiological orientation. All this is present in Marx, and it means a totally unjustified curtailment to reduce his conception of man to an 'environmentalistically' misunderstood formula of the 'sum of the social conditions' as the origin of everything.[10]

Next, what are the accomplishments of Soviet philosophical anthropology in its effort to portray man, the individual, as the subject of his actions and relations?

MAN AS SUBJECT

While declarations about man as the creator of his existence are not lacking in Soviet literature, there is a considerable lack of theoretical articulation in them. In the past few years it has been several times remarked that the problem of the individual person has been badly neglected as a consequence of dominant pre-occupations with the activities of the large social groups.[11] M. B. Mitin states that there is not a single problem of the inner spiritual world of man (joy and grief, creative success, flights of phantasy, feeling of responsibility, loneliness, illness, fear of death, etc.) "which might not be – or has not actually been – the subject of a Marxist analysis – psychological, logical, social or moral".[12] But besides the fact that much *might* be analyzed still, we have to note that much of that which has already been done, has not penetrated to the basic problems of anthropo-sociology.

To accentuate the singular, personal subject more clearly, has been one of the aims which V. P. Tugarinov – following his valuable studies on the categories of dialectical and historical materialism as well as on the value aspects of human life – pursued in his recent booklet *Person and Society* (1965). He defines the single man as a subject, as a substantial unit, as an 'object of nature' and at the same time as an 'element in society', as the 'bearer of the social relations' and agent of socio-historical process. Man acquires the status of 'personality' by the entirety of properties which form in his interaction with society.[13] After exposing these properties, Tugarinov condenses the concept of 'person' into the following formula: "A person is a man who possesses a historically determined degree of rationality and responsibility toward society;

who participates, in accordance with his innate qualities, in certain rights and liberties (or is able to participate in them); who, through his individual activity, contributes to the development of society and leads his life in a way which corresponds to the ideals of his epoch or class."[14] Tugarinov (as well as other authors) emphasizes the receptivity of individuals, and sometimes he does this in terms which manage to mask the opposite constituent, namely the subject's spontaneity. Thus he writes that the subject, the single person, is a 'reflection of society in an individual form'.[15] Or, in reference to the categories of a subject-object-relation: "The person is a subject. But the subject is nothing but an organic element in the object, a small part of it, and its – the subject's – essence is that in every man, and always in its own way, it reflects in itself the totality of the social conditions under which it lives." "The subjective is just the reflection of the objective, and that is why the subject is the more perfect the more completely and profoundly it reflects in itself the objective."[16] But, instead of a recourse from the subject (single person) to the object (society) – a recourse that would actually involve a vicious circle, for, when we further ask what is society and what characterizes it as human, we would have to recur anew to the individuals and to something which we can find only in them – a different recourse seems to be more fruitful: that to some generic essence in which individuals participate individually as well as in a socially organized plurality.

It is significant that Tugarinov postulates the dependence of society on personal subjects – and not only in the trivial sense that society does not exist outside of individuals, but in a normative sense. "Man is subject also because he – more exactly: that they, people, are that 'object' whose needs and purposes society serves, for whom society properly exists. Man makes history in order to realize his own, human aims."[17] Therewith the subject acquires a strong position, it becomes in a certain sense the 'measure' of social relations (far from being only their 'product'), a legislative instance.

The point is not to defend any bourgeois individualism (bound to the private ownership of the means of production), but to formulate the theoretical expression of a personal autonomy which will survive, we hope, every socialist transformation – or will be firmly re-established insofar as it has suffered some damage. The other point is not to oppose

17

personal autonomy to social engagement, but rather to form social engagement as well as society in such a way that personal autonomy could find its fulfilment. Even where the individual receives something from social tradition, other than indoctrination, a kind of free receptivity is possible which cannot be adequately described in terms of the 'formation of the person by society'.

THE DIGNITY AND VALUE OF MAN

More clarity in statements concerning the autonomy and the rights of the subject are to be expected when the person and his dignity are explicitly treated. Soviet writings contain a series of declarations on personal dignity as well as on the 'value of man'. There is, however, some difficulty concerning the concept of the person itself. The Russian word *ličnost'* conveys predominantly the meaning of *personality* as a complex of properties which man acquires in the process of his education and self-education. The complex of properties which make up the concept of personality embraces, as Tugarinov points out, rationality, responsibility, freedom, individuality and personal dignity.[18] This definition suffers at the same time a restriction insofar as not all individuals *eo ipso* have the status of *ličnost'*. This is only proper to the adult and psychically normal man, but not to the child, the insane, or to one who has otherwise lost the capacity of responsible action. But it is held that differences in the color of skin, in sex and in nationality cannot diminish personal dignity.[19]

The difficulty is that no distinction is made between 'person' and 'personality'. But it seems to us that such a distinction has a primordial significance. What matters here is that a definite status should be attributed to man independently of his degree of maturity, the richness and quality of his personality; some autonomy of existence and value which finds its concretization in certain active and passive rights. In our opinion Schaff does not do enough justice to this when he writes "There is no person as a spiritual unit which one might distinguish from the individual as a real being. Personality is only a specific determinateness of the human individual and belongs to it like its physical appearance. To separate personality in the form of a hypostatized 'person' from the individual is as much a mystification as the attempt to deprive the individual of its shape or its shadow…"[20] He arrives at the simple alternative that "either you take personality as a complex of properties of a real subject..., or you take it autonomously as a spiritual person and thereby decide not only the question of personality, but also that of the human individual as such, in the spirit of idealism".[21] A passage from Marx' critique of the Hegelian theory of the state appears to Schaff as an argument directed "against the idealistic (personalist) concept of the person", seeming to justify the following conclusion: "personality is not an independent or autonomous spiritual being (with regard to the material world, also to the world of real human individuals), but a social product, the function of social conditions, of relations between real human individuals". From which follows that the personality of man is not something simply 'given' but something in the process of 'becoming'.[22]

We do not want to deny that in the theories of the person there are cases of spiritualistic curtailment. As for the term '*spiritual* person' we want neither to defend nor to criticize it here. What matters is not the adjective 'spiritual' but the status of *autonomy*, which concerns not only the spirituality of the person but its bodily and social existence as well: the individual in its totality. We cannot understand why Schaff wants to associate so closely autonomy with pure spirituality. Autonomy is already implied in the simple fact that everyone in his singularity is himself, as distinguished from others.[23] And also, *what* a man is like is never reduced to what 'society' has made out of him (and, normatively, it *should* not be reduced to that). As Tugarinov observes, there are a variety of relations between the individual and society, ranging from almost complete coincidence to harsh divergence and opposition.[24] Therefore it is imperative to have a peculiar categorial articulation of that autonomy which the individual may enjoy as a person in a collectivity of persons, notably with respect to its axiological implications, the rights which the person gains by this status. It is imperative to be recognized as a 'self-with-a-purpose'. And it is of great importance to note that this status is not something acquired in the course of the development of personality, but something which man simply possesses as a *character indelibilis* at his entry into a community of persons. There should not be any exception to this rule, not even with regard to those individuals to whom Tugarinov rightly refuses to ascribe the status of 'personality'.

Some Soviet reasonings about the dignity or value of man make it obvious that uncertainty results from the lack of such a concept of the person. In his *Foundations of Marxist Ethics,* A. F. Šiškin proclaims that Communist morals, by virtue of their humanistic principles, highly respect human dignity. The universal development of man, Šiškin says, is the greatest productive force, the main capital is man himself. That is why Marxism demands the abolition of all conditions and relations enslaving and degrading man. Under Socialism everything is aimed at the elevation of man, "man becomes the greatest of all values in the world".[25] These rather ambiguous declarations (because of their strange motivation) are followed by a recitation from the thought of a 're-volutionary democrat', namely a sentence by V. G. Belinskij demanding esteem for the human dignity of every man just because he is a man.[26] The line of though leads further to considerations in which 'human dignity' appears in still another meaning: something is said about a respectable behavior worthy of man, as well as about his self-respect as a feeling of this worthiness. This is a kind of dignity which man is able to lose, and he loses it by conducting himself unworthily. Finally we arrive at the conclusion that real dignity is possessed not by the 'knights of profit' and their lackeys, but by the working men, the fighters for peace and social progress.[27]

Two concepts of 'human dignity' have been projected here one upon the other in such a way that one relativizes the other. This becomes still more explicit in those passages of M. I. Petrosjan's book on humanism. The author conducts a polemic against the English 'revisionist' C. Taylor, who objected against the functionalization of human dignity, demanding that man must have his value simply because he is a man, irrespective of the rôle he plays in the 'development of the human possibilities'.[28] Petrosjan's reply is that this can only mean that parasites and reactionaries have the same value as men of creative work and fighters for peace![29] As regards the value of man, she distinguishes between two 'levels'. On an 'anthropological level' all men are equal, without difference as to race and language. But, since man is also a *social* being, this 'biological basis' should not be 'metaphysically absolutized'. "The value of man, insofar as we speak of him as representative of the human species, is incontest-able... But the notion of value loses its autonomy and absoluteness as soon as something is said about man as a social being." What matters here is the social significance of a person.[30] "Therefore one must seek the criterion of the value of a person in the sphere of the social relations which determine his essence. The dominant principle in this sphere is the work-activity of man as his specifically human activity. Consequently, the criterion of the value of a person lies in his relation to work, in the socially useful work of man."[31]

To transfer axiological equality into an anthropo-biological sphere which is so 'undialectically' separated from the social sphere is, we believe, not an acceptable solution, for it leaves the decisive question unanswered: which are the implications of that equivalence in the *social* sphere, what rights (connected with the dignity of man) should never be restricted in view of differences in social function, be it even relations of political enmity or cases of antisocial conduct? It might be advisable to make a distinction (analogously to that between person and personality) between the *dignity* of man and the *value* of particular *qualities* or *accomplishments* flowing from this personality.

SUBJECT AND HISTORY

The Marxist-Leninist conception of the historical evolution of human society is marked by a polarity of principles which is by no means free of tension. In following Marx and Engels, Soviet theoreticians declare that men make their history themselves. But often enough this is being said only in the second instance, while in the forefront they proclaim the other thesis, that history is an 'objective process' obeying laws not dependent on man as subject. Men make history in accordance with objective laws, and the laws operate and make their way through the activity of men. The authors of one volume on historical materialism, V. Ž. Kelle and M. Ja. Koval'zon, are particularly conscious of the duality of these aspects: they subdivide their book correspondingly into a first part exposing history as the natural-historical process, and a second, characterizing the same history as the result of human activity. (The third part gives a separate account of the 'spiritual side' of the process.) "History is at the same time both a natural-historical process independent of the will and the wishes of men, and a result of the activity of men, guided by their goals, wishes and intentions."[32]

A very questionable construction has been accomplished here in order to give an account of a state of affairs which is capable of being much better accounted for. It is beyond doubt that much has occurred in history which was undesired, and much of what has been desired has not occurred; that history is not an unilinear and coherent teleological process but a rather elementary resultant of innumerable activities competing with each other; that every activity is bound to a range of material means in which it finds the measure and the limits of its possibilities. All this can be denoted by its proper name, but hardly justifies the conceptual construct 'objective process'. The appeal to 'objective laws' (habitual among Soviet theoreticians) is no less problematic. Kelle and Koval'zon believe that this is precisely one of the 'rational elements' in Hegel's philosophy of history: he has rightly observed that something is produced in the actions of men which transcends their conscious aims. But this something is not the march of the *Weltgeist*. "Marxism has demonstrated that, although history is being made by men, the activity of the latter is determined by objective laws of social being, and is a form of the realization of these laws, no matter whether men are conscious of them or not. These laws also determine the objective results of human actions. Men make history, but they make it not arbitrarily, but as they are determined by the material conditions of their life." [33]

It is irritating to see how abruptly this line of thought leads from the evident fact that history cannot be made *ad libitum*, to the concept of 'objective laws' and the hypostasis of an 'objective process', radically cut-off from the natural teleology and conditionedness of human activity. We find this abrupt transition also in G. E. Glezerman's book on the laws of social development. Having stressed the dependence of human activity on definite conditions, he concludes, "Therefore, the course of historical events is determined not only by the conscious actions of men. It is subjected to objective laws ... which during the entire past history have dominated over them like elemental forces of nature." [34]

The introduction of the laws, so insufficiently prepared, is all the less convincing since, with few exceptions, their codex has up to now remained rather undefined. And as regards those few laws which have been formulated *expressis verbis* (e.g. the law of the correspondence between the relations of production and the character of the productive forces), they are far from being able to concretize the concept of history as a process which obeys laws. Laws of social processes – how many or few of them one may be able to formulate – can hardly be anything else than definite correlations between initial situations, behaviours or dispositions of subjects, setting of goals, means of their realization, results of actions and reactions of subjects, and so on. Insofar as the dispositions of the subjects have an essential constitutive part in such laws, it is misleading, to say the least, to call them simply 'objective'.[35]

Having started from subjects and their aims, activities and results, Soviet theoreticians apparently find it more easy to arrive at the construction of the 'objective process' than to find the way back from there to an understanding of social movement based on the activity and teleology (which, although conditioned and limited, split and broken, is nonetheless simply and solely real) of subjects, or their inherent impulses to action and reaction.

A constructive critique of the present conception of historical materialism would have to include the proposal to invert its whole procedure. Instead of integrating the activity of subjects into a prefabricated scheme of the 'objective process', one should remain in the framework of this activity and its motivation and integrate the total ensemble of the conditions, constellations, institutions, etc. into the concept of 'motivated activity'. Such a procedure, by the way, would be consistent with what Marx and Engels wrote (in the *German Ideology* and *Holy Family*) against hypostatizing history, insisting that it is nothing but the activity of men pursuing their purposes. Not a single instance of 'conditionedness', rightly discovered and stressed by Marxism, would have to be lost from sight as a consequence of this recourse to pragmatology. On the other hand it would advance considerably the cause of a rich explication of the subject as a historical entity.

SUBJECT AND SPONTANEITY

The degradation of the subject in many (not in all) constructions of Soviety theory is not such that the subject's activity would be denied. Rather, the moment of spontaneity in human activity is not clarified. The Russian term for 'spontaneity' is *'stixijnost'*. It signifies an explicitly low level of activity, a narrowly reactive behavior without awareness of further connections and consequences. Hereafter, however, we shall mean by 'spontaneity' (consistently with the Soviet *Philosophical Dictionary*) that moment or share of qualitatively definite (generic or individual, reproductive or productive) self-movement or self-activity of the individual which is never reducible to determination from without and wherefore individuals are not to be regarded as mere 'products' but as immediate participants in the factual and normative 'essence' of the species and its historical progress.

It is not difficult to demonstrate that in the Soviet version of historical materialism the necessary room for this element of spontaneity is still to be created. This becomes manifest in all considerations where the originality of the subject is at stake – be it in discussions about the roots of human-social activities in needs and interests, be it in analyses of the axiological aspects of human life, or in the fundamental definition of human freedom. In each of these instances the tendency of Soviet theoreticians is to minimize the originality and autonomy of the subject (or the subjective) and transfer instead the *nomos* into something 'objective', i.e. independent of the subject.

In regard to the possibility of considering the *needs* (or the neediness) of man as something factually and normatively ultimate, V.Ž. Kelle and M. Ja. Koval'zon object that thereby nothing at all is explained: the needs depend on the conditions of life, on the level of production.[36] Another author, A. V. Borzenko, writes: "In fact, the immediate causes of human activity are always the conscious motives and the objectives and intentions resulting from them." But the objectives, he continues, "reflect the external world", are determined by it – although not immediately but "by mediation of the needs of men and the whole complex of their mental world. The needs of men, on their part, form themselves in the process of their interaction with the external world and with each other, they are a product of social life".[37] It is easy to imagine what the author has in mind. Nonetheless, a one-sided and anthropologically wrong point of view results when only those cases are taken into account where needs arise in consequence of some outside stimulation, because most of these merely consist in additions to, and concretizations of, the basic *repertoire* of needs which man simply has and elementarily feels. Moreover, it is impossible to answer by recourse to the external world and the rest of social life the question as to how *new* needs arise for the first time. Here we touch a spontaneity which is inherent to the range of invariant basic needs.

A similar tendency reigns in Soviet discussions about the value of goods, human actions and social institutions. There are authors who, like V. V. Mšveineradze, try rigorously to purge these value characteristics from the stigma of subjectivity. It is true, so we read, that the value of something is relative to some interest of subjects. "But these interests, notwithstanding their subjective form, have themselves an objective foundation and express social, above all economic relations." In the last analysis, it is said, the 'objective measure' of value lies in the 'objective laws of social progress'. Value is defined as a "social category by which to denote the material and spiritual phenomena created by men in their struggle for social progress, freedom and the development of human personality".[38] This formula can hardly conceal that behind all the talk about the 'objective' ultimately there is the reality of a normative, demanding subject.

The position of the subject as the measure of value has been more clearly pronounced by S. I. Popov. "The value-relation of man towards reality forms itself on the basis of his interests and needs: man himself is the supreme and in a certain sense the unconditional value..."[39] But when Popov, after having recognized the constitutive function of the subject, proceeds to define the 'criterion of value', he contradicts another author who stated that the measure of value is man himself. It is more correct according to Popov to base value on the laws of social progress. But the most adequate solution seems to him to be the recognition of 'social practice' (being the motive force of social progress) as the universal criterion of value.[40]

Nowhere else is the subordinative treatment of the subject as obvious as in understanding human freedom as 'insight into necessity'. "Man is free", F. V. Konstantinov proclaims, "when in his socially significant activity he is consciously guided by the objective laws of historical progress."[41] D. I. Kerimov pronounces still more clearly how thoroughly freedom is reduced to obedience: "The freedom of the individual consists in the subordination of his will, intentions and actions under the socially significant objectives of which he has become conscious, which guarantee the domination of reason over feeling, and self-control, organization and discipline... to the advantage of society."[42]

While some of this may be true, it does not constitute the essence of freedom. Rather, it means a dependence of the autonomous, freely acting subject on certain natural and social regularities. The subordination involved here proves to be something subordinate itself. It consists mainly in certain regards which are imperative in the choice of means, procedures, partial goals, etc., which are themselves subordinate to the total and final objectives set or accepted by the subject autonomously. It is sheer folly to substitute this secondary instance of subordination as the quintessence of freedom itself. It would be unjust to blame the Soviet theoreticians for not paying attention to other aspects of the problem of freedom; but the dominant rôle which this formula has received as the core of the philosophical understanding of freedom entails a one-sidedness which is by no means harmless, since it tends to dim the spontaneity proper to the human subject. This is why it is far from trivial when Tugarinov recurs to the original and usual understanding of freedom, as the possibility to act according to one's own will and not under external constraint.[43]

SUBJECT AND PROJECT

Marxism has its roots in a 'philosophy of self-consciousness'. From this self-consciousness as the 'supreme deity'[44], the road led to the proclamation of man as the 'supreme being' and to the formulation of a 'categoric imperative' demanding the overthrow of all conditions under which man is a humiliated being.[45] The projection of a future social order arises as the reaction of an autonomous being to the heteronomy to which it has been submitted – to 'alienation' as a totality of privation, repression and destruction 'against which human nature revolts'.[46] In the early social theory of Soviet Marxism, however, this order of motivation has been turned almost upside-down: we may even speak of an alienation of theory from subject. But, the problems of the subject have attained new actuality in the post-Stalinist era. At present the programmatic declarations of party ideologies are even ahead of the theoretical constructions of philosophers, who are faced with new tasks. The central field of application is the anthropological constitution of Soviet society itself. Here the theoreticians are confronted with the question as to how man as the subject and substance of 'social relations' is the measure of all that is necessary and possible.

Out of a multitude of problems now becoming acute we only wish to touch upon the general problem of the anthropological interpretation of Communism as an ideal of social order. It was not without reluctance and relapses that, in the past few years, the opinion found more and more recognition according to which Communism is above all an 'ideal' based on certain anthropological norms, and will have an evident value for the people who live under its order. But in the following sentences we can see how difficult it has been to clear the way for the new axiological approach against the formerly prevailing construction of the 'objectively-necessary process'. "Socialism", V. P. Tugarinov states, "is the result of the incontrovertible operation of the objective laws of historical development", an "objective, natural-historical phenomenon", and the theory of Socialism "is the scientific expression of this historical necessity". But at the same time Socialism and Communism are "the highest value for millions of working people", therefore "not only historically necessary, inevitable, but also desirable for billions of men".[47] We cannot agree that the author has succeeded in interrelating axiological normativity and 'objective necessity' in a convincing and lucid manner – especially when he further indicates that the axiological quality is to be understood as a derivate of the scientifically established 'objective necessity'.

Here we have to deal with a pragmatological calculus in which axiological and factological, subjective and objective constituents are tightly interwoven in a definite sequence of subordination. The *prius* and central point of reference in any case is a subject with definite aspirations, branching into various directions; these directions are the dimensions of desiring and longing, also of hope, running far ahead of any possibility of practical realization. Something of this sort has always been fundamental for Communism (independently of any scientific analysis of the conditions under which it might be realized), insofar as its final goal has been to establish an order of human life characterized by abundance, equality, freedom and harmony. The 'historical necessity' of this project is axiological by its very nature and origin – and on this level it must be necessary because desirable, and not the reverse. It is not scientific simply to *postulate* a life without want, exploitation, domination and annihilation of man by man. Scientific reflection begins where the anthropological ideal is to be confronted and connected with an entirely sober, realistic conception of human nature and the scale of its possibilities, far from all illusions. Of a scientific order is also the search for the adequate

27

instrumental and institutional prerequisites for realizing desired goals. The most decisive elements in this field are the possibilities of the subject itself, because the material prerequisites are what they are only in correlation with corresponding dispositions on the part of subjects.

As for the projects of Communism, they raise many questions concerning presumptive human behavior, e.g. how people change their attitude to their daily work under new institutional conditions, what norms of distribution of the social product they will regard as normal, what kinds of rivalry can still arise between them, how universal their interest in public affairs will be, etc. In all these instances the question will also be, within what limits the programmatic activity of some will be able to determine the behavior of others. On this level only that can be 'necessary' which is really possible; for a thing to be desirable is not enough.

The subject therefore is legislative in a twofold sense: in what it desires as well as in what it actually is able to do. The 'legislation' of which we are speaking does not consist in arbitrary decisions, as far as vitally important things are concerned. Rather, it is the outcome of a definite striving in the very being of the subject.

In the directions indicated here a wide field of reflections opens up – reflections which would find a worth-while place in the center of the historical-materialist theory of society. The task can be briefly defined as the 'subjectological' and 'pragmatological' reorganization of historical materialism. Or, to put it in the style of the 'slogans' so popular in the Soviet world: the decisive task is now the explication of a theory of the acting subject in historical materialism.

The Free University of Berlin

REFERENCES

* Reprinted from *Studies in Soviet Thought* VI,2 (June 1966). Original title: 'Das Handelnde Subjekt im Historischen Materialismus'.
[1] The German editions are titled: *Marx oder Sartre? Versuch einer Philosophie des Menschen*, 1964, 176 pp., *Marxismus und das menschliche Individuum*, 1965, 349 pp.
[2] *Ličnost'i obščestvo*, 1965, str. 25–26.
[3] *Gumanizm*, 1964, str. 154. Similiarly F. V. Konstantinov, in: *Čelovek i èpoxa*, 1964, str. 89.
[4] *Gumanizm*, str. 156.

[5] *Ibidem*, str. 157.
[6] *Ibidem*, str. 160.
[7] M. Landmann: *Der Mensch als Schöpfer und Geschöpf der Kultur*, 1961, S. 46.
[8] Karl Marx, *Frühe Schriften* I (ed. H.–J. Lieber and P. Furth), 1962, S. 597.
[9] In the chapter on Feuerbach in the *Deutsche Ideologie* there is a passage where the word 'individuals' occurs on almost every line. (*Werke* Bd. 3, 1958, S. 67)
[10] It is probable that Marx only wished to state that the *phenomenon of religion* results from a definite state of society, and not from an extra-historical human essence.
[11] See the editorial in *VF* 1963, 2, 6; V. P. Tugarinov: *Ličnost' i obščestvo*, str. 30–31.
[12] *Čelovek i èpoxa*, str. 65.
[13] *Ličnost' i obščestvo*, str. 24–25, 43.
[14] *Ibidem*, str. 88.
[15] *Ibidem*, str. 29.
[16] *Ibidem*, str. 28.
[17] *Ibidem*, str. 25.
[18] *Ibidem*, str. 45–87.
[19] *Ibidem*, str. 41.
[20] A. Schaff: *Marxismus und das menschliche Individuum*, S. 120.
[21] *Ibidem*, S. 126–127.
[22] *Ibidem*, S. 127–128.
[23] V. P. Tugarinov, *Ličnost' i obščestvo*, str. 43.
[24] *Ibidem*, str. 15.
[25] *Osnovy marksistskoj ètiki*, 1961, str. 321.
[26] *Ibidem*, str. 322.
[27] *Ibidem*, str. 324.
[28] C. Taylor: 'Marxism and Humanism', in: *The New Reasoner*, 1958. 2, 96–97.
[29] *Gumanizm*, str. 190.
[30] *Ibidem*, str. 190–191.
[31] *Ibidem*, str. 188–189.
[32] *Istoričeskij materializm*, 1962, str. 159.
[33] *Ibidem*, str. 162.
[34] *O zakonax obščestvennogo razvitija*, 1960, str. 90; V. P. Tugarinov: *Ličnost' i obščestvo*, str. 25; A. V. Borzenko: *Problema celi v. obščestvennom razvitii*, 1963, str. 7.
[35] *Filosofskij slovar'*, 1963, str. 428–429.
[36] *Istoričeskij materializm*, str. 161, 163.
[37] *Problema celi v obščestvennom razvitii*, str. 11.
[38] "Marksizm i problema cennostej", *FN* 1965, 1, 69.
[39] "Kategorii cennosti i ocenki i marksistskaja filosofija", *FN* 1965, 5, 58.
[40] *Ibidem*, str. 58.
[41] *Čelovek i epoxa*, str. 92.
[42] "Svoboda i pravo", *FN* 1964, 3, 21.
[43] *Ličnost' i obščestvo*, str. 61.
[44] K. Marx, *Frühe Schriften* I, S. 21–22.
[45] *Ibidem*, S. 497.
[46] F. Engels, in: *Werke* Bd. 2, S. 257.
[47] *O cennostjax žizni i kul'tury*, 1960, str. 6.

KARL G. BALLESTREM

THE SOVIET CONCEPT OF TRUTH*

There are two words for 'truth' in Russian: *istina* and *pravda*. *Pravda* is truth as a norm or value for both thinking and acting. *Istina* is truth in the context of theory of knowledge. We deal here exclusively with *istina*.

The theory of truth is a largely elaborated part of Soviet philosophy, due to the fact that Lenin paid considerable attention to this problem, above all in his *Materialism and Empiriocriticism*.[1] Ever since, Soviet theoreticians of knowledge have given similar attention to the problem and tried to clarify, systematize and apply what Lenin said[2], but in this further development a basic opposition to Lenin's views was impossible. It does not seem, therefore, fruitful to distinguish new trends in regard to this theory, particularly as among Soviet philosophers of today there are no really diverging opinions in most cases. One can treat the different contributions as parts of one theory.

What is the place of the theory of truth within Soviet theory of knowledge? If we divide Soviet theory of knowledge into (1) *critique of knowledge* (*an sit cognitio*), (2) *metaphysics of knowledge* (*quid sit cognitio*: 'the basic question of philosophy') and (3) *description of knowledge* (*quomodo fit cognitio*: psychology), – the theory of truth is mainly exposed in (2). It belongs to the general examination of the nature of knowledge, of the relation between being and thought, between knower and known.

GENERAL DEFINITION OF TRUTH

"Truth is the subjective representation of the objective."[3] Or: "Truth is the correspondence of a concept, an idea, to an object; a knowledge which correctly reflects objective reality."[4] In this or a similar way, a general examination of the problem of truth will usually begin. Although these general definitions will always be specified later on, it is already evident at this point that truth means knowledge as such, in its realization through unity with the object. It is a quality of the entirety of knowledge, not of special acts of knowledge.[5] It is a quality of knowledge and not of things (no ontological truth).[6] It is a quality of knowledge and only indirectly of linguistic expressions.[7]

This explains why 'truth' is often used in the same sense as 'knowledge' and always in the same sense as 'true knowledge'. It is necessary to keep this in mind to understand the whole terminology and approach of the Soviet theory of truth. Thus truth is said to be objective, relative and/or absolute, to be a process as well as concrete. These properties of truth make more sense, of course, if one calls them properties of true knowledge.

PROPERTIES OF TRUE KNOWLEDGE

The first property of true knowledge is its *objectivity*. It consists in the adequacy and correctness of the reflection in the knower. This correctness is only given in "such knowledge, whose content depends neither upon man nor upon mankind."[8] In other words: although knowledge is subjective in its form, it must reflect the "object such as it exists outside and independently of consciousness."[9] All kinds of idealism are said to deny this property of truth.

The second and most distinctive characteristic of truth in the Soviet conception is its *relativity* and/or *absoluteness*. These are said to be "the two moments of objective truth".[10] To understand this rather complicated theory one must go back to the basic conception in Soviet theory of knowledge of the reflection of the objective dialectic by the subjective dialectic. The whole of reality develops dialectically. This has (among many others) two meanings: (1) reality reaches ever new stages, overcomes and integrates them in its development; (2) this development is – so to say – not only vertical but horizontal: it is the development to ever greater richness and structural complexity of the same basic reality. The reflective development in consciousness corresponds to the development in reality following both of these meanings. Consciousness or knowledge (both terms have the same meaning in Diamat)[11] of reality is at a certain point of its development either *preliminary*, to be overcome, or *definite*, sure for ever. Therefore, its truth is either relative or absolute in the meaning of (1). But knowledge of reality is also at a certain point of its development either a *partial* or an *all-comprehensive* reflection of reality. Therefore, its truth is either relative or absolute in the meaning of (2).

From this results that both 'absolute truth' and 'relative truth' are used

31

in two different ways. 'Absolute truth' means (a) definite, and (b) all-comprehensive knowledge. 'Relative truth' means (a) preliminary, and (b) partial knowledge.[12] In the light of this conception all truth is somehow relative, because although knowledge may accurately reflect reality, it must change corresponding to reality. "Just as everything changes and develops in the world, also truth changes."[13]

"Relative truth is that knowledge which basically reflects reality truly, but not entirely, only in known determinations, in certain conditions and relations. This knowledge is specified, completed and made concrete in the further development of science."[14] But relative truth is not only completed, but also destroyed by the further development of science. For example, the theory about atoms as indivisible parts of all things was relatively true in this sense.[15]

What is the relation between relative and absolute truth? The following text gives a first answer to this question: "What is absolute truth? Absolute truth is a truth which cannot be refuted in the future. . . . Absolute truth is related to relative truth as the whole to the part. . . . Human knowledge changes and develops from relative to absolute truth."[16] Thus, absolute truth appears as the sum of relative truths and the (ideal) limit toward which the (infinite) development of human knowledge goes.

But is there no actual absolute truth? "Absolute truth exists not only as limit toward which our knowledge tends, but which it actually never reaches. Knowledge is absolute if it develops on the path of objective truth and it only finds its absoluteness in this development. . . . in all domains of scientific knowledge there are absolutely true statements which cannot be refuted in the further development of science. In each objective truth there are certain moments, sides, of absolute [truth]. Thus, our knowledge about the physical structure of matter is, on the whole, not complete, absolute, but there is much absolute in it (for example, the statements that the atom is divisible, that electrons, protons, neutrons are elements of the atom are absolutely true)."[17]

Referring to the schema given above, one can say that Soviet philosophy accepts *absolute truth* in the sense of (b) only at the end of the development of reality and of knowledge through *relative truths* in the sense of (a) and (b). It nevertheless holds that actual human knowledge can be *absolute true* in the sense of (a) and at the same time *relative* in the sense of (b): knowledge – although partial – may accurately reflect something so basic in reality that it will not be changed. The above given statements of physics and even more the laws of the dialectic are absolutely true in this sense. In this also consists the 'dialectical unity' between absolute and relative truth.[18]

In a further interpretation we shall come back to this question of the relativity and absoluteness of truth. At this point – only looking at the direct textual context in which the subject is treated – much seems to remain obscure in regard to this theory.

The third property of truth (true knowledge) is its being a *process*. With 'truth as process' two things seem to be meant: first that knowledge goes through different stages from sensation up to reasoning. In this sense, the "coincidence of a thought with an object is a process."[19] But secondly, and above all, this expression refers to the fact that knowledge is the historical development of human consciousness to absolute truth. We found this idea already expressed in the texts on relative and absolute truth. The following texts state it explicitily: "Knowledge is not a short, one-time acceptance, but a long-lasting, complicated, infinite process ..."[20] And again: "Dialectical materialism, contrary to metaphysical materialism, understands truth as the historically conditioned process of reflection of reality."[21]

Truth is, finally, said to be *concrete*. "An abstract approach to truth is a distortion of truth, its being ignored. The only correct approach to it is the concrete approach, i.e. to examine all essential sides of a phenomenon in its historical circumstances."[22]

This means that true knowledge reflects an object in its surroundings and in its historical determinations (how it came to be). Otherwise it is considered isolated and abstract. "Each object is related to all other objects of the world through an infinite number of threads. To know an object, one must examine all its connections, all its sides, but without separating the single sides of the object from the general coherence."[23] But there is also the other characteristic of concreteness: "Marxist philosophical materialism considers the concept of concreteness of truth in connection with the category of historicity. A concept is only really concrete if it reflects certain historical conditions, takes them into account, is related to them."[24]

Truth in the Soviet conception appears at this point as determined by four main characteristics: *objectivity* (adequacy of the reflection); *relativity and/or absoluteness* (preliminary versus definite, partial versus all-comprehensive reflection); *process* (development toward truth in consciousness); and *concreteness* (coherential and historical determination).

FORMS OF TRUE KNOWLEDGE

Soviet theory of knowledge attributes truth to knowledge as such, not to a special form of knowledge and its linguistic expressions. Consequently, if asked what forms of knowledge can be true, the answer is: all of them. Thus, *sense knowledge* (in its different forms), *concepts, judgments* and *reasonings* are equally considered bearers of truth. In all of them something objective is reflected and, therefore, they can all be true.

As to the truth of *sense knowledge*, the following text is categorical: "Not only the forms of rational or theoretical knowledge – concepts, judgments and syllogisms –, but also the forms of sense knowledge – sensations, perceptions and representations – contain objective truth." [25] The text – as so many others – goes on explaining that already Lenin attributed truth to sense knowledge and that this had to be so, because sense knowledge objectively reflected reality.

With regard to the truth of *concepts*, the Soviet theory is somewhat more difficult to understand. As all knowledge – insofar as it reflects something objectively – is true, so are concepts. K. S. Bakradze, for example, says that to deny truth to concepts is to confuse them with words (which can be only true in the composition of a sentence).[26] But a concept is true if its content is real (one could say: if it is exemplified). But if something real must be thought in a concept, it is of course difficult to distinguish it from an existential judgment. Indeed all concepts seem to not only imply, but to be constituted by judgments.[27]

The examples of true concepts one finds in Soviet theory of knowledge are always extremely complex concepts, like capitalism, Marxism, etc. In this sense, concepts are said to be "results of many judgments" and – repeating Lenin – the "result, sum . . . of the history of the knowledge of the world."[28] Thus 'concept' is very often used like 'theory' in this context (as we talk of the Soviet concept of truth).

No Soviet philosopher would deny the truth of *judgments*. But some among the logicians – to the great indignation of all others – attribute

34

truth exclusively to judgments. The Polish philosopher A. Schaff, whose book on *Some Problems of the Marxist-Leninist Theory of Truth* has been translated into Russian, holds that to talk about truth or falsity in all other forms of knowledge besides judgment makes no sense.[29] I. D. Andreev tries to refute this classical view and continues by saying[30] that even in the Soviet Union this opinion is shared by V. F. Asmus[31] and the editors of the *sbornik* on logic of 1956.[32]

Soviet philosophy also speaks about the truth of *inferences* as such. In some cases this is not taken very formally. One repeats this theory with regard to the 'unity of the laws of being and thought'. But it means rather that an inference from true premises to a true conclusion is true, because its parts are true and itself leads to true knowledge. Thus if V. I. Evčuk categorically states that "the inferences of natural sciences are objective truth"[33] it does not seem to mean much more than that. But others take it more formally. V. I. Čerkesov, for example, says that just as the content of thought reflects the content of reality, so do the formal sides of thinking reflect the formal sides of reality. He leaves the question unanswered as to what should correspond to the syllogistic form in reality. But he goes on explaining that form and content are inseparable in reality as well as in thought. Wrong conclusions, drawn from wrong premises with logical correctness are impossible; in this case one will soon discover a logical error too.[34]

Čerkesov's theories are, on the whole, coherent with the system of Soviet theory of knowledge. Nevertheless, some Soviet philosophers certainly hold the opposite view. Apart from K. S. Bakradze, whom Čerkesov attacks in this context[35], there is L. B. Baženov, who keeps truth and logical correctness clearly separated[36] and exposes the Aristotelian view on their mutual relation (*ex falso sequitur quodlibet*, etc.).[37]

Concluding the remarks about the forms of true knowledge, one must say that the majority of Soviet philosophers (and among them the most faithful interpreters of the 'classics') hold that all forms of knowledge – from sense knowledge up to reasoning – can be called true.

LIMITATION OF TRUTH: FALSITY

One may be astonished that the question of *falsity* has not been touched until now. Usually one finds an explanation of falsity alongside with an explanation of truth. A concept of falsity might even serve to throw a better light on a certain concept of truth and thus be a primary factor of explanation.

In the Soviet context – and we are at this point still following the direct context in which our subject is treated – this is certainly not the case. The question of falsity is introduced so hesitantly, the expression itself (*ložnost'; ošibka* – error) used so rarely, that one asks whether there is a theory of falsity at all.

Certainly, no Soviet philosopher would deny that there is falsity, that truth is difficult to find, etc. But there seems to be no explanation for it, as there was an explanation as to why, how and when we have truth. Is it necessary to have an explicit theory of falsity? Is it not sufficient to state that falsity is the opposite or the lack of truth?

A theory of falsity is always desirable, but in the Soviet context it seems even necessary. It is indeed difficult to understand how in a theory, where truth is objective reflection, but the same definition is given for knowledge as such, falsity could be explained. Falsity must then be the same as ignorance. False knowledge reflects nothing at all. Indeed, this position is adopted more or less explicitly. (That is why we said at the beginning that 'truth' often has the same meaning as 'knowledge' and always the same as 'true knowledge').

There are texts where 'falsity', 'error' and 'ignorance' (*neznanie*) are used without distinction.[38] But, as one cannot explain falsity without knowledge, one talks about the 'dialectical unity of truth and falsity (error)'.[39] Thus falsity appears more and more as the partial character of a knowledge, as its limitation. This limitation can be double: (a) from the side of the *object*: because of the complex character of an object, knowledge does not reach it entirely[40]; (b) from the side of the *subject*: because of the limited capacities of the subject, knowledge itself will be limited.[41]

This, of course, makes falsity very similar to relative truth, as discussed above; we can see it in the following text of the *Filosofskaja Enciklopedija* "...even errors on the path of knowledge, resulting from the one-sidedness of relative truth, are signs of the insufficiency of former [knowledge] and the awareness thereof permits the development to a higher step of knowledge."[42]

In summary one must say that the identification of truth and knowledge (truth as the essential property of knowledge) reduces falsity to the limitation (relativity) of truth, to the partial ignorance of an object in an act of knowledge.

CRITERION OF TRUTH: PRACTICE

The rôle of practice in man's life, more precisely of the working upon the objects of nature, was one of the main problems of Marx and has remained such for Soviet philosophy. We cannot go into this problem deeply, because on the one hand it involves a number of the most basic philosophical views Marxism-Leninism has to offer (but the consideration of which would lead us too far), and on the other the problem seems to be dealt with by Soviet philosophers (contrary to the treatment by Marx) at a level that makes even a well-read Sovietologist shiver. Thus, we shall shortly sum up.

Practice is the origin of knowledge. Knowledge is acquired through working upon things. All theory is a generalization from and directed by the needs of practice. But practice is also the finality of knowledge. Knowledge tends to its application and verification in practice. Herewith, practice is the only criterion of truth. This criterion is said to be absolute, insofar as it is objective, relative insofar as it never completely verifies (or falsifies) a theory (theory and practice are in evolution).

Practice is not (or only secondarily) understood as sense knowledge (or experience). Contrary to the materialism of the seventeenth and eighteenth century, practice is understood as an *active* principle of transforming the world.[43] As well at the beginning (origin) as at the end (criterion) of knowledge, practice appears as an active principle: knowledge is realized through working on an object, the object is realized (as changed) through thinking practice.

Practice is not (or only secondarily) understood as individual activity. It is *social practice*, as M. N. Rutkevič – the specialist on the question – strongly underlines.[44] The following text sums up the Soviet concept of practice: "Marxism-Leninism understands by practice the socio-historical activity of people, which is directed toward changing the surrounding world."[45]

INTERPRETATION

Considering again the Soviet theory of truth, as it results from the explicit texts on the subject and as it was exposed above, there remain a number of problems, the Soviet answer to which must be disclosed in a further interpretation of partly the same texts, partly of the more remote contexts of Soviet theory of knowledge. The remaining problems, as we see them, can be formulated in the following way: (1) How can the Soviet conception of the relation between *truth* and *knowledge* be further determined? (2) What is the real *subject* of true knowledge in Soviet philosophy? (3) What is the proper *form* of true knowledge in Soviet philosophy?

From the answer to these questions, as given by Soviet philosophy, an *implicit theory of truth* will result, which can explain most of the obscurity that is left after an examination of the explicit texts.

(1) We said that in the Soviet theory truth appeared as the essential property of knowledge. Both truth and knowledge are defined as objective reflection. 'Truth' is thus often used in the same sense as 'knowledge'.

We already saw the consequences of this view in the theory of the forms of true knowledge and the concept of falsity. We now ask why truth is attributed, as the essential property, to knowledge as such.

One of the reasons is that Soviet philosophy makes no distinction between *meaning* and *denotation*. For them, objective reflection is the reflection of an existing reality.

That a concept is intentionally related to a meaning (*conceptus objectivus*) or that a linguistic expression has a meaning, and that this meaning is not the same as the object to which it may or may not be attributed – such a theory cannot be found in the Soviet context. Concepts reflect reality – that is all.

That factual judgments (or sentences) affirm or deny the unity of several meanings in an existing object – this a Soviet philosopher would never admit. Judgments reflect reality in a more complex way than (simple) concepts – that is all.

Consequently, that truth is the property of that knowledge in which the unity of several meanings in an object is affirmed or denied and the facts correspond to this affirmation or denial – this statement will not be accepted by Soviet philosophers. *All* forms of knowledge, insofar as they objectively reflect reality, are true.

Consequently, the explanation of *falsity* as the property of that knowledge in which the unity of meanings in an object is affirmed or denied, while the facts do not correspond to this affirmation or denial, will not be accepted by Soviet philosophers. Contrary to this theory, in which false knowledge has meaning too, they will maintain their view about falsity as partial ignorance of an object, which is really no falsity at all.

These remarks are merely intended to show, that the confusion between truth and knowledge, the attribution of truth to all forms of knowledge and the impossibility of explaining falsity in Soviet philosophy, is based – last not least – upon the lack of distinction between meaning and denotation. When Soviet philosophers discuss this distinction, they treat it as idealistic, because the meaning of signs are not objectively existing things.[46] Instead, Soviet philosophy describes knowledge as a simple mirroring of existing things.

On the other hand, this primitive correspondence-theory of truth, which explains hardly anything, is not the real theory of truth in Soviet philosophy. Although it is widely exposed in all the explicit texts, its real importance is minor, as we shall see in the following.

(2) The texts which discuss the question of the objectivity, absoluteness and relativity of truth, suggest an examination of the question: what is the subject of true knowledge? One first thinks that the subject of true knowledge should of course be the individual knower. But soon one realizes that there is predominant talk of the knowledge of mankind, of social consciousness. Every-day knowledge of individual persons is hardly ever used as an example.

In fact, already the definition of objective truth as that knowledge whose content is independent of consciousness, i.e. of man and mankind (cf. quotations 8 and 9) shows this ambiguity. The subjective side of knowledge is twofold, of man and of mankind. Soviet philosophy consequently distinguishes *individual* and *social consciousness*. As 'consciousness' is the same as 'knowledge' (cf. quotation 11), the distinction is between *knowledge of man* (individual knower) and *knowledge of mankind* (social knower). But does this really mean a distinction between two different types of subjects of knowledge? Is it not the same individual knower who is on one side individually conscious (as being one), on the other side socially conscious (as being related to others)?

39

The relation between individual and social consciousness depends upon the relation between individual and society in general. Soviet philosophy affirms that society consists of nothing but the individuals and only exists through its individuals. But each individual is almost completely determined by society, above all in those sides of his being which are different from material nature – his intellect and will.[47] One says that "certain forms of society produce a concrete historical person" but that the person is "not only a product of history, but also an immediate participant in the historical process . . ."[48] The text goes on explaining, following Marx, that the person "is the totality (*sovokupnost'*) of all social relations" and finally that it is "the product of the law-bound (*zakonomernogo*) development of society."[49] Apparently, society relies on the individuals as on its material and conditional causes, but individuals are in their essence determined by society. Their relation is quite analogous to that of an organism to its members.

For the relation between individual and social consciousness, this idea is even more clearly expressed. G. M. Gak, a recognized authority on the subject, says the following: "As society, although it consists of individuals and is inconceivable without them, is a reality different from the totality of the individuals, neither can social consciousness, although it too does not exist without the consciousness of the individuals, be identified with the totality of individual minds, but has its special qualitative characteristics. . ."[50] As to individual consciousness, one can read the following determination: "Individual consciousness is the consciousness of an individual who lives in a society and is related to a certain class and is therefore in its essence, in its idea-content (*idejnomu soderžaniju*) an expression of social, of class-consciousness."[51]

Individual and social consciousness must be distinguished. Social consciousness only exists through and is conditioned by individual consciousness. But individual consciousness is determined in its essence and content by social consciousness. The picture of an organism is again the most appropriate to explain what is meant: all movements of my finger are my movements, but all my movements are not the movements of my finger. In this consists the 'special qualitative characteristic' of the whole over its parts.

Social consciousness is understood as the knowledge of mankind ('consciousness' and 'knowledge' are again identified in this context[52]).

All that X knows, belongs (provided that it is expressed) to the knowledge of mankind and is determined by it. But all the knowledge of mankind does not belong to and is not determined by the knowledge of X. Thus, the knowledge of X plays an instrumental rôle in relation to the knowledge of mankind.

A closer examination of the texts on relative and absolute truth and on truth as a process shows the relation between individual and social consciousness in a *dynamic* context. These texts describe the development of knowledge toward absolute truth. It is evident that in most cases one refers to the knowledge of mankind.

In the dialectic of relative and absolute truth, one talks about the historical process of knowledge toward absolute truth. This process is infinite. "Knowledge is an eternal, infinite approximation of thinking to the object", Lenin said.[53] This means "that the total human knowledge moves from relative to absolute truth, from less comprehensive and less exact, to more exact and more comprehensive knowledge."[54]

This shows quite clearly, that 'truth as process' and the 'development of knowledge from relative to absolute truth' do not refer to individual knowledge. They refer to the reflection of the objective by the subjective dialectic. But as this reflection is an infinite historical process, 'subjective dialectic' cannot have the meaning of 'individual knowledge'. In fact, knowledge by an individual knower is neither eternal, nor infinite, nor a historical process. Whilst knowledge of mankind continually progresses (following the development in reality) individual knowledge always has a limited start, can regress, stop, etc. Anyhow, 'as great and genial as a thinker might be, his knowledge cannot significantly transcend the limits of a given historical epoch."[55]

But individual knowledge is of course related to the development of the knowledge of mankind, as the following text of S. L. Rubinštejn shows. "Talking about the process of knowledge, one obviously cannot limit oneself to the individual process of knowledge, to the individual knowledge of the world, one must thereby also view the process of historical development of knowledge; the process of knowledge of the world by the individual is mediated through the development of knowledge of the world by mankind, through the historical development of scientific knowledge, just as on the other hand the process of the historical development of scientific knowledge is mediated through the knowing activity of individuals. . ."[56]

From this text follows that 'social consciousness' is indeed understood as the 'knowledge of mankind' in our context. The development of knowledge is determined by a mutual 'mediation' (*oposredstvovanie*) of individual and social knowledge. But knowledge of mankind remains the determining, individual knowledge the instrumental factor in this mutual relation – as we saw above. Knowledge of mankind is also at each point of its development a more comprehensive reflection of reality than the individual contributions to it.

(3) Mankind as such obviously does not think. "Each thought originates and exists only as the thought of somebody, as the thought of one or another man. There are no other thoughts and cannot be." [57]

But mankind as such possesses knowledge in the form of all objectivized individual knowledge, which is organized in a system. This is the 'system of scientific knowledge' (*sistema naučnogo znanija*), which is the *proper form of the knowledge of mankind*. The following text – again by S. L. Rubinštejn – is perhaps the most significant expression of this theory: "The system into which enter – thereby transformed – the thoughts of the individual, the product of his knowing activity, is the system of scientific knowledge, which is built in the process of socio-historical development. For the thinking of the individual it appears as 'objective reality', which he finds (*prednaxodit*) as independently, already-existing, social property and which he must *acquire* through his knowing activity. In the process of learning, the continuous, socially-organized knowledge of man, the system of scientific knowledge, which matured in the process of historical development, appears to the individual as an object of acquisition." [58]

The system of scientific knowledge is given to each knower as an 'objective reality', which he must acquire, conform himself to. This is not only so in relation to the whole system, but "each member (*člen*) of this system appears no more as the thought of an individual but as its ideal object." [59]

In this way we have not only the knowledge of mankind as a specific type of knowledge. Mankind also has a special form in which its knowledge is embodied: the system of scientific knowledge. As the knowledge of mankind is, in its comprehensiveness, more absolute than the knowledge of the individual, so is the form of an objectivized system more absolute, more true, than the forms of individual thinking: "Concrete knowledge of an object always forms a determined system, a totality of particular judgments, in which [totality] objective truth is contained. Judgment and concept disclose particular properties, sides, laws in an object, but a system of scientific knowledge reflects an object in the unity of its multiform sides, relations, mediations."[60]

It thus seems that the system of scientific knowledge appears as the form of true knowledge *par excellence* and that individual knowledge has to conform itself to the system of scientific knowledge of a given epoch (because the system itself develops), in order to be true.

Engels had said that it was impossible to construct systems after Hegel. Although the world is certainly one system, a totality of many interrelated parts, it would require a comprehensive knowledge of the world to construct systems. As we don't have such knowledge – he said – the one who constructs systems must fill many gaps with his imagination, remains on the level of phantasy, of ideology.[61] Nevertheless, Soviet theory puts the stress on the construction of scientific systems (including philosophical systems) and even talks about the system of scientific knowledge, the expression of the knowledge of mankind. This system of scientific knowledge is in progressive evolution. Thus individual knowledge must be coherent with the actual level of science.

In this way we come to the coherence-theory of truth in Soviet philosophy. Individual knowledge is true, insofar as it is coherent with the actual knowledge of mankind, which is expressed in the actual level of science. A new concept of falsity appears: knowledge is false (or erroneous) if it is not coherent with the actual knowledge of mankind.

This is an implicit theory. But is it not too implicit to be called a Soviet theory of truth? Are the theories, on which it is based (above all the distinction between the knowledge of the individual and the knowledge of mankind) generally accepted, or only by a minority of Soviet philosophers? Is this theory ever applied in a field of Soviet philosophy? The answers to these questions determine indeed, whether this can be called a Soviet theory, or just a speculation based upon certain tendencies of Soviet philosophers.

It is true that not all Soviet philosophers would make the distinctions on which our analysis was based as clearly as those we chose. Nevertheless, one could call the group we described the Hegelian right, which includes practically all the 'dialectical logicians' and many others.

As to the other question, one must say that the coherence-theory of truth (and falsity) is *applied* by practically all philosophers in the Soviet Union. It is mainly applied in two domains: historiography of philosophy and critique of bourgeois philosophy. To judge theories as *progressive* or *reactionary* is a clear application of the coherence-theory of truth.

Marxism-Leninism considers the history of philosophy not as a gallery of philosophers, but as the development of the philosophical ideas of mankind (part of the *obščestvennoe soznanie*), which reflect the development of reality and of society (*obščestvennoe bytie*). Furthermore, Soviet historiography of philosophy does not just describe ideas, it judges them. And yet, it is hard to find a place in this context where a theory is called true or false. Among other qualifications, theories are usually called progressive or reactionary. Whenever we met the terms they were given the same meaning: knowledge is progressive if it is coherent with the actual knowledge of mankind and helps its (historically determined) development. Knowledge is reactionary if it is incoherent with the actual knowledge of mankind and retards its development. Thus a theory like nominalism was at one point of the development of human knowledge (at the end of the middle-ages) progressive, but is today considered reactionary, against the development of science. The same is said, for example, about the theory of mechanism.[62]

But this is further specified. As knowledge not only reflects reality but also society, and as society is divided into classes, knowledge is progressive if it is coherent with the knowledge of the progressive class in society. E.g., today knowledge is progressive if it is coherent with the knowledge of the proletariat, expressed in the system of Marxism-Leninism (some types of knowledge are said to be 'neutral' in this regard). The 'principle of party-mindedness in Marxist history of philosophy' explains this theory.[63] This leads to results such, that relatively unknown philosophers are explained extensively, not because of the level of their philosophical writings, but because of the progressive character of their philosophy.

Progressiveness thus receives the meaning of truth as coherence, as explained above. To be reactionary, means to be false in this theory. "To see the truth, one must look forward, defend the progressive and help the ascending line of history." [64] This coherence-theory of truth does not reduce Soviet theory of knowledge to an implicit idealism. The knowledge of mankind as a whole reflects reality objectively and develops from relative to absolute truth. Therefore, the knowledge of mankind as such is always true, it develops and is modified, but on the whole this process is described as a progressive continuous evolution to ever more exact, more accurate and more comprehensive knowledge.[65]

Truth is – to conclude – the correspondence between the objectivized subjective dialectic and the objective dialectic. Objectivized subjective dialectic is the knowledge of mankind, which is embodied in the system of scientific knowledge. Individual acts of knowledge are only true through their coherence with the knowledge of mankind. 'True' is, above all, the system of scientific knowledge and this at the end of its development.

HISTORICAL REMARKS

It would be very interesting to make a thorough comparative study, analyzing the Soviet concept of truth in its dependence upon and similarity with other concepts of truth in the history of philosophy. In this regard, we must limit ourselves to a few concluding remarks.

In its basic realism and the definition of objective truth, the Soviet theory seems very close to the Aristotelian concept of truth. In fact, Soviet philosophy praises the Aristotelian definition of truth as materialistic and progressive, although it hardly ever uses this definition in its own theory of truth. Attributing truth to all forms of knowledge (also sense knowledge and concepts), the Soviet theory of truth departs from Aristotle. It consequently no longer has a theory of falsity in the Aristotelian sense and follows Hegel in the conception of falsity as limited, isolated and incoherent knowledge.

Dealing with relative and absolute truth, it completely follows Hegel (and Spinoza) by holding that ultimately only a system of ideas can be called true, and one idea can only be so through coherence with and determination in the system. As with Spinoza and Hegel, this coherence and determination constitute the concreteness of an idea for Soviet philosophy. Hegel and Diamat teach that this system of ideas develops towards complete, absolute truth.

Hegel, Spinoza and Diamat would agree on the statements: true is a whole system of ideas (*das Wahre ist das Ganze*); true knowledge is concrete knowledge. Hegel and Diamat would agree in saying: the system of ideas is true at the end of its development (*das Absolute ist wesentlich Resultat*).

The similarity between the Hegelian and the Soviet concept of truth is at this point just formal, as for Hegel the system of ideas is reality itself, whilst for Diamat it is the objectivized subjective dialectic reflecting the objective dialectic. Our analysis shows truth in the Soviet theory as logical, not ontological. Hegel's seems either logical or ontological, or both.

Only a further analysis of the theory of practice as basis and criterion of truth and of the Soviet answer to the 'basic question of philosophy' in general can clarify the ontological relation between subjective and objective dialectics and therefore explain our subject from a content point of view: is truth in Diamat just logical, or both logical and ontological as in all metaphysical monism? [66]

Notre Dame University

REFERENCES

* Originally published in *Studies in Soviet Thought* IV,1 (March 1964).
[1] Lenin, V. I.: *Materializm i empiriokriticizm*. Moskva. 1961. Str. 107–128.
[2] We shall not analyze Lenin's conception of truth as such. A special study on this subject is prepared at the Fribourg Institute of East-European Studies by F. Selvadoray.
[3] Cereteli, S. B.: '*K leninskoma ponimanija dialektičeskoj prirody istiny*'. *VF* 1960, 4, 74.
[4] *Kratkij filosofskij slovar'*. Pod red. M. Rozentalja i P. Judina. Moskva. 1954. Str. 201.
[5] Cf. Levin, G. A.: *Voprosy teorii poznanija v proisvedenii V. I. Lenina 'Materializm i empiriokriticizm'*. Minsk. 1960. Str. 149.
[6] *Filosofskij slovar'*. Pod red. M. M. Rozentalja i P. F. Judina. Moskva. 1963. Str. 176.
[7] Cf. *ibid.*
[8] *Osnovy marksistskoj filosofii*. Moskva. 1963. Str. 258. Henceforward: *OMF*.
[9] *Filosofskaja enciklopedija*. T. II. Moskva. 1962. Str. 345. Henceforward: *FE*.
[10] *OMF*. Str. 261.
[11] Gak, G. M.: *Učenie ob obščestvennom soznanii v svet te teorii poznanija*. Str. 6 – shows that Lenin and Soviet philosophy always gave the same meaning to 'soznanie' and 'poznanie'.
[12] The explicit distinction of the different meanings of 'absolute' and 'relative truth' is ours. Nevertheless, it results from an analysis of the direct context in which this subject is treated.
[13] Evčuk, V. I.: 'Konkretnost' istiny i ee značenie v processe poznanija'. *Voprosy marksistso-leninskoj filosofii*. Moskva. 1956. Str. 123. Cf. also Xasxačix, F. I.: *O poznavaemosti mira*. Germ. ed. Berlin. 1953. p. 94.

[14] *OMF.* Str. 261. Cf. Andreev, I. D.: *Osnovy teorii poznanija.* Moskva. 1959. Str. 250–251.

[15] Cf. *Dialektičeskij materializm.* Pod red. A. D. Makarova i dr. Moskva. 1960. Str. 346–347.

[16] Xasxačix, F. I.: *loc. cit.* Str. 87.

[17] *OMF.* Str. 260.

[18] Cf. Gabriel'jan, G. G.: *Marksistskaja logika kak dialektika i teorija poznanija,* Erevan. 1963. Str. 389.

[19] *OMF.* Str. 260.

[20] Andreev, I. D.: *loc. cit.* Str. 252.

[21] *FE* II. Str. 347.

[22] Vartapetjan, K. B.: *O nekotoryx osnovnyx voprosax marksistskoj-leninskoj gnoseologii.* Erevan. 1963. Str. 239–240. Cf. *ibid.* Str. 262.

[23] Xasxačix, F. I.: *loc. cit.* Str. 102.

[24] Evčuk, V. I.: *loc. cit.* Str. 127.

[25] *Dialektičeskij materializm. Loc. cit.* Str. 127.

[26] Bakradze, K. S.: *Logika.* Tbilisi. 1951. Str. 96–97. Cf. Andreev, I. D.: *loc. cit.* Str. 281–282.

[27] Reznikov, L. O.: 'K voprosu ob istinnosti ponjatii'. *Voprosy logiki.* Leningrad. 1960. Str. 45. Cf. Bakradze, K. S.: *loc. cit.* Str. 99.

[28] Reznikov, L. O.: *loc. cit.* Str. 43.

[29] Schaff, A.: *Nekotorye problemy marksistsko-leninskoj teorii istiny.* Moskva. 1953. Str. 12.

[30] Andreev, I. D.: *loc. cit.* Str. 283–284.

[31] Asmus, V. F.: *Logika.* Moskva. 1947. Str. 70.

[32] *Logika.* Pod red. D. P. Gorskogo i P. V. Tavanca. Moskva. 1956. Str. 72.

[33] Evčuk, V. I.: *loc. cit.* Str. 122.

[34] Čerkesov, V. I.: *Materialističeskaja dialektika kak logika i teorija poznanija.* Moskva. 1962. Str. 98–113.

[35] *Ibid.* Str. 101–102.

[36] Baženov, L. B.: 'O prirode logičeskoj pravil'nosti'. *Voprosy logiki* (sbornik). Moskva. 1955. Str. 107.

[37] *Ibid.* Str. 117.

[38] Cf. Andreev, I. D.: *loc. cit.* Str. 259–260.

[39] Cf. *ibid.;* Xasxačix, F. I.: *loc. cit.* Str. 91.

[40] Cf. Andreev, I. D.: *loc. cit.* Str. 246–247; *Dialektičeskij materializm. loc. cit.* Str. 301–302.

[41] Cf. Andreev, I. D.: *loc. cit.* Str. 245.

[42] *FE* II. Str. 347.

[43] Cf. Oiserman, T. I.: *Zur Geschichte der vormarxschen Philosophie* (germ. transl.). Berlin. 1960. S. 110; Cf. Rutkevič, M. N.; *Dialektičeskij materializm.* Moskva. 1960. Str. 261 (attributes the opposite view to Feuerbach).

[44] *Ibid.* Str. 262, 264.

[45] Kasakov, A. P., El'meev, V. Ja.: 'Ob absoljutnosti i otnostitel'nosti praktiki kak kriterija istiny'. *Dialektičeskij materializm.* Leningrad. 1958. Str. 180.

[46] Cf. Brutjan, G.: *Teorija poznanija obščej semantiki.* Erevan. 1959. Str. 135.

[47] Cf. *OMF.* Str. 132.

[48] *Istoričeskij materializm.* Pod red. M. Ja. Koval'zona i D. I. Košelevskogo. Moskva. 1963. Str. 122.

KARL G. BALLESTREM

49 *Ibid.* Str. 123.
50 Gak, G. M.: *loc. cit.* Str. 28.
51 *OMF.* Str. 561.
52 Gak, G. M.: *loc. cit.* Str. 29.
53 Lenin, V. I.: *Filosofskie tetrady.* Moskva. 1933. Str. 168.
54 Xasxačix, F. I.: *loc. cit.* Str. 90.
55 *Ibid.* Str. 92.
56 Rubinštejn, S. L.: *Bytie i soznanie.* Moskva. 1957. Str. 53.
57 Tavanec, P. V.: *Voprosy teorii suždenija.* Moskva. 1955. Str. 53.
58 Rubinštejn, S. L.: *loc. cit.* Str. 43–44.
59 *Ibid.* Str. 43.
60 Kopnin, P. V.: *Dialektika kak logika.* Kiev. 1961. Str. 391.
61 Engels, F.: *Dialektik der Natur.* Berlin. 1952. pp. 419–420.
62 Cf. *OMF.* Str. 255.
63 Cf. *Istorija filosofii.* Pod red. M. A. Dynnika i dr. T. I. Moskva. 1957. Str. 22–25; *Kratkij očerk istorii filosofii.* Pod red. M. T. Iovčuka i dr. Moskva. 1960. Str. 9–10.
64 Vartapetjan, K. B.: *loc. cit.* Str. 255.
65 *Ibid.* Str. 259–260; Cf. Andreev, I. D.: *loc. cit.* Str. 257; Cf. Xasxačix F. I.: *loc. cit.* Str. 90.
66 For a further elaboration of this problem cf. K. G. Ballestrem: 'Dialectical Logic', *SST* 1965,3, 139–172 and *Die sowjetische Erkenntnismetaphysik und ihr Verhältnis zu Hegel*, D. Reidel, Dordrecht, 1967.

48

RICHARD T. DE GEORGE

THE FOUNDATIONS OF MARXIST-LENINIST ETHICS*

Marxist-Leninist ethics has at last come into its own. After a decade of sporadic Soviet discussion concerning a course in the subject, the Ministry of Higher and Special Secondary Education of the USSR has designated an ethics text for students of higher educational institutions. The book, the first to be so characterized, is Professor A. F. Šiškin's latest work, *Osnovy marksistskoj étiki* (The Foundations of Marxist Ethics).[1] This and the *Xrestomatija* (Reader) of Marxist ethics[2] (which was produced under Šiškin's general editorship) provide ample textual material for a course in the Foundations of Marxist Ethics – a course which has until now been conspicuously absent from the Soviet philosophical and general university program of studies. Such a course has recently been recommended for inclusion in the curriculum of all institutions of higher education.

The first draft program for a course in Marxist-Leninist ethics was drawn up by M. I. Lifanov and appeared in *Voprosy Filosofii* in 1951.[3] A report of the discussion of the draft program was printed several months later.[4] Though hailed as a welcome first attempt the draft was quite severely criticized by a number of philosophers, among whom was A. F. Šiškin who suggested, as did others, an alternative plan for the course. Following the discussion, interest in establishing the course seems to have waned and during the next several years nothing more appeared about it. In 1955 Šiškin published his *Foundations of Communist Morality*[5], which in content largely coincided with his suggestions for the organization of a course, but which was not specifically designated as a text. His proposed criticism of bourgeois ethics was largely missing from the book, however, as well as the proposed neat division of ethical categories into principles, norms and moral qualities. Of course, whereas he had suggested in 1951 that the theme of Stalin's Party as the embodiment of the "mind, conscience and honor of our epoch" be developed, this gave way to a chapter (IV) entitled "The Communist Party – The Mind, Conscience and Honor of our Epoch".

The impetus for a course in ethics was generated anew by the Twenty-First Congress of the CPSU in 1959 (Jan. 27-Feb. 5) which declared that the Soviet Union had entered the period of the full-scale building of Communist society and that one of the major tasks was educating the masses in the Communist spirit of collectivism, Soviet patriotism and internationalism, and the other "lofty principles of Communist morality".[6] On March 18–21, 1959, a conference was called by the IF AN SSSR, the Ministry of Higher and Special Secondary Education SSSR and the Leningrad Department of Philosophy to discuss a new draft program for a course in the Foundations of Marxist Ethics. The speeches, discussions and draft program were published in book-form under the title *Voprosy marksistsko-leninskoj étiki* (Problems of Marxist-Leninist Ethics)[7] and reported on in *Voprosy Filosofii*[8] and *Filosofskie Nauki*.[9] One of the three main papers at the conference was given by Šiškin, in which he began by pointing out the absence of courses and texts in ethics and the generally intolerable situation with respect to the lack of both books and specialists in the field, given the task of Communist education underlined by the Twenty-First Party Congress. The draft program, which had been prepared by a committee under the direction of Professor Šiškin, outlined a thirty-two hour course. It had been discussed previously by the philosophy departments of Moscow, Leningrad, Kiev, Sverdlovsk and other cities. Yet it is interesting to note that the ten themes presented and the order of their presentation correspond so closely to the course plan sketched by Šiškin eight years earlier in his criticism of Lifanov's plan that his direction is clearly evident in the resulting product.

Despite a good number of disagreements the members of the conference recommended approval of the draft program with instructions that a committee of the Ministry of Higher Education study the various suggestions in completing the final course program. Also discussed was the publishing of a *Xrestomatija* and the preparation of text-books in ethics by 'author-collectives'.

How much the discussed draft program was changed as a result of the conference is difficult to ascertain. A draft program – possibly the revised one – prepared by a Committee on Higher Education SSSR and the IF AN SSSR under the direction of A. F. Šiškin was published in *VF* 1959, 6, 178–185. Some of the wording describing the course content in this draft varies slightly (though the themes and the overwhelming portion of the text are identical) from the text published as the draft discussed in March. The uncertainty concerning the status of the *VF* text arises from the fact that though it appeared in June, which is three months later than the conference, the text of the conference and the presumably original draft did not appear until 1960, and the report of the conference did not appear in *VF* until issue 7 (July) of 1959. The matter is somewhat complicated by the fact that the *Xrestomatija* which was published in 1961 and "compiled in conformity with the draft program of the course 'Foundations of Marxist Ethics'"[10] is divided into seven sections whereas a division into nine sections would have been expected, unless the course program had been changed. The division, moreover, differs significantly from Šiškin's book (13 chapters) which, though recommended as a text and though it coincides quite well in content with the draft program, does not conform specifically to the thematic division of the program. It has in fact been criticized by Soviet reviewers as a text-book because it handles in too much detail as well as too tediously many of the questions of ethics.

The two Soviet reviewers, Arxangel'skij[11] and Sadykov[12], both refer to Šiškin's book as a step forward, despite its shortcomings. As the author admits, it covers a great deal of what he had already covered in his earlier book, though the structure is different (and improved) and the concern with the inculcation of the masses with Communist morality is more pronounced and developed. Šiškin makes a greater attempt to clarify the meaning of terms such as 'morals', 'ethics', 'custom', 'principle of morality' and the like than any other Soviet philosopher previously. He develops the notion of the 'relative' independence of the development of morals *vis-à-vis* the material conditions of society and the other elements of the social superstructure, and he gives a reasonably clear presentation of the unity of moral goals and the means of their achievement. He attempts to show how the morals of collectivity, the new morals of the new man in Communist society, follow from the development of the new society. Central questions, such as the moral freedom of the individual person, the relation of personal and collective conscience and obligation, the derivation and justification of ethical categories, the relation of the simple norms of morality to the notion of the development of moral progress, and the elaboration of such categories as 'good' and 'evil' are quite poorly and inadequately treated and have in some cases

51

received better treatment at the hands of other Soviet philosophers (e.g. in Tugarinov's *O cennostjax žizni i kul'tury*[13]). The book is best in its earlier sections dealing with theoretical questions, most tedious in the presentation and application of moral norms and qualities.

As the major statement of Marxist-Leninist ethics, published in an edition of 100 000 copies, and destined as a text for general use in institutions of higher education it is intended to serve as a presentation of the *foundations* of Marxist ethics. It may so function for Soviet students. For anyone except a Marxist, however, it cannot so serve because it assumes and proceeds from the 'truth' of the Marxist-Leninist classics: it assumes the validity of the Marxist interpretation of history, of the distinction between base and superstructure, of the inevitable triumph of Communism, of the coincidence of the aims of the proletariat and those of 'all mankind', of the position of the Communist Party as the vanguard and defender of the aims of the proletariat, and so on. These assumptions are not generally made explicit, but it is within their framework that Šiškin proceeds.

The book begins with a discussion of the subject-matter of ethics (ethics is the science of morals; its proper study is moral teachings, the explanation of the origin of morals, the nature of moral ideas and judgments, the criteria of morals, etc.[14]) and with a statement that the materialist understanding of history is the basis for a scientific theory of morals. This is followed by a general discussion of different types of morals (those of primitive society, slave holding society, feudal society, etc.). There then follows a chapter on the relation of morals to politics, law, art, science, and religion. The three chapters form a unit and are the most interesting portion of the book. From a brief discussion of freedom and necessity Šiškin then presents Communism as the moral ideal of mankind and as the criterion of morality. This is the basis for deriving the basic principles of Communist morality, the highest of which is devotion to Communism; this in turn is the basis for collectivism. Love of the socialist fatherland, love of other socialist countries and solidarity with workers of all countries are presented in one chapter, conscientious work for society in another, Communist humanism in a third, and the moral basis of marriage and family in a fourth. Having dealt with moral principles, Šiškin in Chapter X summarily and perfunctorily turns to the Marxist understanding of the concepts of duty, conscience, honor, and

52

happiness. These are clearly subsidiary considerations for him, as are (surprisingly) the simple elementary laws of society and (not surprisingly) questions of decorum, propriety, good form and etiquette. Then follows a list of the moral virtues and character traits of the fighters for Communism. The last chapter is devoted to the means of educating workers in the spirit of Communist morality.

Šiškin's book raises a number of points which could be discussed at length. His misstatements and oversimplifications of Western philosophical and religious positions are especially disturbing to the Western reader, as are his caricatures of capitalist society in terms of Marx's nineteenth-century descriptions and predictions without the least effort to document their present-day factual applicability. He completely ignores many ethical questions, such as 'why should I be moral?', individual freedom, and the distinction between material, formal and subjective rightness. Even the Soviet reviewers complained that too often Šiškin presents his position rather than arguing to it or defending it. The Communist Party, the supposed vanguard of the progressive elements of mankind, is quoted by Šiškin with authority in moral questions. But he does not make clear whether what the Party prescribes is right because it prescribes it, or whether it prescribes what it does because it is right. This latter seems to be Šiškin's position, but he does not disclose the method by which the Party discovers the needs of mankind, how it determines the moral demands of a given situation, nor how it decides which qualities are the moral ones that should be aimed at by the new man.

There are only two points, however, that I shall examine in any detail. I choose these because they are central and peculiar to Marxist-Leninist ethics. The first is the basis of ethics, the second is the claim that Communism is the moral ideal of humanity and the criterion of morals.

I. BASIS OF ETHICS

According to Marxism-Leninism, as presented by Šiškin, morals have their origin in customs or dispositions[15] based upon the material conditions of life and the relations existing between persons, as well as between an individual and his society, class, state, country, family, and so on.[16] Morals appear only with society because only then do men have real relations with others. In working together men develop thought, speech, society, and customs necessary for working together.[17] Moral views and feelings which thus developed became expressed in principles or norms of conduct.[18] Social necessity and norms of conduct became in turn the subjective need of the individual, his moral duty.[19] As society developed into classes, different classes developed different moral customs. Each change in the conditions of life, moreover, brought about corresponding changes in customs and so in morals, though social consciousness lagged behind social being, especially when a class either within or without a country conserved remnants of the old order.[20] Historical variations in moral concepts, feelings and norms are thus the result of varying economic relations. Each epoch had its ruling morality which expressed and defended the interests of the ruling class and which was imposed on the ruled or exploited class, and accepted by them if they were not conscious of their own needs. If they were made conscious of their needs, however, they formed new norms and traditions. Marx and Engels in discovering the laws of social development discovered those moral ideas which are founded on the development of reality and are expressive of its future.[21] They found this truly human morality, which will eliminate the exploitation of man by man and which will create a society of truly human relations, in the morality of the working class.[22] The founders of Marxism then gave the workers a clear consciousness of their condition and a goal towards which to struggle, namely the goal of Communism wherein there would be no exploitation and every person would receive enough for his all-round development.[23] Thus Marxism, while admitting the class character of morals, holds that Communist morality expresses the highest ideals of humanity.[24] Communist morality is not a relative morality because it is an objectively true, just, truly human morality.[25] Just as mankind will progress to a classless society, so it will progress morally to the state of Communist morals, which will embrace all of humanity.

Now in this presentation there are three major claims which I shall consider: (1) morals are the result of material (primarily economic) relations; (2) morality is relative to historical conditions, though this relativity is of a special type since it is determined by material conditions of life; (3) there is an all-human morality, discovered in its roots by Marx and Engels, which will eventually triumph.

With respect to (1) what Šiškin really means is by no means clear. If he merely means that, for instance, there must be private property before there can be theft and so before theft can be considered wrong, then his claim is certainly – though trivially – true. But he gives no indication of whether, for example, stealing property is wrong because the property owner does not like it, or because the propertied class as a whole does not like it or because of some other reason. Šiškin neither clearly specifies the meaning of 'determine' nor does he show in any concrete case or in any detail how the economic conditions determine morality. The situation is complicated by the fact that he admits that politics, religion, philosophy, education, etc., also influence morality [26]; and that these are also supposedly determined by economic relations does not help matters. Unless the *meaning* of the alleged determinism is clarified, the truth of the claim cannot be fruitfully discussed.

(2) The difficulty just stated infects the second claim also. We know that customs change and that moral norms vary from society to society and from age to age. Šiškin is on firm ground in pointing this out, and he is certainly correct that the concrete circumstances of time and place to some extent affect what is held to be right and wrong. But when he claims that morality is *determined* by historical conditions he must demonstrate it. This he does not do (and indeed cannot do until our first difficulty of meaning is cleared up). Furthermore his oversimplified thesis does not adequately explain the differences between the morality advocated by Stoicism and by Epicureanism in Greek society, for example, nor the continuity of Christian morality in slave societies, feudal societies and capitalistic societies. Nor does he explain differences among individual members of a class with respect to their moral judgments. Citizen "A" may know that his class considers action x to be good and yet believe that it is bad. Clearly what "A" means here by 'good' is not that his class feels a certain way. I am not sure what he can mean on Šiškin's thesis. But it seems clear that Šiškin must explain how the economic relations of his society produce this non-conformist – and in the stablest societies there seem to be such people. The closest Šiškin comes to explaining this is to refer to the influence of past morality. Though this accounts for some divergencies it does not account for all; and these latter are not considered by him.

(3) Behind the relativism of morals, Šiškin seems to claim, there is an absolutism or a morality expressive of the interests of all mankind and

in conformity with developing reality. This morality emerges historically as Communist morality. The difficulty with his position, however, seems threefold. First, to speak of progress implies a criterion by which to judge it. If there is an absolute or ideal norm of morality (and it seems that there must be one if progress is to be judged), then in fact what is moral is not dependent merely on economic relations or conditions. A capitalist may think exploitation of his workers is good because it brings him wealth; and his class might think it good; and together they might convince the workers of it also. Yet it would not in fact be good, if by 'good' we mean anything other than how a given class is 'determined' to react towards certain relations as a result of socio-economic conditions. If the proletariat and the capitalist differ about the morality of exploitation it is not true that each is correct from his point of view and there is no possibility of deciding between them. For Šiškin the proletarian judgment is more correct because more progressive and more expressive of the aims of humanity. It seems therefore that there is a dual meaning of 'good' in Šiškin's position. There is a relative sense of 'good', held by a class or individual, and a truer, ideal sense of 'good' which historical actions fall short of, but towards which the progressive elements of humanity are moving. The relationship of these relative meanings and of the ideal meanings of 'good', 'right', etc. are not dealt with by Šiškin but they clearly pose a problem to which he must speak if his position is to be tenable. Furthermore it seems that both the relative and the ideal moments of the moral judgment must be explained in terms of the economic determinism governing morality. Whether this can successfully be done remains to be seen. My only point here is that it must be considered, and is not in this book.

The second point to be made is that the basis of the ideal of morality in terms of which progress is judged by Marxist-Leninist morality seems to be the "interests of mankind". But neither 'interests' nor 'mankind' is explained in such a way as to render it useful in making moral judgments. There seems to be the assumption that mankind is for some unspecified reason the same as the historically exploited classes (exploiters express their own interests, not those of mankind). Concretely speaking any given individual might be thought to express his own interests. But, according to Šiškin, it seems that while this is true of exploiters, the exploited either express not their own interests but those of mankind or in expressing their own interests they in fact express those of mankind. It is not clear whether this is an *a priori* statement based on the nature of man (which is doubtful since Šiškin seems opposed to any notion of man's 'nature') or whether it is an empirical generalization (how Šiškin has learned of 'mankind's' interests is not clear, unless it was from Marx and Engels) or whether it enjoys some other unexplained status. A hint as to the meaning of 'interests' seems to be given by the claim that all men desire freedom from exploitation. But what else humanity desires or the means by which one determines this is not stated.

Thirdly, we are concerned with the factual claim that Communist morality alone expresses the interests of mankind and is in conformity with developing reality. This claim presupposes certain knowledge of how reality is developing (as well as the intelligibility and truth of scientific socialism). Insofar as the future development of humanity seems problematic Šiškin here seems to introduce an element of Communist faith. Moreover, the coincidence of the aims of Communism and the interests of mankind are at best vaguely stated, and the claim amounts to little more than the statement that both are opposed to the exploitation and oppression of man by man and aim at the free development of all men. These are certainly noble and worthy aims. But Šiškin's appropriation of them for Communism alone is *a priori* and can, I think, be empirically challenged.

II. COMMUNISM AS THE MORAL IDEAL OF HUMANITY AND AS THE CRITERION OF MORALITY

It is on the basis of the claim that Communism is the moral ideal of humanity and the criterion of morals that Šiškin derives his moral principles (principles of morality are its most general and important norms[27], though how one decides exactly which norms are principles is not clear since Šiškin himself has given varying lists), such as collectivism, devotion to Communism, and humanism. It is thus basic to the Marxist-Leninist system of morality, as Šiškin presents it, and so worthy of examination here. Šiškin claims that Communism is the moral ideal of humanity because it creates those social conditions in which the free development of each man is the condition for the free development of all[28] and because only a Communist society (in which man is no longer dominated by personal property, no longer fears other men or sudden ruin or unemployment) can make possible the all-round development of the human person. Insofar as Communism is man's moral ideal the struggle for Communism is the objective standard of the valuation of human acts.[29] What helps the struggle is good; what hinders it is bad.

Now here also there seem to be three points that require discussion. For the claim to stand, the following are required: (1) a clear notion of what is meant by Communism; (2) a demonstration that this is truly what humanity desires (or should desire); (3) the assurance that this criterion can be fruitfully used in making concrete moral judgments.

(1) Unfortunately precisely what Šiškin means by 'Communism' is not made clear. It was of course not made clear by Marx, Engels or Lenin, and has not been delineated in detail by the Program of the Twenty-Second Congress of the CPSU. We cannot therefore blame Šiškin for his lack of precision here. Communism is a future condition, not a present one. Yet if it is in fact a moral ideal from which moral principles and virtues are to be drawn, it must have content. Under conditions of Communism, we are told, there will be no private property, no exploitation or oppression, and each man will be free to work towards the all-round development of his personality. If we were to grant that these are the essentials of man's moral ideal (whatever that may mean), there is still a major difficulty for Šiškin. For, following Marx, Engels and Lenin, he seems to hold that the ideals mentioned above which are realized under the conditions of Communism result necessarily when there is no private property and the remnants of bourgeois society have been eliminated. That the free all-round development of each person follows from the social relations of a non-private property society is not demonstrated by Šiškin (nor by his predecessors). Nor is it clear how it could be demonstrated since the conditions do not exist. That a society in which private property no longer exists automatically leads to conditions favorable to the free all-round development of each person in society, however, must be *shown* if this ideal is to serve as the moral ideal of all humanity and if it is not merely a tenet of faith. More concretely this means that the content must be known so we can judge when we are approaching it. And if someone else, for example, the Communist Party is leading society to this goal, it is necessary that we know how they determine the content of the ideal, lest whatever they determine become in fact the content of humanity's ideal.

(2) If we were to accept the vague content of Communism as meaningful, we would still have to examine whether it is in fact the only and proper moral ideal of mankind. It must be shown that people in fact do desire this (a problem comparable to that on pages 56–57) and that they should desire it. This latter requirement asks for some justification for basing the moral ideal on any given set of 'human' interests as opposed to another set. It is to ask for some criterion by which we decide what is properly 'human' and what improperly human, and it is to ask for some discussion of values, especially of the value of each person. Such discussion is lacking in Šiškin's book.

(3) That the criterion of any moral system be applicable and that it be applicable in all cases is a necessary requirement for any criterion. For if it is not applicable it cannot be used in making moral judgments and so some other standard will have to be used; likewise, if it is not applicable in all instances, wherever it is not applicable another standard will be required. But wherever another standard is required either both will be derivative from a prior standard (in which case Communism could not be the ultimate standard as it is in Marxist-Leninist ethics) or we would have a dual (or multiple) standard, which is quite obviously not Šiškin's intent. But our prior discussion concerning the vagueness of the content of Communism as an ideal infects as well the struggle for it and so creates (at best) uncertainty in the latter's application as a criterion of moral judgment. In many cases it will serve, and these are developed by Šiškin. But in a great many others, including cases (as raised by Firsov in *Voprosy marksistsko-leninskoj étiki*)[30] of sexual morality, for example, the struggle for Communism seems an extremely remote and little useful criterion. The proximate criterion in fact becomes the Communist Party and its pronouncements. But how they utilize so vague a criterion in making their decisions remains unanswered by Šiškin.

My brief analysis does not demonstrate that Marxist-Leninist ethics is untenable. This was not my intent. I do hope, however, to have shown that Šiškin's presentation of Marxist-Leninist ethics leaves a great many questions unanswered which will have to be dealt with either by him or by others. Marxist-Leninist ethics has come into its own, but it still has, it seems, a long way to grow.

The University of Kansas

REFERENCES

* The study resulting in this publication was made under a fellowship granted by the Ford Foundation. However, the conclusions, opinions and other statements in this publication are those of the author and not necessarily those of the Ford Foundation. Originally published in *Studies in Soviet Thought* III,2 (June 1963).

1 Šiškin, A. F.: *Osnovy marksistskoj étiki* (The Foundations of Marxist Ethics.) Moskva. 1961. 528 Str.

2 *Marksistskaja étika, Xrestomatija* (Marxist Ethics. A Reader). (Oščaja redakcija A. F. Šiškin.) Moskva. 1961. 512 str.

3 Lifanov, M. I.: 'Marksistsko-leninskaja étika (Proekt programmy speckursa dlja filosofski fakul'tetov' (Marxist-Leninist Ethics [Draft Program for a Specialist Course in the Philosophy Faculty]). *VF* 1951, 2, 192–196.

4 Čudnovskaja, E. Ju.: 'O proekte programmy speckursa po marksistsko-leninskoj étike' (On the Draft Program of the Specialist Course in Marxist-Leninist Ethics). *VF* 1951, 6, 218–226.

5 Šiškin, A. F.: *Osnovy kommunističeskoj morali* (Foundations of Communist Morals). Moskva. 1955. 320 str.

6 *History of the Communist Party of the Soviet Union*. Moscow. 1960. pp. 719 and 726.

7 Moscow, 1960.

8 Efimov, V. T.: 'Naučnoe soveščanie po voprosam marksistsko-leninskoj étike' (A Scientific Conference on Questions of Marxist-Leninist Ethics). *VF* 1959, 7, 187–190.

9 Lejman, I. I.: 'Soveščanie po marksistsko-leninskoj étike' (A Conference on Marxist-Leninist Ethics). *FN* 1959, 4, 183–186.

10 *Marksistskaja étika. Xrestomatija*, p. 4.

11 Arxangel'skij, L. M.: 'Tvorčeskoe issledovanie osnov marksistskoj étiki' (Creative Research on the Foundations of Marxist Ethics). *VF* 1962, 10, 150–153.

12 Sadykov, F. B.: 'Novyj naučnyj trud po marksistskoj étike' (A New Scientific Work on Marxist Ethics). *FN* 1962, 6, 95–96.

13 Tugarinov, V. P.: *O cennostjax žizni i kul'tury* (On the Values of Life and Culture). Leningrad. 1960).

14 Šiškin, *Osnovy marksistskoj étiki*, p. 14.

15 *Ibid.*, p. 8.

16 *Ibid.*, p. 7.

17 *Ibid.*, p. 58.

18 *Ibid.*, p. 7.

19 *Ibid.*, p. 58.

20 *Ibid.*, p. 109.

21 *Ibid.*, p. 147.

22 *Ibid.*, p. 40.

23 *Ibid.*, p. 36.

24 *Ibid.*, p. 43.

25 *Ibid.*, p. 41.

26 *Ibid.*, p. 109.

27 *Ibid.*, p. 7 fn.

28 *Ibid.*, p. 176.

29 *Ibid.*, p. 185.

30 Firsov, B. A.: 'Glubže raskryvat' ideal kommunizma, lučše otvetit' na voprosy molo-deži' (The More Profoundly the Communist Ideal is Revealed, the Better the Questions of Youth Will Be Answered), in *Voprosy marksistsko-leninskoj étiki*, pp. 82–83.

THOMAS J. BLAKELEY

MARXIST-LENINIST SCIENTIFIC ATHEISM*

I. CONTEMPORARY MARXIST-LENINIST PHILOSOPHY ON THE NON-EXISTENCE OF GOD

Because there is no God and the concept of God is but a pathological indicator of man's alienation in an immoral society, contemporary Marxist-Leninist philosophers do not deem it necessary to pay much attention either to the demonstration of this non-existence or to the refutation of proofs to the contrary. Their attitude is a combination of 'socialist indifference' (it is destined to disappear, anyway) and 'revolutionary activism' (but, the Party requires that one fight it), and their mode of argumentation shows it. There are three principal areas of proof and disproof: the *via negativa* is made up of a quasi-systematic affirmation of the impossibility of the properties and functions traditionally assigned to the Supreme Being, with a rather off-hand use of pseudo-scientific data; the *via positiva* is a simplified presentation of the Feuerbach-Marx argument from alienation; the *via negationis* consists of counter-proofs, each of which is to counter one of the traditional philosophic proofs for the existence of God.

The *via negativa* suffers from one defect which is rather to be expected in the Marxist-Leninist context. The arguments brought against the properties and functions usually attributed to God are said to be based on the data of the natural sciences. This is only partially so. In each case, it is easy to see that the scientific data in question have been given a Marxist-Leninist interpretation before being turned to practical use.

For example, the God of tradition is presented as being immaterial or spiritual. Scientific atheism asserts that such a being cannot possibly exist since contemporary science has shown that all that exists is material. There are two latent premises in this argument. First, the science in question is natural science by which the Soviets usually understand physics, biology and chemistry, but especially the first.

And, this science – so goes the Marxist-Leninist argument – has found no evidence (i.e. sense-verifiable proof) for the existence of any immaterial beings. The second latent premiss is that this 'conclusion' of the empirical sciences is in perfect accord with the basic principle of the 'scientific' philosophy, dialectical materialism, according to which all is matter or a function thereof.

Similarly, contemporary Marxist-Leninist philosophers argue that God as creator of the world is an impossibility. Not only is all that exists material, but matter as such is eternal: it contains its own motion (in the form of real contradictions) and has no need of an external creative agency. Again, contemporary empirical science is invoked as having uncovered no (sense-verifiable) evidence for a former non-existence and subsequent coming-to-be of the material world. And, again, this agrees with dialectical materialism, the basic category of which is self-sufficient and eternally existing matter.

Among the more Marxian arguments for the non-existence of a God, we find that based on man's absolute self-sufficiency. Here it is held that God is not the creator of man because man makes himself through the exercise of productive work. The basic anthropological materialism of dialectical materialism – derived from *Homo homini Deus est* and *Der Mensch ist was er isst* – affirms that what man is is produced in the course of his efforts to form the material world in his image: man humanizes himself at the same time as he humanizes matter and as a result of doing so. Therefore, on two counts man needs no creator. As the culmination of the evolution of the material world, he shares in matter's self-sufficiency and auto-dynamism. As autocreative, he is himself sufficient to explain his own existence.

By the same token it is unnecessary to postulate a God as the creator and guarantee of values. The sole value is man and his aspirations as expressed in the goals of the proletariat and its Marxist-Leninist Party. Only the bourgeois world of metaphysically fixed values, serving to perpetuate the position of the exploiters in class-society, had need of a creator. Man as the proletarian value is not only historically variable but also sufficient unto himself.

Finally, the God of tradition is shrouded in mystery. Even those philosophers who offered philosophic proofs for His existence did not pretend to prove more than mere existence: nothing positive could be affirmed of the nature or operations of this so-called Supreme Being. And, in fact, most believers have, in the past, wallowed in rank irrationalism, maintaining that nothing could be known of the object of their adoration until the 'beatific vision' in the 'hereafter'. Such a being – so argue the Marxist-Leninists – is non-existent. All that exists is knowable (intelligible); if this God existed He would — after so many centuries of religion and theology – be known; He is not; therefore, He does not exist.

There are other arguments of this type used by contemporary Marxist-Leninist scientific atheists, but these major instances suffice to exhibit the basic form: God is traditionally said to be immaterial, to be the creator of the world, of man, and of values, and to be shrouded in mystery. But, science and dialectical materialism have demonstrated that a being with such properties and operations is both superfluous and impossible. Therefore, God does not exist.[1]

In the *via positiva* it remains only to show the origin of the concept of God. Contemporary Marxist-Leninist scientific atheists do this with the help of a watered-down rendition of the Feuerbach-Marx notion of alienation. Alienation itself is rarely discussed as such in the works of contemporary dialectical materialists although it has come into vogue since the West started putting emphasis on the 'young Marx'. In the context of scientific atheism, it is a question rather of the epistemological and sociological consequences of alienation (which we take up in detail below). Briefly stated, the Soviet argument runs as follows: inhuman class-society puts unbearable burdens on man; the only real way of escaping these burdens is the abolition of class-society with its exploitation of man by man; but, previous to the development of the true, Marxist-Leninist explanation of the causes of exploitation and to the formation of the proletariat as the most advanced incorporation of historical progress, this was impossible; man, therefore, sought escape in a figment of his imagination, an imagined ideal man which he projected, objectified and worshiped – as God. This is why God came to be: as an escape-mechanism from the burdens of class-society. This is what God is: a figment of man's collective imagination.

The *via negationis* contains the contemporary Marxist-Leninist philosophic responses to the diverse proofs for the existence of God which have been offered in the history of (Western) philosophy. There are many of them and we will limit ourselves to the list contained in the *Short Scientific-Atheist Dictionary*.[2]

The *cosmological* proof concludes to the existence of God on the basis of the affirmation that the existing world must have been created by someone. It includes Aristotle's argument from the existence of motion to the existence of a prime-mover as well as proofs from the limited, conditional and accidental character of the phenomenal world to the existence of an unconditionally necessary being. A basic flaw of the cosmological argument is that it is logical to ask for the cause of this cause of all things. Besides, if there is something eternal and uncaused then it is material nature, the existence of which is completely evident, rather than a God whose existence has to be proved. But, the untenability of the cosmological proof became fully evident with the advent of dialectical materialism which demonstrated the falsity of the view that a cause is purely and simply external to its effect.

The *teleological* proof is based on the fact that there is purposiveness in nature. It is affirmed that this purposiveness could only be the work of an intelligent agent who, therefore, is the creator of reality. This proof is mortally weakened already by the fact that alongside of a relative purposiveness in nature there is frequent non-purposiveness, squandering and imperfection. Further, in society there is little purposiveness in evidence since the just, religious and innocent (especially, young children) suffer as much or more from social inequity as do the so-called 'sinners'. The invalidity of the teleological argument was demonstrated for nature by Darwin who showed that the so-called purposiveness of nature is due to natural and not supernatural causes. It was Marx and Engels who gave a scientific explanation of the course of history and the causes of social phenomena, removing thereby any basis in fact that the teleological proof supposedly had.

The *ontological* proof was formulated by Anselm of Canterbury and developed in diverse ways by Descartes and the members of the Leibniz-Wolff school. It is a sophism based on the following line of argument. God is conceived as the absolutely perfect concept. If this concept lacked a note (*priznak*) as essential as being, then it would be imperfect. But, since all conceive it as perfect it must have this note. Therefore, God must exist. But, this is all rank scholasticism. In essence, the ontological proof argues from the existence of a concept or idea of a perfect God to the existence of a real being corresponding to this idea. This is illegitimate. At most, the ontological proof establishes the existence of the concept of God, which no one really cares to deny.

The *historical* or *psychological* proof for the existence of God was developed by Descartes. It is based on the 'universal extension' of the notion of God, i.e. on the fact that all people are religious and have a notion of God. It is further postulated in this context that our knowledge is imperfect and limited. Whence the idea of God cannot be its product but must be the product of another, a perfect being, i.e. God. This so-called proof suffers from a fatal defect. In addition to believers, there are in the world a significant number of atheists. What is more, the majority of the world's believers have as the object of faith not a unique, all-perfect God but a series of anthropomorphic and zoomorphic supernatural sub-stances, the existence of which cannot be proved in this way since they do not possess the properties involved in the proof. In addition, science has shown that *de facto* incomplete and limited knowledge is responsible for ideas on the supernatural; but, it has further shown that with the constant perfecting (accumulation) of knowledge belief in God disappears.

The *ethical* proof for the existence of God was developed by Kant. It is based on Kant's affirmation that each man has a knowledge of the universal and immutable ethical law. But, man himself is incapable of reconciling the demands of duty with the search for happiness. The equilibrium between these two can only be established by the completely ethical being, God. Marxism-Leninism makes it clear, however, that there is no universal and immutable ethical norm. Ethical norms come to be in society on the basis of the social conditions in which social groups and classes live. They are dictated by the interests of these social groups and classes, and they vary through the course of history. Society itself is the source of morality which, therefore, requires no supernatural being to explain its existence.

Contemporary Marxist-Leninist scientific atheists use analogous arguments to disprove the existence of an immortal soul (no immateriality), of religious mysteries (all is knowable), of angels and saints (a mythical 'holy family'), and to demonstrate the inanity of religious rites (they are offered to a non-entity). In general, however, the futility of all religious phenomena is considered established when it is shown that they have no object.

65

Parenthetically, we might note that of late a new disproof of the existence of God has made its appearance on the Soviet philosophic scene. It could be called the *cosmonautological proof of the non-existence of God*. This consists in affirming that if there is a God in Heaven, Gagarin *et al.* should have found some traces of God and – more importantly – of Heaven. Since they did not, there is new evidence for His non-existence.

II. THE 'ROOTS' OF RELIGION IN DIALECTICAL AND HISTORICAL MATERIALISM

One of the more progressive elements in contemporary Marxist-Leninist scientific atheism has been the realization that the continued existence and great popularity of religion cannot be denied but must be explained. If God is non-existent and religion without object, then the fact that there are large numbers of believers poses the problem of how man can faithfully adhere to a totally false set of theories and practices. It is to the credit of contemporary Marxist-Leninist philosophers that they have sought out the answers to this question in the classics of Marxism-Leninism and have come up with a more or less systematized doctrine on the causes or 'roots' of religion. As a matter of actual fact this doctrine deals with the 'roots' of both idealism and religion, since idealism is conceived as the refined, philosophic expression of religion. There are two major classes of 'roots' of religion and idealism: the epistemological and the social.

The *epistemological* roots of idealism and religion fall in the area of dialectical materialism's theory of knowledge where all the fundamental categories are defined in terms of the 'basic question of all philosophy'. The basic question of all philosophy is whether matter or spirit is primary. Materialists maintain that matter is primary and that spirit (therefore, thought, God, soul, etc.) is secondary or derived: idealists maintain that spirit (thought, God, soul, etc.) is primary and matter secondary. Thought is both a reflection and a function of matter: as a function of matter, thought is the natural operation of the most complex and highly developed of all matter, the brain. As a reflection, thought is the subjective dialectic, that is, the dialectical reproduction of the objective dialectic (material reality as structured according to the three 'basic laws of the dialectic').

66

Knowledge is sense-knowledge or logical (rational) knowledge; the former is basically concrete, the latter is basically abstract. Truth is relative or absolute. Practice is both the basis of knowledge and the criterion of its truth.

The epistemological roots of idealism and religion are those aberrations of thought due to an illegitimate prolongation of an otherwise normal cognitive function. In other words, the epistemological roots are pathological but the pathology consists not in a basic malfunction but in the non-observance of the limits of a perfectly normal function. The contemporary Soviet doctrine on the subject[3] isolates three series of epistemological roots: those dealing with sense-knowledge; those centered around logical knowledge; and those involving an opposition between the metaphysical and dialectical ways of viewing reality.

In the description of *sense-knowledge* dialectical materialists are adherents of the strict interpretation of *nihil in intellectu nisi prius fuerit in sensibus*, recognize a certain element of subjectivity in sensation, and admit that the subject exercises a synthesizing function in the formation of perceptions. Extremism in the interpretation of each of these leads to a peculiar type of opening for idealism and religion.

The *absolutization of sensation as the primary and unique cognitive given* is one of the commonest causes of idealism and religion. Its basic syllogistic form is as follows: sense-perceived things are ideas; ideas exist only in minds; therefore, sense-perceived things exist only in minds. By absolutizing sensation the idealists arrive at the denial of the existence of anything outside of sensation. Since we know only sensations, it is senseless to talk of things outside of sensation: there is no such thing as objective reality, as matter. Although it, too, holds sensation to be the primary and unique cognitive given (of itself logical knowledge cannot reach material reality), dialectical materialism insists that sensation is sensation of something, that its primacy and uniqueness are relative to the matter which it reflects. On the basis of this absolutization, idealism denies the existence of matter, gives primacy to the subjective, that is to spirit. Thus, the path to religion is cleared of any major obstacle.

In the *absolutization of the subjective element of sensation* idealism commits the cognate error of forgetting that alongside the subjective element there is the objective aspect of sensation, that is the fact that it is the reflection of objective, material reality. Idealists elevate subjectivity to the

67

level of *the* essential mark of sensation. This alienates sensation from its external, material source and turns the thing into a complex of sensations. Dialectical materialism, on the other hand, teaches that the subjective moment in sensation is but the necessary correlate of the more fundamental, objective moment which is its reflection of the material world. The subjective moment is necessary since sense-knowledge is the work of an individual knower whose personal traits and existential situation influence the mode of his receiving external stimuli. But this subjective moment is, by its very nature as a reflection, secondary to that material objectivity which makes up the fundamental aspect of sensation. The idealist stress on the subjective leads – as in the previous instance – to the engulfing of the objective by the subjective and, consequently, to the affirmation of the primacy of subjective spirit over objective matter. The result is an abdication to religious obscurantism.

By the *absolutization of the subject's synthesizing function in the formation of perceptions* idealists arrive at making all that is unique in sensation the product of the subject. Unlike simple sensations which are direct and univocal reflections of the material properties of things in the subjective dialectic, perceptions are groups of reflected properties which have been analyzed and then synthesized by the knowing subject. Ignoring the material source of the data involved and the analytic process which necessarily precedes the synthesizing function, idealists maintain that the essence of the percept is produced by the subject and that, therefore, the subject is the creator of perception. Dialectical materialism recognizes the synthesizing rôle of the subject in the production of perceptions, but insists that this has significance only in the whole context of the formation of percepts where one must take into account the preliminary analytic function which, in turn, can only be based on data from the objective, material world, of which all knowledge is but a reflection. Idealism's isolation of the synthetic function attributes to the subject responsibility for the creation of all that is contained in sensation, thus affirming again the primacy of the subjective, the spiritual, and paving the way for religion's Creator.

Logical (or rational) knowledge has sense for dialectical materialists only on the basis of and in dialectical unity with sensation; it is abstract but nonetheless derived from and a reflection of matter; and although it possesses a certain creativity it is no kind of fantastic distortion of the material reality which it reflects. Idealism and religion can arise precisely through distortion of these basically correct views.

The *absolutization of the distinction between sense-knowledge and logical thought* is one of the most widespread causes of idealism and religion. The dialectically contradictory character of the cognitive process makes it easy for the undiscerning to lay stress on one type of knowledge to the exclusion or denigration of the other. Exaltation of sensation over logical thought, or concentration on the sense-particular to the exclusion of the abstract-general, leads to nominalism and the denigration of abstract thought in general. Over-emphasis on the abstract-general to the exclusion of its source in the sense-particular leads, on the other hand, to idealism of the Platonic variety. Dialectical materialism teaches that the sense-particular and the abstract-general are mutually complementary dialectical contradictories. In addition to the real, individual, material thing, there exists in objective, material reality the universal in the form of the universal laws and bonds which connect all real things into one harmonious whole. And, on the other hand, in addition to the abstract-general, there exists in thought, in the subjective dialectic, the concrete-singular which is a representation in the subjective dialectic of the objective dialectic in all its ontological and historical detail. Thus, there is an interpenetration of the two dialectics such that any separation of the functioning of the two types of cognition implies the destruction of both. Both forms of distortion of the distinction between sense-knowledge and logical thought lead to idealism and religion. The nominalist variety is forced to attribute to sensation qualities proper only to logical thought and, thereby, falls into one of the absolutizations of the functions of sensation described in the previous section. The Platonic variety is, of course, the epitome of idealism. The abstract-general is given an existence apart from its material source and matter is made to depend essentially on thought. This type of philosophy is ready-made for the defense of religion.

In the *absolutization of thought's abstractness in reference to its material source* a basically correct thesis – that logical thought isolates that which is essential in objective, material reality, leaving aside what is non-essential or accidental – is distorted to read that logical thought deals with ideas or concepts of such a level of abstraction that their relationship to the matter which they reflect is no longer of any essential significance.

Concepts are given an independent existence and are treated as if they were the simple creations of the mind, having no necessary relation to any material reality. For dialectical materialism, thought is a reflection and what is reflected in thought – even logical thought of a high degree of abstraction – is always and in every case the external, material, objective reality around us. Even sciences such as higher mathematics draw their basic operators and functors from no source other than material, objective reality. The idealists have been deceived by appearances. Because some sciences can operate for some time on a high level of abstraction, that is, without any immediate reference to a material correlate, the idealists and religionists conclude that 'matter has disappeared', that is that it is no longer necessary as the unshakeable foundation of all human knowing. But, as Lenin has shown, this error grows out of their inability to grasp knowing as an essentially reflective operation. Such an absolutization, of course, eliminates matter as an obstacle to religion and puts religious pseudo-concepts on the same footing as the concepts of science.

The *absolutization of the creativity of logical knowledge* is the counterpart on the level of logical knowledge of the absolutization of the subject's synthesizing function in the formation of perceptions. That it is more serious than the latter is due to its abstractness and, above all, to the great distance by which it is separated from everyday practice. The idealists isolate thought's creative function from its reflective nature and maintain that the contents of thought are the free creations of the knowing subject. This eliminates not only the material, objective world as concrete correlate of thought but also practical, human activity as criterion of the validity of knowledge. The theory of knowledge of dialectical materialism teaches that there is a strong element of creativity (i.e. freedom to separate and combine) in the operation of logical thought. But, it also teaches that, despite this relative freedom, thought remains essentially a reflection of the material world: creativity means freedom to combine only that content which is a reflection of the real, material world. Further, Marxist dialectical materialism has shown that practical human activity, that is, human practice, is the base of all knowledge and the ultimate criterion of the truth of all knowledge. This means that logical knowledge is creative only because of the needs of practice and that the results of its creativity are legitimate only in function of this same practice. By giving free rein to this creative aspect of logical thought, idealism gives respectability to religion's most fantastic creations, such as God, angels, and saints.

Metaphysics and dialectics as used in the context of the epistemological roots of idealism and religion refer to the metaphysical as opposed to the dialectical mode of thought. The dialectical mode of thought is the seizing of reality in its dialectical essence (as presented in Marxist-Leninist philosophy) and is characteristic only of dialectical material-ism. The metaphysical mode of thought ignores motion, isolates aspects which should not be isolated, and is generally one-sided and fixed in its views of things: it was and is characteristic of most non-dialectical-materialist systems of thought. Because they are primarily methodological, the roots of idealism and religion included under this heading cut across the previously treated groups and – to some extent, at least – serve to explain them. The major epistemological roots of idealism and religion which are attributed by the Marxist-Leninists to the use of a metaphysical mode of viewing reality are the artificial separation of the universal and particular, of the ideal and real, and of the absolute and relative.

Metaphysical *separation of the universal and the singular* is due to an inability to see that just as the universal exists in the singular, so the singular exists in the universal. Dialectical materialism was the first to find this, the only solution to the traditional philosophic problem of the one and the many. The singular and universal are contradictories, but interpenetrating contradictories: their nature is such that neither can exist in the absence of the other. Elimination of the universal in favor of the singular leads to nominalism and the inability to give a satisfactory explanation of knowledge and its relationship to reality. This was the course of vulgar materialism. Elimination of the singular in favor of the universal leads to Platonism, divorce from reality, and a rank idealism which neither sees the real, material world nor is able to cope with its problems. One and the other (nominalism and Platonism) lead to religion: the former by its inability to explain the problems which give rise to religion (mainly epistemological) and to defend itself against the on-slaughts of idealism and religion; the latter by its open espousal of a non-realistic, anti-materialistic and fundamentally idealistic position.

Metaphysical *separation of the ideal and the real* is founded on a mis-understanding of the real nature of the relationship between real, material being and the ideal concepts of thought. Here there is no question of an interrelation of interpenetrating categories of relatively the same status – as in the case of the universal and the singular. Dialectical materialism teaches that the ideal is essentially secondary to real, material being of which it is a reflection. Thus, only one side of the categorial pair really lends itself to an essentially idealist distortion. Over-emphasis on the real, objective material world can lead to trouble of the idealist and religious variety only if it is pushed to the absolute extreme of denying the existence and/or validity of the ideal. This is an ultra-empiricism which can lead to elimination of cognition and to idealism by default. But, it is over-emphasis on the ideal with consequent denigration or rejection of the real and material which leads to absolute rationalism of a type which renders understanding of reality impossible and thereby engenders an irrationalism even more dangerous than that consequent on ultra-empiricism. This fundamentalist irrationalism is the progenitor of religion.

Metaphysical *separation of the absolute and relative* is analogous to that of the singular from the universal since it consists in separating two contradictory but interpenetrating categories. Dialectical materialism teaches that the absolute cannot exist except in and through the relative, just as the relative can have no existence except in and through the absolute. This is especially the case in reference to truth. Truth in general is historically determined and limited by the individual knower and, therefore, relative. But, an accumulation of relative truths can constitute an absolutely true statement. Thus, the growth of knowledge is a constant interplay of relative and absolute truths. The same is true of reality where there is an absolute – the essence – and a relative – the properties or accidents. There is no essence without the accidents and no accidents without the essence. Throughout reality dialectical materialism sees the interplay and interpenetration of contradictories opposed to each other as absolute to relative. Over-emphasis on the absolute to the exclusion of the relative leads to dogmatism, which is a peculiar distortion of the mind's ability to know reality insofar as it leaves out all the essential, dialectical relations. On the other hand, exclusion or denigration of the absolute and exclusive emphasis on the relative is relativism, whereby any clear understanding of reality is rendered impossible. Both dogmatism and relativism destroy the ontological and epistemological premisses of a correct, dialectical-materialist understanding of reality, thereby preventing a consequent a-religious explanation of the world.

These epistemological roots of idealism and religion are best viewed as *possible* aberrations in the operation of man's cognitive apparatus. They are propensities which have to be activated in order really to give rise to idealism and religion. Their activation is explained by Marxist-Leninist scientific atheists in terms of historical materialism's interpretation of the structure and development of society. The activating elements are called the social roots of idealism and religion. Historical materialism teaches that human society is in constant evolution. In the course of that evolution social consciousness (the ideologies) lags behind social being (the forces of production and the relations of production). The resulting tension expresses itself in the formation of antagonistic social classes which are defined by their relationship to social being. The reactionary class owns the means of production but is essentially bound up with social consciousness. The progressive class uses the means of production but is alienated from social being because it does not own what it uses. When the exploitation of the progressive class by the reactionary class becomes unbearable, there is a social revolution. History is the history of class-struggle from the classless, primitive society through the slave-holding and feudal eras to the present, capitalist period and on into the final, classless, Communist society. Each of the great religions has come to be in a period of great social upheaval and sharpened class-conflict. Thus, it is generally true that any aspect of historical class-conflict can be and is construed as a cause of religion. There are, however, certain factors to which contemporary Marxist-Leninist theoreticians give greater importance and these are called the *social roots* of idealism and religion.

Fear of nature is the most universal and influential of the social roots of idealism and religion. Especially in societies where science is still in its rudimentary stages, ignorance of the forces at work around him makes man unsure of himself and leads him to seek escape. Ignorance of the forces of nature has a double consequence. First, man is unable to understand and control the natural catastrophes which threaten his existence. In the face of storms, earthquakes, fires, etc. his ignorance renders him incapable of doing anything but running away. More importantly, man is dependent for his existence on the success of his endeavors to transform and control his natural milieu. Disarmed by ignorance, he can but run when nature proves intractable in the face of his best efforts. Helpless before nature, man is incapable of preventing the activation of one or another of the epistemological roots. Thus fear of the forces of nature not only drives man to seek escape from reality, it also releases the cognitive forces which lead him to escape into idealism and religion.

Fear of the blind forces of social development is equally as potent a root of idealism and religion. Before the advent of Marxism-Leninism with its scientific explanation of the working of the forces of social development, man was able neither to understand nor to control the development of production and, therefore, of social being and society as a whole. Man's existence is intimately tied up with the production of material goods, a process which he should be able to control. Ignorant of the true nature of the productive process, he has no choice but to try to escape. Throughout the history of class-society man has been plagued by over-production, economic crises, famines in the midst of plenty and other social catastrophes. In addition, the exploitation of man by man in class-society has stunted culture, caused wars and, in general, tended to frustrate man's self-fulfillment. Rendered unhappy and existentially uncomfortable by all these pathological phenomena he falls prey to blind fear. With the growth in complexity of social relations, his situation becomes completely untenable and fear of the unknown causes him to panic. Ignorance of the laws of social development and panic before their apparent capriciousness force escape into religion and paralyze man's ability to resist the operation of one or another of the epistemological roots.

Class-pressure, that is, the burdens which man must bear in class-society, is also a social root of idealism and religion. The exploitation of man by man brings with it inequality and hatred between classes. This inequality exists not only between the exploiting and exploited classes but also between the politically powerful and powerless, the intellectually endowed and the uneducated, etc. The feelings of superiority and inferiority, and the consequent hatreds, make man's social existence precarious. As long as he does not understand the workings of society, there is nothing he can do to change the situation. His helplessness finds expression in an escape into religion and in a lowered resistance to the operation of the epistemological roots of idealism and religion.

74

Another social root of idealism and religion is the *relative independence and activity of ideology*. Although Marxist-Leninist determinism has demonstrated the essential dependence of social consciousness (ideology) on social being (forces and relations of production), the unnatural separation of mental work from physical work in class-society renders ideology relatively independent of the social being which it reflects. In terms of classes this means that the classes which monopolize mental work are out of direct contact with the productive process and, therefore, are able and tempted to develop theories which do not correspond to the actual state of affairs. This renders possible the development of religion – ideology in its most characteristic form – independent of its lack of reference to any reality, material or social. The way is thereby clear for a relatively independent realization of the epistemological roots of idealism and religion.

Class-interest also plays a rôle as a social root of idealism and religion. Every man in a class-society is a member of one class or another. Because of his social position he tends to defend what he sees as the interests of the class to which he belongs. It is in the interests of the exploited class that the truth about reality and society be known and understood in order that they be controlled by and for the majority. On the other hand, the exploiters are interested in the maintenance of the *status quo*. One major element of this *status quo* is religion, which not only serves to justify the exploiters in their nefarious work but also distracts the exploited from their revolutionary goals. Therefore, party-mindedness demands that the exploiter encourage the development of religion in all ways; for example, by facilitating the activation of the epistemological roots of idealism and religion as well as by increasing the intensity of the other social roots of idealism and religion.

These are the major roots of idealism and religion as presented in contemporary Marxist-Leninist exposés on scientific atheism. The social roots serve as occasions for the development of the epistemological roots which are essential in determining the origin and character of religion as a false ideology. So far, there have been no indications of an attempt to cor-relate the two more closely. Recently, however, some Marxist-Leninist philosophers have begun mentioning a third class, the *historical roots* of religion. Although there has been little discussion of them, there seem to be two main types. The first is the attempt of religious fanatics and leaders to adapt religion to the new requirements of successive historical eras as, for example, the development from polytheism to monotheism. The second is religion's tendency to preserve traditional forms and values, which appeals to man's natural preference for the tested and proved.

In the contemporary Marxist-Leninist doctrine on the epistemological and social roots of idealism and religion we are aware of being confronted with something which is very specific to Marxism-Leninism: few other philosophies even discuss the matter, and none do so in this way. It is legitimate, therefore, to ask if religion can be interpreted at all in these terms. It is true that religious thoughts and acts have human beings as their vehicles. And, since these humans think and are social, it makes sense to ask about the influence of their cognitive activities and social structures on their religious views and doctrines (and vice versa). On the other hand, religion is not just a cognitive operation; nor is it exclusively social. Religion is a totalistic phenomenon: it encompasses the whole man and relates to all of his functions. Why, then, do the Marxist-Leninists isolate the epistemological and social aspects of it for special analysis? It seems that this can best be explained in terms of the nature of Marxism-Leninism itself. Marxist-Leninist philosophy is – when it comes to essentials – an epistemology. All of its terms are defined in reference (direct or indirect) to thought: its terminology is predominantly epistemological; and its enemies are almost always condemned for epistemological aberrations. In addition, Marxist-Leninist philosophy is peculiar in having a doctrine on society as an integral part. Philosophy is, for it, the 'science of the most general laws of nature, *society* and human thought'. It is only natural, then, that Marxism-Leninism should view religion – its exact counterpart – as essentially constituted by these same two factors.

The epistemological factors which contemporary Marxist-Leninist philosophy lists as roots of religion are as valid as Marxist-Leninist epistemology in general, and we have examined this in detail elsewhere.[4] Although it is not worthwhile to consider each of the epistemological roots in detail, it is possible to isolate a principle fundamental to them all, the weakness of which vitiates the whole analysis. Each of the roots is the breach of one or another 'dialectical unity' in the operation of man's cognitive processes. They reduce, then, to the opposition between the 'dialectical' and 'metaphysical' as contemporary Marxist-Leninist philosophers conceive it. The 'metaphysician' views reality in terms of fixed concepts, without motion, without seeing the essential connections between things. If this means anything at all, it says simply that the metaphysician is thinking. I defy the Soviets to produce an unfixed, moving concept! More, let them try to describe the ebb and flow of reality and thought without using fixed and relatively motionless concepts. All the mystical anointment of the dialectic cannot change the brute fact that when one thinks one must use relatively stable concepts or (to keep the anti-concept group happy) univocally defined terms. If the dialectical materialists have discovered a new way in which to think, all we can say about it at present is that it is incommunicable and, therefore, irrelevant to science.

The social roots of idealism and religion are, again, as valid as Marxist-Leninist historical materialism. But, as in the case of the epistemological roots, there is a common denominator, the validity of which conditions the validity of each of the social roots. This is the notion that some kind of fear is at the basis of all of man's religious beliefs and activities. It may be the case that fear plays a not-insignificant rôle in the religious lives of many people: authority uses fear and religion is authoritarian, and it has been observed that the number of conversions rises during and after great catastrophes such as wars. Emotions and feelings have their place and are useful in those places. But they have no place in philosophic discourse. While one may justifiably invoke fear as the initial impulse for turning to religion, this is sadly insufficient when it comes to explaining both the complexity of the religious experience and the tenacity of its hold on man. In other words, if there is absolutely no factual basis to religion and religious thought – if they are purely products of fearful fantasy – then one has to abandon the search for a rational explanation or else conclude that the vast majority of mankind has been composed of whimpering idiots. This account of things, which is merely an extension *ad absurdum* of historical materialism's description of class-society, leaves one in no position to offer a 'scientific' (i.e. unemotional) explanation of many obvious historical facts, such as progress in the arts and sciences, in industry, etc. This is, perhaps, the fatal flaw in the whole of scientific atheism and particularly in its account of the causes of religion: it is fundamentally pessimistic with regard to the basic soundness of human character, and with regard to man's ability to adapt to and control his environment. It is difficult to see how this weakly man is going to be refashioned in order to produce an idyllic society, especially since the refashioning is to be carried out according to the specifications of Marx, Engels, Lenin, *et al.* who were, after all, mere men.

Boston College

REFERENCES

* Originally published in *Inquiry* 9 (1966) 1.
1 For a bibliographical and doxological introduction, see T. J. Blakeley, 'Scientific Atheism: An Introduction', *SST* IV,4 (1964) 277–295, and 'Soviet Writings on Atheism and Religion', *ibid.*, 319–38.
2 *Kratkij naučno-ateističeskij slovar'*, Moskva, 1964. The editor-in-chief is I. P. Camerjan.
3 The best description is to be found in P. Čerkašin: *Gnoseologičeskie korni idealizma* (The Epistemological Roots of Idealism), Moskva, 1961. 238 str. See also the bibliography cited in note 1.
4 Cf. T. J. Blakeley, *Soviet Theory of Knowledge*, D. Reidel, Dordrecht, 1964, 203 pp.

DAVID DINSMORE COMEY

PHILOSOPHICAL LOGIC IN THE SOVIET UNION
1946–1966*

I have been asked to write a survey of logic in so far as it is part of Soviet philosophy, so I shall not discuss Soviet mathematical logic except to mention some basic points about it. Russian mathematical logicians have developed a constructivist school of logic that shares certain methods with modern intuitionism but rejects the somewhat mystical epistemological bases of the latter. Constructivism is interesting philosophically because it insists on using finitary methods and rejects the use of the law of the excluded middle and *reductio ad absurdum* arguments in proving the existence of mathematical entities. Such proofs must be entirely constructive. That is to say, they must use methods like mathematical induction that involve no gaps or points at which an arbitrary choice must be made. Hence there is a strong interest in problems of decidability, computability, algorithms, and recursive function theory. The Russians have made numerous contributions to these fields, many of which have been novel and brilliant.[1] These contributions have long been admired and appreciated by leading Western mathematical logicians.

When one turns to the field of philosophical logic, however, the situation is different. There have been fewer Soviet contributions, and even these have been virtually ignored by Western philosophers. In this article I shall try to point out some of the many developments in Soviet philosophical logic that are likely to be of special interest to Western philosophers. I shall also try to sketch the broad trends that have occurred in Soviet logic during the last two decades.

One reason for both past and present interest in Soviet philosophical logic is that it encompasses two different views of logic, which Soviet logicians refer to as 'formal logic' and 'dialectical logic'. Up to 1956, what was meant by 'formal logic' was more or less the classical syllogistic logic of Aristotle, Port-Royal, and Mill. Since 1956, Soviet philosophers have become quite conversant with the propositional and functional calculi and other developments of modern symbolic logic, and these have become part of what they continue to call 'formal logic'.

What Soviet philosophers have meant by 'dialectical logic' cannot be so readily described, especially to Western readers. One difficulty is that the whole topic of the dialectic now lies outside the mainstream of contemporary Western philosophy. Much of it is couched in a special vocabulary that is unfamiliar to most Westerners except contemporary neo-Hegelians and Marxists. A more basic difficulty is that as of today dialectical logic has no really concrete body of doctrine that can be codified and presented in a concise form. While the Marxist version of the dialectic is more than a century old, the treatment of it as a specifically logical discipline, that is, as a dialectical *logic*, really got under way only fifteen years ago.

The principal reason for this was that until very recently, Soviet philosophy has been largely an exegesis on the 'classics' of Marxism-Leninism: the writings of Marx, Engels, Lenin, and, while he was alive, Stalin. In taking over large parts of Hegel's philosophy for his own system, Marx kept more or less intact the Hegelian dialectic with its three 'laws': the identity and struggle of opposites, the transformation of quantitative into qualitative, and the negation of the negation. Marx intended to write a book on dialectics that would have been a study of logic and a methodology of the social sciences, but his concentration on *Capital* prevented him from writing it. Engels also intended to do a book on the use of dialectics in the natural sciences, but he never completed the manuscript. The notes for the book were finally published in Moscow in 1927 as the *Dialectics of Nature*. Lenin also spent part of his exile in Switzerland writing an analysis of Hegel's logic and dialectics, but dropped the project when revolution broke out in Russia in 1917 and he returned to take over political leadership. His notes were later published in 1929 and 1930 and are known as his *Philosophical Notebooks*. Thus the Marxist-Leninist 'classics' on dialectics and logic are really a relatively small number of short passages from these two notebooks and from Engels' *Anti-Dühring*. Throughout these passages in the classics, there is a strong undercurrent of contempt for classical formal logic, but not so strong as to constitute an outright denial of its validity. Engels admitted that formal logic was applicable to static situations, but insisted that change and development was far more prevalent and demanded the use of dialectics for an accurate description. Plekhanov took a similar view: formal logical reasoning was a special case of dialectical thinking in the same way that rest is a 'special case' of motion. Lenin's writings also regard dialectics as a higher form of logic but do not explicitly reject formal logic if it is used in certain contexts.

Although Soviet philosophers continued to debate the mutual relations of dialectics and formal logic after Lenin's death in 1924, there was very little clarification of how dialectics was to function as a science of thinking. In the Stalinist period after 1931, when philosophical debate virtually ceased, the general attitude toward logic was reflected by the linguist Marr's remark that formal logic was a bourgeois remnant that had been swept away by proletarian dialectics. In a way this was true, for formal logic disappeared from the Soviet educational curriculum. In 1944 and 1945, however, several articles calling for increased attention to logic were published, and in November 1946, the Communist Party's Central Committee decided to begin teaching formal logic in certain Soviet universities and secondary schools.

The logic program quickly turned out to be overly ambitious, for both logic teachers and textbooks were not available. Various textbooks were tried and condemned as 'idealistic'. At a conference in 1948, the logicians promised to make logic into 'a sharply pointed ideological weapon in the struggle against the bourgeois ideology alien to us'.[2] Another conference in 1949 urged logicians to determine the relationship between logic and dialectics and to base their work on the Marxist-Leninist classics instead of bourgeois logical theorists. When Stalin made his famous proclamation on linguistics in the summer of 1950, however, he removed language from the Marxist base-superstructure schema and denied its 'class' nature. The logicians interpreted this as applicable to logic as well, so they quickly recanted their views of the previous two years, indulged in the obligatory self-criticism of that era, and said 'only ignorance ... can explain the attempts of some comrades to call formal logic a partisan, class-bound science (either bourgeois or Soviet)'.[3]

In November 1950, the chief Soviet philosophical journal, *Voprosy filosofii*, tried to resolve the relationship of dialectics and logic by calling for a discussion in print. The series of articles that followed was the first systematic Soviet attempt to delineate what dialectical logic is. It marked the beginning of a fifteen-year evolution that is still going on. The original series consisted of 13 articles that were published, plus a summary of 42 other contributions that were submitted.[4] There were numerous different points of view, but two were more influential than any of the others.

The first view admitted that both formal and dialectical logic existed, but not as two separate logics. Formal logic was said to deal with simple, stable phenomena, which it views in an abstract and static way. Dialectical logic, on the other hand, was considered capable of dealing with a complex and developing reality and could so account for motion and change; thus it was a higher form of thinking. Formal logic was said to be a lower level of logic, being to dialectical logic what arithmetic is to the integral calculus.

The second point of view was a defense of formal logic undertaken by K. S. Bakradze and N. I. Kondakov. They maintained that there are not two logics, one dialectical and one formal; rather, there is only one logic, and it is formal logic. It is concerned with the *forms* of correct reasoning. Dialectical logic is nothing more than dialectics, and coincides with the theory of knowledge, as Lenin had pointed out repeatedly in his *Philosophical Notebooks*. Thus dialectics is concerned with the *content* of thought rather than its form.

An editorial in the final issue of *Voprosy filosofii* for 1951 attempted to give an official decision on the discussion by more or less upholding the first view and its contention that dialectical logic was qualitatively a higher form of thinking.[5] Nevertheless, the editorial took note of the value of formal logic as well, so that as a result formal logicians had the opportunity to continue with their work. During the next few years, the dialectical logicians tried to work out the details of the field for which they had secured official support. Meanwhile, the formal logicians increased their published output, and within a few years of Stalin's death in 1953 had produced a number of texts. The most important of these were by D. P. Gorskij, P. V. Tavanec, Bakradze, and Kondakov. All were basically expositions of formal logic as it was just prior to the introduction of symbolic logical methods. The books by Kondakov and Bakradze were severely attacked by the pro-dialectic editors of *Voprosy filosofii* in 1955, but a number of formal logicians supported them, and Bakradze and Kondakov wrote spirited defenses of their views and got them published in *Voprosy filosofii* under the title 'Against Unscientific and Malevolent Criticism'.[6]

In September 1956, a regularly scheduled seminar on formal logic began meeting at the Institute of Philosophy in Moscow. I have attended a number of its sessions, beginning in 1957; a surprisingly broad range of topics in both pure and applied logic are discussed carefully, and the quality of the papers presented is uniformly high. In 1958 a conference was held to discuss a re-organization to improve the logic program at Moscow University, where most of the logicians were being trained. A rigorous five-year logic curriculum, far more ambitious than any existing American one, was proposed but has not yet been fully implemented.[7] At the same conference the logicians expressed a desire to publish a journal of their own, but that also has yet to appear. Instead, most articles on logic continue to be published in *Voprosy filosofii* or in collected volumes of essays on logic that have been appearing at the rate of about one per year since 1959.

Simultaneous with these developments in formal logic during the late 1950s, the Soviet Union rapidly increased its interest in the field of cybernetics. The Soviet usage of the term 'cybernetics' is quite broad, and covers not only electronic computers and automated control systems, but information theory in communication networks and biological organisms, programmed learning, economic input-output theory, information retrieval, operations research, and a number of other technologically important fields.[8] Inasmuch as many of these fields involve application of symbolic logical techniques, the importance of formal logic rose correspondingly during this period.

This has been reflected in the changing attitudes of the dialecticians who had been quite critical of formal logic during the 1950–51 discussions. There is no longer criticism of formal logic or its methods, but rather of what are considered to be unwarranted generalizations concerning its scope and capabilities in the philosophical and scientific realm. A broadly based consensus has been reached among dialectical logicians concerning the relationship between dialectical logic and formal logic. It evolved during the late 1950s and has received its most persuasive presentation in two collective volumes published in 1962.[9]

According to this viewpoint, which is basically epistemological in its orientation, formal logic is an abstraction from the constant change and motion in the objective real world. By making such abstractions, it provides us with forms of thought that are free from contradiction and uses concepts that are stable and precisely defined. Thus formal logic is a valuable tool, but should not be considered as a complete or final schema for representing reality. To assume that the real world operates according to the laws of formal logic and that material entities are as static as the concepts that formal logic uses would be an unwarranted and metaphysical 'absolutization' of formal logic. The correct viewpoint is regarded as the following. In order to describe the change that takes place in the real world, it is necessary to have a dialectical logic that uses 'plastic', 'flowing' concepts. Moreover, when formal logic completely eliminates contradictions from its systematic formulations, it prevents itself from dealing with the 'objective contradictions' in the real world that are considered the root of all motion and change. Therefore a logic incorporating the laws of the dialectic is necessary to supplement the abstract and essentially restricted methods of formal logic. The latter remains, however, the logic of correct reasoning and it is useful in providing deductive systems and other means of analyzing relationships between 'fixed' concepts.

This consensus is shared to a large degree by the formal logicians themselves, most of whom are interested in non-epistemological topics that are amenable to formalization, and they readily leave other problems to the dialectical logicians. Moreover, it should be emphasized that the dialectical logicians and formal logicians are not members of opposing camps. Several logicians, Gorskij and Tavanec especially, are equally versatile in both fields and have written on some of the more important problems in dialectical logic.

The formal logicians have been working on many different types of problems during the last eight years. Some of their work, such as A. A. Zinov'ev's articles on the logic of connections, and the numerous writings on the cybernetic applications of formal logic, are in the same class as the works of the Soviet mathematical logicians.[10] Some of the technical works are closely related to traditional philosophical problems, however. Zinov'ev has raised some intriguing philosophical questions about many-valued logics in two books and several articles.[11] He has also given attention recently to problems of entailment and strong implication, and has proposed a set of axiomatized systems of entailment abstracted from informal logical intuition.[12] Causal implication has also received attention from V. S. Švyrev, whose work on inductive logic and other problems is consistently outstanding.[13] Modern algebraic treatments of syllogistic have been worked out in several articles by Zinov'ev, A. L. Subbotin, and V. A. Smirnov, another consistently good writer.[14] Zinov'ev has explored the possibilities of applying modal logic to scientific methodology, and there have also been similar studies of probability logic.[15] V. N. Sadovskij has done several analyses of the relationships between the axiomatic and deductive method and its significance for scientific methodology.[16]

Besides these contemporary topics, there is a good deal of interest in the history of logic, especially in the works of pre-revolutionary Russian logicians like Poreckij and Vasil'ev who respectively developed canonical normal forms and many-valued logics before these were treated in the West.[17] Aristotle's logic, as treated using modern symbolic methods, and Frege's logical works have been the subject of numerous studies. The logical views of Western positivists, pragmatists and operationalists continue to be given close attention from both an historical and a critical philosophical viewpoint. There are half a dozen studies on the semantic conception of truth alone.[18]

Let us return now to the dialectical logicians, who spent the latter half of the 1950s endeavoring to define the subject-matter of their activities. In April 1958 a conference was held in Moscow on 'The Problems of Dialectical Contradictions in the Light of Contemporary Science and Practice'.[19] Since 1959 there has been a steady flow of works on dialectical logic, the most important of which are by M. N. Alekseev, P. V. Kopnin, and B. M. Kedrov.[20] There is still no uniformity of opinion among them on exactly what dialectical logic is, but one can summarize some of the basic points of difference.

One group contends that there is a specifically dialectical type of thinking, and that dialectical logic studies the special forms of dialectical concepts and dialectical reasoning. The most outspoken supporter of this viewpoint is V. I. Čerkesov, but his latest work has been subjected to a great deal of criticism by other dialectical logicians. S. B. Cereteli is said to be working on a dialectical logical calculus, but the project is accorded little chance of success. The most viable version of this viewpoint has been developed by Alekseev, whose basically epistemological interests lead him to differentiate between dialectical thinking and the dialectic of thought, a complex but potentially interesting distinction.

The predominant viewpoint among the dialectical logicians, shared in varying degrees by Kopnin and Kedrov, is that the subjective dialectic in the mind 'reflects' the objective dialectical processes in the real world, and that dialectical logic is concerned with developments in both realms, as well as how they relate to each other. This essentially correlates logic with epistemology, which is in accordance with Lenin's thesis that logic, dialectic and the theory of knowledge coincide.

When one looks at these developments in general outline, one gets the impression that the basic conception of the dialectic in its current form is not radically different from the stage in which Engels and Lenin left it. Given the veneration with which Engels and Lenin are officially regarded in the Soviet Union, many dialecticians would consider this to be correct.

While there may not have been major innovations in the basic doctrines of the dialectic, there have been recent trends that tend to emphasize certain developments more than others. For example, there is less of a fixation on contradictions and the central rôle they are said to play in nature and society. The three laws of the dialectic still receive a good deal of attention from certain philosophers, but there is also growing interest in exploring the wide variety of regularities and interconnections among the natural phenomena discovered by modern science that may not be fully exhausted by concentration on these three laws.

A number of dialecticians have also stated that many of the categories of the dialectic, such as necessity and chance, abstract and concrete, possibility and actuality, could benefit from some reworking in the light of modern scientific knowledge. A schema of categories of this sort is not generally part of the working technique of most modern Western philosophers except for the neo-Thomists, but there is no intrinsic reason why such a schema might not be fruitfully applied given sufficient imagination and flexibility. Contemporary Soviet dialecticians are confident that their categories incorporate this flexibility, and they have made numerous pledges to not only rework the traditional categories and make concrete applications of them to science, but also to investigate new categories that more closely reflect some of the problems of modern science.

One volume of such investigations has already been published.[21] In a cautious but original fashion, it deals with continuity-discontinuity, attraction-repulsion, finity-infinity, symmetry-asymmetry and a number of other categories not usually mentioned in the dialectical literature.

However, there is still a considerable way to go before the pledges mentioned above can be considered to have been successfully fulfilled.

There is also more of a tendency to provide concrete scientific evidence to support and illuminate philosophical theses concerning the dialectic. For example, a recent book on dialectical logic and scientific knowledge makes novel use of data from psychology, anthropology and other sciences.[22]

The most interesting trend, however, is one that bears resemblances to the trend that has been taking place among Western logicians. A recapitulation of the Western trend may be helpful before we start to make comparisons.

In the last twenty years, English-speaking philosophers have become increasingly disenchanted with the logical positivists' views on logic and language. Not only has language turned out, upon close examination, to be a far more subtle instrument of communication than the positivists had thought, but these subtleties, which the positivists were content to ignore, are extremely important. Moreover, language has turned out to have a far greater variety of significant uses than can be compressed into any formal calculus of statements. The relevance of formalized logic to the solution of most philosophical problems is now regarded as quite questionable.

There is also growing evidence that formal calculi have limits even as models of logical reasoning. As Strawson and Toulmin have carefully shown, certain attempts to reduce perfectly good arguments to a formalized version using the ordinary quantifiers and connectives of symbolic logic often result in paradoxes or even plain absurdities. Both feel that 'logic' must be understood in a much broader sense than it has been recently, and Toulmin in particular believes that the future development of logical theory will involve a *rapprochement* between logic and epistemology.

When faced with this rebellion, some logicians took the position that what they were really doing was developing formal constructions that had intrinsic interest even if they were not representative of any natural language or process of reasoning. But other logicians, Quine being one example, have contended that their calculi should be regarded as attempts to reconstruct schematically the language of science, which they say is more precise and systematic than natural languages. It is the contention of these formal reconstructionists that scientific theories are best

87

understood by recasting them in neat formal calculi whose properties can then be explored by applying the techniques of modern symbolic logic.

Yet in recent years, even this position has come under fire, and many philosophers of science have come to the reluctant conclusion that the many years of extensive efforts to formalize scientific theories have contributed very little to our understanding of the way in which those theories are developed or the nature of the rôles they play in science. Most of the problems that we are really interested in solving, such as the nature of scientific explanation, remain without definitive solutions. The attempts at formalization have tended instead to generate problems that are irrelevant to the issues at stake.

The formalizers claim that the simpler logical calculi *avoid* many of the problems inherent in the non-formalized versions. But it is a moot point whether a language can be complex and rich enough to perform adequately the tasks demanded of it without simultaneously containing the snares that produce the puzzles and problems. It is likely that if a theory is simple enough to be accurately represented by a formal calculus, then the formalization is probably superfluous: the structure of the original theory will be perspicuous enough to begin with. On the other hand, if the original theory is highly complex, then the formal calculus will probably have to have such a correspondingly high degree of complexity as to sacrifice whatever advantages the formalization was supposed to gain.

Moreover, avoiding a problem is not the same thing as solving it. Since most of the problems in the methodology of science concern the normal usage of scientific language, the problem will probably have to be solved within the contexts of that usage. The tactic of 'avoiding' them by switching to some artificial calculus on another level is at best a temporary expedient that only postpones the inevitable.

Instead of resorting to formalization, the leading philosophers of science today like Putnam, Bromberger, Feyerabend, Hanson, Toulmin and Scriven prefer to use more informal methods. Their informal approach tries to pay close attention to the contexts in which the theory or concept under consideration is being used. It then compares that usage with other similar contexts in order to illuminate the basic function and nature of the theory or concept. This approach also emphasizes that scientific theories are not static and completed things: they develop, and are related to lots of other things that are going on. As theories change, their functions change too, and so do the meanings of the concepts that are embedded in them. Knowing a theory's history is often important in discovering how the theory's key concepts and hypotheses relate both to each other and also to other theories at various times in its development.

When one looks at the recent work of Soviet logicians, both dialectical and formal, one finds that they also have come to realize that formalized techniques have definite limits and that it is desirable to try more informal methods in logic. The convergence of the Western and Soviet attitudes is all the more remarkable because they have developed independently of one another. Soviet dialectical logicians, of course, have always maintained that the positivist program was doomed to failure. More recently, however, they have developed within their own field a range of informal techniques that puts them in a position similar to the anti-positivist attitudes that have evolved in the West.

For their part, Soviet formal logicians have spent a great deal of time examining the various formalizations attempted by the logical positivists, and have reached their conclusions about the limits of this approach independently of the criticisms that have been made here in the West. (The exception is the critiques made by Hempel, whose work is frequently cited by Soviet philosophers, whereas that of Toulmin, Hanson and more informal logicians remains ignored.)

Švyrev, who has written a number of excellent critiques of the positivist attempts to develop a logic of science, has concluded that the positivists' principal error lay in their almost complete reliance on mathematical logical methods to investigate scientific knowledge.[23] Since Soviet formal logicians have no such illusions[24], it is unlikely that they will get involved in any such fruitless ventures as trying to symbolically axiomatize biology, etc.

Soviet logicians of science are currently working on a wide range of problems. For example, many of them feel that the positivists were wrong in dismissing the problem of scientific discovery as a totally psychological and therefore non-logical problem. They are trying to determine whether or not there can be any sort of 'logic of discovery'.

They are also investigating how models and modeling techniques are used in scientific theorizing, and some studies are being made of reasoning by analogy.[25] Gorskij has written a very worthwhile book on the rôle of abstraction in concept formation, and has followed it up with studies on the types of abstraction and idealization that are used in science.[26] His latest work deals with different methods of definition and their relative significance in scientific theory construction.[27] The logical relationships between the theoretical and empirical levels in science, as well as the question whether the distinction is a meaningful one, have received extensive attention from Zinov'ev, Smirnov and Švyrev.[28]

In general, the sorts of problems that Soviet dialectical and formal logicians are probing in the logic of science are very similar to current research in America and Britain. The chief exception is the problem of scientific explanation, but the one Soviet study done so far is quite promising.[29]

As the interest in informal methods in the logic of science has grown, dialectical logic has played its rôle through three trends that will be significant also for its future development. These trends have emphasized the rôle of dialectical logic (1) as a *content-oriented* logic (as contrasted with formal logic which is basically form-oriented) that considers contexts and other semantic and pragmatic factors[30]; (2) as a *genetic* logic that takes into account the historical aspects of what it analyzes; and (3) as a logic and methodology of science as science *develops*, instead of as a 'logic of the finished research report' (to use Hanson's terms).[31]

The convergence of these trends with the informal and anti-positivist movement in contemporary Western logic and methodology of science is worthy of close attention from both Western and Soviet logicians.

Another encouraging trend is the strong effort to involve Soviet scientists in solving problems of scientific methodology. Seminars on methodology now meet regularly at all the scientific institutions of the Academy of Sciences. There have been four national conferences on logic and scientific methodology: two in Tomsk in 1960 and 1963, one in Kiev in 1962, and one in Novosibirsk in 1964. Half a dozen volumes on scientific methodology have appeared in the last three years. As a result of these efforts, there is now a great deal of contact between scientists and the logicians and methodologists. Such close contacts cannot help but result in more significant contributions to the logic of science.

In conclusion, when one looks at the status of Soviet logic today and compares it with that of fifteen years ago, the progress that has been made is truly remarkable. Soviet logicians faced some difficult problems in

1950, most of which have now been successfully overcome. Today the Russians have a thriving school of logicians that outranks that of any other nation except America. Its methodological pluralism is basically a healthy advantage, and what is most significant is that the problems Soviet logicians are working on are the really important ones that face logic today.

Cornell University

REFERENCES

* Originally published in *Inquiry* 9 (1966) 1, under the title: 'Current Trends in Soviet Logic'.

Soviet philosophers have published more than a thousand articles and a hundred books on dialectical and formal logic since 1946. In order to keep the references down to a printable size, I have restricted most of my citations to articles printed either in the chief philosophical journal or in the two collections of essays cited in the bibliography, both of which are being translated into English. The abbreviations follow the notes below.

[1] Comprehensive reviews of these contributions by myself and others may be found in the *Journal of Symbolic Logic*.

[2] *VF* 1949, 1, 368.

[3] *VF* 1950, 2, 211.

[4] See *VF* 1951, 5, 153–63 for a summary of the discussion.

[5] *VF* 1951, 6, 143–9.

[6] For the editorial attack, see *VF* 1955, 3, 158–71; for replies by Bakradze and Kondakov and the editors' rebuttal, see *VF* 1956, 2, 218–36.

[7] For complete details of this 1958 conference and the proposed curriculum, see my article in *SST*, II,1, 21–36.

[8] For further references to Soviet work in cybernetics, see my bibliography in *SST*, IV,2, 142–61.

[9] See the articles by P. V. Kopnin and P. V. Tavanec (pp. 7–62) and B. M. Kedrov (pp. 63–218) in *Dialektika i logika – Zakony myšlenija*, Izd. Akademii Nauk SSSR, Moscow 1962, 336 pp. See also the articles by D. P. Gorskij (pp. 5–41) and Kedrov (pp. 42–141) in the companion volume *Dialektika i logika – Formy myšlenija*, Izd. Akademii Nauk SSSR, Moscow 1962, 312 pp.

[10] For a list of Zinov'ev's articles on the logic of connections, see pp. ix–xi of the English translation cited in the next note.

[11] A. A. Zinov'ev, *Filosofskie problemy mnogoznačnoj logiki*, Izd. Akademii Nauk SSSR, Moscow 1960, 139 pp. Zinov'ev prepared a special edition of this book which was translated by Guido Küng and myself. A. A. Zinov'ev, *Philosophical Problems of Many-Valued Logic*, D. Reidel, Dordrecht 1963, 155 pp.; see also A. R. Turquette's review of it in the *Journal of Symbolic Logic*, 29,4, 213–14. Other articles by Zinov'ev on many-valued logic appear in *VF* 1959, 3, 131–6, and *FVSFL*, pp. 111–39.

[12] A. A. Zinov'ev, *Logika vyskazyvanij i teorija vyvoda*, Izd. Akademii Nauk SSSR, Moscow 1961, 152 pp.; see also his article on logical and physical entailment in *PLNP*, pp. 87–150.

[13] See Švyrev's article on causal implication in *Logičeskie issledovanij*, Izd. Akademii

Nauk SSSR, Moscow 1959, 466 pp., pp. 139–58, and his article on inductive logic in *VF* 1961, 3, 74–85.

[14] On syllogistics, see Zinov'ev's article in *Problemy logiki*, Izd. Akademii Nauk SSSR, Moscow 1963, 151 pp., pp. 38–65; Smirnov's article on pp. 64–83 of the same volume; Smirnov's article in *Naučnye doklady vysšej školy – Filosofskie nauki*, 1959, 3, 80–88; and Subbotin's article on pp. 89–94 of the same issue.

[15] Zinov'ev's article on modal logic is in *VF* 1964, 8, 88–95; G. I. Ruzavin has an article on probability logic in *PLNP*, pp. 200–49.

[16] For Sadovskij's articles on deductive method, see *VF* 1963, 3, 63–75; *FVSFL*, pp. 215–62; and *PLNP*, pp. 151–99. See also Smirnov's article on the 'genetic' method in logic in *FVSFL*, pp. 263–84.

[17] See Smirnov's article on Vasil'ev in *Očerki po istorii logiki v Rossii*, Izd. Moskovskogo Universiteta, Moscow 1962, 258 pp., pp. 242–57; for a favorable appreciation of Vasil'ev as progenitor of many-valued logic, see my review in the *Journal of Symbolic Logic*, 30,3, 402–4.

[18] For example, Tavanec's article in *FVSFL*, pp. 140–51. For bibliographies by W. F. Boeselager on general Soviet works on neopositivism, see *SST*, III,3, 230–42, and IV,1, 81–84.

[19] A commentary on the conference and German translations of some of the papers by Zinov'ev and others appear in N. Lobkowicz (Ed.), *Das Widerspruchsprinzip in der neueren sowjetischen Philosophie*, D. Reidel, Dordrecht 1959, 89 pp.

[20] M. N. Alekseev, *Dialektika form myšlenija*, Izd. Moskovskogo Universiteta, Moscow 1959, 282 pp.; P. V. Kopnin, *Dialektika kak logika*, Izd. Kievskogo Universiteta, Kiev 1961, 448 pp.; B. M. Kedrov, *Edinstvo dialektiki, logiki i teorii poznanija*, Gospolitizdat, Moscow 1963, 295 pp. See also the two volumes cited in note 9.

[21] *Nekotorye kategorii dialektiki*, Rosvuzizdat, Petrozavodsk 1963, 134 pp. Produced by the philosophy department at the Gorky University of the Urals in Sverdlovsk. The circumstances of its publication are somewhat reminiscent of the earlier *magnum opus* on categories that was first tried out shortly after Stalin's death under the title of *Kategorii dialektičeskogo materializma* as a publication of a pedagogical institute in Jaroslavl'. (*Učenye zapiski Jaroslavskogo gosudarstvennogo pedagogičeskogo instituta imeni K. D. Ušinskogo*, Vypusk XVI (XXVI), Jaroslavskoe knižnoe izd., Jaroslavl' 1954, 292 pp.) After some of its sections had been omitted or reworked, it was accepted and republished in Moscow in 1956 by Gospolitizdat in a 390-page edition under the title of *Kategorii materialističeskoj dialektiki*.

[22] Ž. Abdil'din, A. Kasymžanov, L. Naumenko, M. Bakanidze, *Problemy logiki i dialektiki poznanija*, Izd. Akademii Nauk Kazahskoj SSR, Alma-Ata 1963, 385 pp.

[23] V. S. Švyrev, 'K voprosu o putjah logičeskogo issledovanija myšlenija', *Doklady Akademii Pedagogičeskih Nauk RSFSR*, 1960, 2, 69–75; see p. 73.

[24] See for example V. A. Smirnov, 'Rol' simvolizacii i formalizacii v naučnom poznanii', *Nekotorye voprosy leninskogo filosofskogo nasledstva* (*Trudy Tomskogo gosudarstvennogo universiteta imeni V. V. Kujbyševa*, Tom 149, Tomsk 1960, 192 pp.), pp. 61–65. See also Zinov'ev's article on pp. 223–70 of the second volume cited in note 9 above, and the following article by V. S. Švyrev, 'Nekotorye problemy primenenija simvoličeskoj logiki k analizu estestvennonaučnogo znanija', *Problemy metodologii i logiki nauk* (*Učenye zapiski Tomskogo Gosudarstvennogo Universiteta imeni V. V. Kujbyševa*, No. 41, Tomsk 1962, 193 pp.), pp. 64–72. This volume contains the papers given at the first national conference on logic and methodology, held in 1960. For an account of the conference, see my article in *SST*, II,1 (March 1962), 21–36. Other articles on the

possibilities and limitations of formal logical techniques in philosophy and scientific methodology appear in *FVSFL* by Tavanec (pp. 3–15) and Subbotin (pp. 91–110); by Tavanec in *VF* 1964, 3, 69–77; by Švyrev in *VF* 1963, 7, 97–109; by Tavanec and Švyrev in *VF* 1962, 10, 10–21 and in *PLNP*, pp. 3–22.

[25] See A. I. Uemov's articles on analogy in *FVSFL*, pp. 186–214, and *PLNP*, pp. 250–93.

[26] The book is D. P. Gorskij, *Voprosy abstrakcii i obrazovanie ponjatij*, Izd. Akademii Nauk SSSR, Moscow 1961, 344 pp.; his articles on abstraction and idealization are in *VF* 1963, 2, 50–60, and *VF* 1961, 9, 65–78. See also A. L. Subbotin's, article in *PLNP*, pp. 357–74.

[27] Gorskij's article on definitions is in *PLNP*, pp. 294–356.

[28] Zinov'ev's article on the empirical-theoretical distinction appears in *Dialektika – teorija poznanija: Problemy naučnogo metoda*, Izd. 'Nauka', Moscow 1964, 502 pp., pp. 236–51; Smirnov's article is in *PLNP*, pp. 23–52; Švyrev's article is also in *PLNP*, pp. 53–86.

[29] E. P. Nikitin, 'Struktura naučnogo ob"jasnenija (formal'nologičeskij očerk)', *Metodologičeskie problemy sovremennoj nauki*, Izd. Moskovskogo Universiteta, Moscow 1964, 245 pp., pp. 197–225.

[30] G. P. Ščedrovickij, 'O različii ishodnij ponjatij 'formal'noj' i 'soderžatel'noj' logik', *Problemy metodologii i logiki nauk*, pp. 81–92. (See note 24 above.)

[31] See Kopnin's articles in *VF* 1962, 10, 3–9, and *VF* 1964, 3, 55–68; also Alekseev's article in *VF* 1962, 11, 76–85.

ABBREVIATIONS

FVSFL   *Filosofskie voprosy sovremennoj formal'noj logiki* (Philosophical Problems of Modern Formal Logic). Izdatel'stvo Akademii Nauk SSSR, Moscow 1962, 364 pp.

PLNP   *Problemy logiki naučnogo poznanija* (Problems in the Logic of Scientific Knowledge). Izdatel'stvo 'Nauka', Moscow 1964, 410 pp.

W. F. BOESELAGER

SOVIET DIALECTICAL METHODOLOGY*

'Dialecticians' vs. 'Aristotelians': this opposition of two lines of thought has been observed in almost every branch of Soviet philosophy. Yet nowhere has it been more visible and decisive than in the fields of logic and methodology. Since the great discussion about formal logic in 1950/1951[1], the contributors to these fields can be adequately classified in the following simplified way:

(1) Scholars who know and use the formal methods of mathematical logic, who defend the validity of formal logic in all fields of rational knowledge, and present and/or discuss the detailed methodological problems of science – as they are discussed by Western analysts – with the help of these formal means. Such authors are, for instance: K. S. Bakradze, A. A. Zinov'ev, D. P. Gorskij, N. I. Kondakov, P. V. Tavanec.

(2) Philosophers who show little interest and competence in contemporary formal logic and insist on the possibility and necessity of developing a 'dialectical logic'[2], i.e. of posing and solving the problems of knowledge in a way which is to be completely different from and superior to the formal methods of the 'Anglo-Saxon neopositivists'. Some of the leading dialectical logicians are: M. N. Alekseev, B. M. Kedrov, P. V. Kopnin, M. M. Rozental', V. I. Čerkesov. However, the new non-formal approach was always more demanded and praised than developed or applied, and one became accustomed to look for careful and detailed work exclusively among the followers of the first tendency. The impression was frequently gained that a Soviet author would insist on the superiority of dialectical logic – if not for dogmatic reasons – mainly because he was not competent in mathematical logic or did not like it. "Dialectical logic is really no logic"[3] and many observers would add: It does not seem to be relevant for *methodology* at all.[4] If anything of real interest for the understanding of science is to come out of the Soviet Union, it was expected to come from the 'Aristotelians', and therefore it was hoped that they would increase in number and in influence.

However, this writer believes that such expectations were wrong and

that things have developed in a different way. (1) A dialectical methodology, i.e. an application of 'dialectical logic' to methodology of science
is being developed. It has already reached some detail and technical
competence and, in collaboration with formal logicians, it occupies the
first place in Soviet methodology. (2) This dialectical methodology gives
senseful answers to many questions connected with the understanding of
science within the general system of contemporary Marxism-Leninism.
Some of the work of the 'Dialecticians' in this field seems to be valuable
even from a non-Marxist-Leninist point of view.

This development certainly deserves a detailed and comprehensive
analysis. However, in the present note only a sketch of dialectical methodology will be given in order to draw attention to its existence and interest
and to provoke further studies in the future. There will be two sections to
this study, following the two points made above: (I) a presentation of
some elements of dialectical methodology and schematic analysis thereof;
(II) an appreciation of its meaning and value within Marxism-Leninism
and of some of its merits for an observer from the outside.

I. PRESENTATION OF DIALECTICAL METHODOLOGY

One can consider a collective work published recently as a representative
example of the most recent dialectical methodology: *Logika naučnogo
issledovanija* (Logic of Scientific Research), edited by P. V. Kopnin and
M. V. Popovič.[5] Kopnin is the director of the Institute of Philosophy of
the Ukrainian Academy of Sciences at Kiev (several of his collaborators
are also at Kiev, e.g., Žarikov and Krymskij). He is one of the best known
Soviet philosophers and an advocate of 'dialectical logic'.

Kopnin says in his introduction that wholesale declarations about the
dialectically lawful nature of scientific procedure are no longer sufficient,
and that his intention is a detailed analysis thereof.[6] In this still relatively
new and underdeveloped field of study, Kopnin wants to use both formal
and dialectical logic.[7] Indeed, the formal methods of mathematical (i.e.,
formal) logic and Anglo-Saxon methodology are to some extent known
and used by the authors of the book; Soviet formal logicians as well as
Western logicians and methodologists like Braithwaite, Carnap, Nelson,
Pap, Popper, Quine, Stegmüller, etc., are quoted and their technical work
of formal analysis is considered as valuable. But a 'limitation to formal-

logical studies' is rejected as insufficient to explain the complex phenomena of science. Formal logic is to be wedded to many other forms of
study (philosophical, psychological, socio-historical) in order to understand science in its totality. Formal considerations are thus present
in the book, but never for their own interest. E. S. Žarikov even uses
arguments of Gödel and Church to show the limitations of formal
systems.[8]

The articles of the carefully edited collective work[9] can be grouped in
three parts: (1) The main steps of scientific research: problem, fact and
system. This part includes a chapter each on scientific problem and fact
by E. S. Žarikov; one by V. V. Kosolanov on abstraction; and one by
P. F. Jolon on theoretical systems in general. (2) Function and change of
theories. Here S. B. Krymskij writes on interpretation of theories;
Popovič, on verification of theories; Kopnin, on the step from probable
knowledge and hypothesis to certainty, and on the rôle of practice;
Popovič again, on logical contradictions as the 'limits of development of
theories' vs. dialectical contradictions; I. V. Byčko and Žarikov, together,
on 'scientific search' (this chapter would have better been included in the
first part); and Krymskij with A. T. Artjux, on the 'logical' principles for
the replacement of one theory by another. (3) 'General methodological
presuppositions' of science. The first chapter of this part is written by
Kopnin himself and it is on the nature of science and its functions in
general and on materialist dialectic as its method; the second chapter by
V. F. Černovolenko deals with the highest steps of systematization:
Weltanschauung and the 'scientific picture of the world'.

More interesting perhaps than this list of contents is an analysis of how
they are treated. Here is a schematized presentation.

(a) First, the authors have a strong bent towards *phenomenological
description* of science. Starting from the firm conviction *that* science works,
they undertake to describe and define, distinguish and combine the steps
and methods of science in order to show *how* it works, whereas Western
methodologists are more concerned with simplified and formalized aspects and forms of science in order to solve the logical problems of *if*
and *why* it works.

An example for the preference given to phenomenological description
is Žarikov's analysis of what he calls a 'fact' (i.e., in the usual Western

language, an 'individual statement of fact'). He describes and classifies 'facts' and shows, for instance, that they have a partly theoretical character and cannot be reduced to an expression of sense data. But at the same time he does not go at all into the problems of how such partly theoretical 'facts' are justified as true statements about the world.[10]

A second general tendency of the dialectical methodologists is to look at scientific knowledge in a *'concrete'* (i.e., comprehensive) way, and not to abstract and isolate aspects of it. There are different forms of this 'concreteness':

(b) One is to see science *genetically*, dynamically, as in development, and not as a ready-given system. This genetic approach to methodology had already been advocated earlier, e.g., by V. S. Švyrev in a *sbornik* on neopositivism three years ago.[11] The system of scientific theory as it exists at a given moment (and as it can be formalized) is only an aspect of the whole living reality. Already the title of Kopnin's collection 'Logic of Scientific *Research*' and the interest in processes rather than in formal structures throughout the book are indications of the preoccupation with development. An example of where this preoccupation leads: Kopnin says that verification can of course never be final and definite, because it is a historical process[12] exactly like truth itself.[13]

(c) Another form of 'concreteness' which follows partly from the first is manifested in the consideration of the *psychological* side of science. According to this, it is wrong to limit one's attention to the formal and formalizable ideal relations among facts and theories, because these relations are only important aspects, and what really counts is to understand the whole process in which the subject comes to know what it comes to know. Psychology in this context is not concerned with physiological and associational conditions, but like philosophical psychology it deals, for instance, with the epistemological analysis of science. Thus Kopnin's *sbornik* contains – as has been seen above – special chapters on abstraction and intuition; probability is understood as psychological probability (i.e., the degree of subjective conviction), great attention is paid to the heuristic importance of how problems are posed and to that of the *Weltanschauung* which guides the scientist.

(d) As a third form of 'concreteness' one can consider the attention given to *practice*. Practice is to be understood in the widest possible sense as 'sensual-material activity', ranging from scientific experiment[14] to political action. Intellectualism (pure theory) and utilitarianism or operationalism (overestimations of the practical) are both wrong. Theory and practice are to be considered as a unity.[15]

(e) Finally, science should not be considered as individual knowledge, but rather as *social*, collective knowledge. E.g., Kopnin insists that scientific research is directed towards that which is new to the whole of humanity, to the *'sub"ekt voobše'* (subject in general).[16]

All these elements of dialectical methodology make it a very specific approach to science. But it is senseful to call it 'methodology'. The meaning of 'logic' in the title of Kopnin's *sbornik* is far from that of the same word in Western terminology, for instance in the title of Popper's *The Logic of Scientific Discovery*. It is equivocal and confusing that the same name 'logic' is being used in both cases. But as for 'methodology' the situation is different: if this term denotes the study of methods (of science) then there seems to be no reason not to apply it to phenomenological descriptions and to genetic, psychological, practical and sociological studies of such methods. On the contrary, it would seem rather artificial to restrict the meaning of 'methodology' to their logical (formal logical) analysis and justification. Before offering a further appreciation, a brief report on *non*-dialectical writings must be given for the purpose of comparison.

There are also publications in the Soviet Union which are concerned with formal logical analysis for its own interest, e.g., the majority of articles in two recent collections edited by P. V. Tavanec.[17] In one of them, Tavanec and Švyrev say that the subject matter of their work is "those aspects of scientific knowledge that are connected with the use of the means of formal logic".[18] This is obviously very different from the interest of Kopnin and his collaborators. But the two directions do not exclude each other, and between the two groups there does not seem to be any 'antagonistic opposition', such as existed some years ago. The *sborniki* edited by Tavanec are published by the same publishing house (Nauka) which published the work of Kopnin, and the two groups are in perfect harmony and sometimes even collaboration. E.g., the man who wrote the article quoted above together with Tavanec is the same V. S. Švyrev who insisted very eloquently on the necessity of a dialectical methodology in another place.[19]

The collections of Tavanec contain articles by Tavanec himself, Švyrev, A. A. Zinov'ev, V. N. Sadovskij, D. P. Gorskij, A. I. Uëmov, I. S. Narskij, Ju. A. Petrov, A. I. Subbotin and others. These philosophers have shown interest in formal logic and some degree of competence in it. Some of their work – e.g., that of Zinov'ev – may even be considered as a valuable contribution to formal logic. But what Soviet methodologists with a principal interest in formal logic do in the majority of their works is to report and discuss Western opinions without much originality or to elaborate in very technical detail problems mostly connected with mathematics or cybernetics and therefore hardly relevant for general methodology. Thus, it seems that the more interesting part of Soviet methodology – one is tempted to say *the* methodology in the Soviet Union – is the work of the 'dialecticians'.

II. APPRECIATION OF DIALECTICAL METHODOLOGY

There is much to be said about the insufficiencies and the large areas of darkness in dialectical methodology. But within the limits of this article it is more interesting to point to some of its positive aspects.

It seems that the described approach actually fits the whole system of contemporary Marxism-Leninism very well (maybe better than any formal analysis does) and that some of the crucial problems of methodology can be sensefully solved (or eliminated) within this system by that approach.

Marxism-Leninism has inherited from Hegel much of his ontology: dialectical monism, relationalism and evolutionism.[20] In the framework of this ontology, knowledge is explained as the 'knowledge of mankind in its historical development', the distinction of ideal and real being is dissolved in the 'unity of the logical and the historical' and in the 'unity of theory and practice', truth is a process and resides in the whole system of knowledge understood as a Hegelian 'concrete universal'.

Keeping the ontological premises of 'dialectical logic' in mind makes it easier to understand the specifics of dialectical methodology: it seems to be only consistent with these premises that the procedure of science is to be first of all described phenomenologically. A proper description of the steps and forms of its development shows at the same time its inner logical structure, because the two are basically one. The demand of 'concreteness' in methodology, or in other words, the refusal to study one 'abstract' side of science independently of the whole is a consequence of the general relationalism. All the forms of this 'concreteness': the genetical, psychological, practical and social point of view, follow naturally from the ontological premisses.

The reasoning may look like this for the example of induction: the existence in science of factual statements with universal and predictive meaning is a fact. The process of formulating such statements must be described and they find their justification in their historical and psychological development, in their practical and social function, and in their systematic effectiveness. The problems of formal inductive logic are precisely caused by the isolated abstraction of the formal side of knowledge and the failure to see the whole phenomenon. Thus, in dialectical methodology this central problem disappears.

To see the Hegelian premisses is a necessary condition for the understanding of Soviet dialectical methodology. But to disagree with those premisses is not sufficient reason to reject the methodological work. First, it may happen that valuable work is done with wrong premisses (*ex falso sequitur quodlibet*) and second, the system of premisses, although wrong as a whole, may have true elements that lead to valid conclusions independently of the systematic connection with other false elements. Both these possibilities allow Soviet methodology to come to some valuable results.

(a) First of all, the *phenomenological* description of the procedures of science is interesting in itself. Kopnin's collection contains many examples of it. If such descriptions cannot replace logical analysis they nevertheless allow a better understanding of science.

(b) The *genetic* approach preserves dialectical methodologists from possible mistakes. E.g., Western methodologists were for a long time convinced of the strict alternative between analytical and individually verifiable, synthetical statements in science because they analyzed the fiction of ready-given, complete scientific systems into which such a strict alternative can indeed be introduced. Western methodologists have since criticized and rejected the erroneous alternative in the face of such problems as implicit definitions and dispositional predicates.[21] But to dialectical methodologists this mistake could not have happened. They see every scientific system in its genetic context, and it was precisely the neglect of the genesis of science that led to the acceptance of the aforesaid alternative.

(c) In a similar and closely connected way the *psychological* approach saves Soviet methodologists from some faults of early Western methodologists. For the development of formal logic it was decisive that 'psychologism' in logic was condemned and the fields of psychology and logic were clearly distinguished. But it seems that Western methodologists were frequently led by this anti-psychologism in logic to illegitimately exclude psychological considerations from methodology as well. Methodology as the analysis of the methods of scientific knowledge cannot do without a study of the nature of knowledge itself, and this study is precisely done by a branch of philosophical psychology. To give only one example: The refusal of psychological considerations by the young Carnap – he would have called them 'metaphysical' – led him to his failure in *Der logische Aufbau der Welt*. His 'psychic objects' as empirical foundations of science were later rejected as misconceptions and as unable to found anything.

(d) *Practice* is the link between theoretical and empirical concepts and propositions. It is in the human activity that the insight into essences and necessary structures of reality is made possible for man. A Cartesian static subject-object relation together with a general mechanist view makes the fact of knowledge and science unintelligible. Practice is the dynamic transcendental relation between consciousness and material world which makes knowledge possible. This is certainly an interesting idea (and a long way from the Marxian concept of *Praxis* in the direction of something like Whitehead's 'causal efficacy').

(e) A last word about the *social* nature of science. Even without the assumption of a monstrous, real *sub"ekt voobše* (subject in general), one is left with something relevant: there is no doubt that scientists act and

101

think in many respects as if there were a great totality of science in general, an organism of scientific systems, of which any individual scientist and his knowledge are only a part. This 'as if' is an important aspect of scientific procedure and it is certainly decisive for the planning of the scientific division of labour and for the direction of scientific progress. Thus, the social considerations, as well as the other specific approaches of Soviet dialectical methodology, seem to be of relevance and interest.

University of Fribourg,
Inst. of East-European Studies

REFERENCES

* Originally published in *Studies in Soviet Thought* VI,2 (June 1966).
[1] *VF* 1950, 2, to 1951, 6. For a survey of the decade after 1950, cf. J. M. Bocheński: 'Soviet Logic', *SST* I (1961) 29–38. A study on the discussions about formal logic is being prepared by J. Hänggi.
[2] For a presentation of dialectical logic, see: K. G. Ballestrem: 'Dialectical Logic', *SST*, V,3 (1965) 139–172.
[3] *Ibid.*, p. 139.
[4] T. J. Blakeley speaks about "the inability of the dialectical materialist to take a methodological point of view", in his review of A. F. Begiašvili: *Metod analiza sovremennoj buržuaznoj filosofii* in *SST* III, 3 (1963) 216 f. Cf. also his *Soviet Theory of Knowledge* (Sovietica, Dordrecht, 1964), pp. 80f.
[5] *Logika naučnogo issledovanija*, Ss. Red. P. V. Kopnin i M. V. Popovič. IF AN USSR, Izd. Nauka, M., 1965. 360 str. A year before, Kopnin had already edited another *sbornik* with M. B. Vil'nickij, treating some of the same problems in a similar spirit and with many of the same contributors, but in a more superficial, handbook fashion: *Problemy myšlenija v sovremennoj nauke* (Problems of Thinking in Contemporary Science), Ss. Red. P. V. Kopnin i M. B. Vil'nickij. IF AN USSR, Izd. Mysl, M., 1964. 470 str.
[6] *Logika naučnogo issledovanija, op.cit.*, str. 18.
[7] *Ibid.*, str. 12f.
[8] *Ibid.*, str. 44.
[9] The articles look more like chapters of a monograph than like collected articles, and they are followed by a common bibliography and indices.
[10] *Logika naučnogo issledovanija, op.cit.*, str. 50–54.
[11] V. S. Švyrev: 'O neopozitivistskoj koncepcii logičeskogo analiza nauki' (The Neopositivist Conception of the Logical Analysis of Science) in *Filosofija marksizma i neopozitivizm* (The Philosophy of Marxism and Neopositivism), Ss. Red. T. I. Ojzerman i dr. (Izd. MGU, M., 1963. 543 str.), str. 315–341, here mainly str. 340f.
[12] *Logika naučnogo issledovanija, op.cit.*, str. 194.
[13] *Ibid.*, str. 178. On truth, cf. also K. G. Ballestrem: 'The Soviet Concept of Truth' in *SST* IV,1 (1964) 1–19 (reprinted above, pp. 30–48).
[14] *Logika naučnogo issledovanija, op.cit.*, str. 197.

[15] *Ibid.*, str. 14, 32f., 57, 163f., 192ff. On practice, cf. N. Lobkowicz: 'Is the Soviet Notion of Practice Marxian?', *SST* VI,1 (1966) 25–36.

[16] *Ibid.*, str. 9.

[17] *Problemy logiki naučnogo poznanija* (Problems of the Logic of Scientific Knowledge), Ss. Red. P. V. Tavanec. IF, Izd. Nauka, M., 1964, 410 str.; and *Formal'naja logika i metodologija nauki* (Formal Logic and Methodology of Science), Ss. Red. P. V. Tavanec, IF, Izd. Nauka, M., 1964, 301 str.

[18] *Problemy logika naučnogo poznanija, op.cit.*, str. 11.

[19] Above, p. 97, and reference 11.

[20] This has been emphasized by many observers. Recently, however, the Hegelian heritage has been found to be the determining factor in contemporary Soviet metaphysics of knowledge by K. G. Ballestrem. Cf. his articles 'The Soviet Concept of Truth', *op. cit.*, and 'Dialectical Logic', *op. cit.* A book by Mr. Ballestrem is forthcoming in German in the Sovietica series: *Die sowjetische Erkenntnismetaphysik und ihr Verhältnis zu Hegel*, D. Reidel, Dordrecht, 1967.

[21] Cf. A. Pap: *Analytische Erkenntnistheorie*, Vienna 1955, pp. 27–57.

T. R. PAYNE

ON THE THEORETICAL FOUNDATIONS OF
SOVIET PSYCHOLOGY*

In common with the other sciences in the Soviet Union, Soviet psychology must conform to the demands of ideology. In psychology, as elsewhere, ideological considerations have exercised a determining influence on the formation of basic theory with the result that over the years a body of scientific and philosophical principles has gradually emerged which is officially recognized as the obligatory basis for Soviet psychological theory. The principles in question have been drawn from two sources: the philosophical doctrines of Marxism-Leninism and the scientific works of I. P. Pavlov. Soviet psychology is, therefore, heir to two distinct and independent traditions, the one owing much to Hegel and the other a continuation of pre-revolutionary Russian physiological psychology. Official Soviet literature, however, presents them as two complementary sources of psychological theory, ascribing to the former the general philosophical foundations for psychology, while the latter is said to provide the scientific methodology. The respective rôles of Marxist-Leninist philosophy and Pavlovian psychology in the formation of psychological theory are expressed in the current *Philosophical Dictionary* as follows: "Psychology as a science founded on dialectical materialism came into being in the USSR. It represents a new historical stage in the development of psychology. Scientific psychology takes as its starting point the Marxist-Leninist theory of knowledge and has as its natural-scientific basis the reflex theory of the psychic put forward by Sečenov and elaborated by I. P. Pavlov."[1]

The aim of this article is to give a brief critical examination of the content of these two traditions, to determine what they say that is relevant to the basic philosophical problems of psychology, and to see whether they can justifiably be called complementary.

The course of Soviet psychology has been largely determined by the continuous effort to bring it into line with the principles of Marxism-Leninism. The most influential factor in the formation of Soviet psychological theory has, in consequence, been dialectical materialism. Here psychology has shared the common fate of the sciences in the Soviet Union; for in keeping with the now generally accepted view, one of the most important tasks of philosophy is to provide a general methodology of scientific knowledge and to give a philosophical interpretation of the data of science. The history of psychology in the Soviet Union has, therefore, been characterized by the repeated attempt to found that science on the principles of dialectical materialism. Judging from the frequent discussions by Soviet psychologists and philosophers on this point, the task has not yet been accomplished to their satisfaction.

None of the 'Classics' of Marxism-Leninism wrote a work on psychology and their writings contain only passing references to psychological problems; and these references have for the most part been concerned with the problem of the relation of mind to matter. Yet, on the basis of these passing and often cryptic remarks and on their general philosophical works, Soviet psychologists have attempted to construct a theoretical framework for their science. Of the general body of philosophical doctrine contained in the writings of the 'Classics', three elements in particular have been influential in the formation of psychological theory: materialist monism, the doctrine of the dialectical nature of reality and, to a lesser extent, the so-called Marxist-Leninist theory of reflection. These three doctrines have exercized their influence on Soviet psychology in that order; Soviet psychologists having successively concluded that psychology must be (1) materialist, (2) dialectical, and (3) must take account of the implications of Lenin's theory of reflection.

(1) *Materialism.* The significance of materialism for psychology is self-evident. Ontological materialism, especially as it appears in the works of Engels and Lenin, implies a monistic conception of man and excludes the possibility of spiritual substances. According to Engels and Lenin, all that exists is matter and what depends on matter. "The real unity of the world consists in its materiality".[2] From the eternal movement of matter arises "every finite mode of existence of matter whether it be sun or nebular vapor, single animal or genus of animal, chemical combination or dissociation" right up to "animals with brains capable of thought".[3] The material unity of the world admits of no exception: "no spiritual world exists separately, besides the material world".[4] The espousal of materialism in this sense would seem to exclude not only spiritual substances but any non-material phenomenon whatsoever, and consequently

105

imply that psychic phenomena too, are material, i.e. merely higher-order material phenomena. But both Engels and Lenin avoid drawing this conclusion. Engels variously speaks of thought and consciousness as "products of the human brain"[5] or as "forms of the motion of matter"[6], while Lenin explicitly states that "to say that thought is material is to make a false step towards confusing materialism with idealism".[7]

(2) *Dialectics.* The key to this apparent contradiction is to be found in the second element of dialectical materialism, namely, dialectics. The Marxist-Leninist doctrine of the dialectical nature of reality finds its most important application in ontology and theory of knowledge. However, as Soviet psychological theory is closely connected with these last mentioned disciplines, it also has important implications for psychology. It permits the reconciliation of dialectical materialism's monistic ontology with the recognition of the special irreducible nature of psychic events. The combination of dialectics and materialism adds a new dimension to materialism. Matter is no longer a homogeneous property of all reality. Within the material unity of the world there is room for specific differences, so that the materialistic monism of the 'Classics' is combined with a form of categorial pluralism. Engels in particular conceives of reality as hierarchically divided into different levels, each with its own specific laws. The laws of a higher level cannot be explained by, or be reduced to, the laws of a lower level since transition from one level to another is achieved through a dialectical 'leap' and consequently something new is added. These levels are usually conceived of as different forms of the motion of matter, beginning with simple mechanical change, ascending through chemical and organic change to the highest form of the motion of matter which is consciousness or thought.

(3) *Theory of Reflection.* The special, irreducible nature of psychic events is further stressed by the so-called Marxist-Leninist theory of knowledge. Though the idea that thought or consciousness is a reflection of the material world is already present in the writings of Marx and Engels, it was further elaborated by Lenin in his polemic with the Russian Machists. The first effect of the Marxist-Leninist theory of knowledge is to underscore the non-materiality of the psychic. In *Materialism and Empirio-Criticism*, Lenin begins by saying that the concepts "being and thinking", "matter and sensation", "physical and mental" are the "ultimate" and "most comprehensive" concepts in epistemology.[8]

This in effect makes them ultimately undefinable and implies that the realities which they express are themselves irreconcilably opposed. Thus, Lenin's theory of reflection not only affirms the peculiar nature of psychic events but implies a duality of matter and spirit. Lenin, however, qualifies this first proposition by stating that the opposition and consequent duality of matter and spirit is realized or is valid only within the limits of epistemology. "To operate beyond these limits with a distinction between matter and mind, physical and mental, as though they were absolute opposites, would be a great mistake."[9] Lenin further qualifies his first statement by adding a second element to his theory of reflection by postulating that the ability to reflect, which is characteristic of human consciousness or thought, is realized in some faint way by all material reality.

The theory of reflection is significant for psychology mainly because it seems to offer a formula for reconciling the transcendent nature of thought with dialectical materialism's monistic ontology. By admitting a duality of matter and consciousness on the level of epistemology the Leninist theory of reflection skirts the 'mechanist' danger of reducing thought to matter, while by restricting this duality to epistemology it safeguards the material unity of the world.

The materialization of psychology was accomplished relatively quickly in the first years following the October Revolution. Between 1917 and 1924 the older introspectionist schools which had existed in Russia since the second half of the nineteenth century were eliminated on the grounds of their incompatibility with new Marxist ideology. In the first years of the nineteen-twenties, when Soviet philosophers were still divided on the principles of Marxist-Leninist philosophy, there was a general consensus of opinion among the new generation of psychologists that Soviet psychology must be 'materialist' in order to be 'Marxist'. Introspectionist psychology was branded as 'idealist', 'subjectivist' and 'dualist', the leading introspectionists were deprived of their posts in universities and schools and their places taken by supporters of the new line.

If the acceptance of 'materialism' as a necessary element in Soviet psychology was achieved relatively rapidly, it was only after a long period of debate that the significance of dialectics was recognized. During the second half of the nineteen-twenties the dominant trend in Soviet psychology was one of pronounced mechanism and reductionism. This was due in large measure to the general predominance of mechanism in Soviet philosophy and to the presence of a number of behavioristically oriented schools in Russia. The works of Pavlov and Bexterev were widely known in Russia and abroad long before the Revolution and the elimination of the introspectionist schools left them in almost undisputed possession of the psychological field. It was only as a result of the condemnation of mechanism at the All-Union Conference of Marxist-Leninist Scientific Institutes in 1929 and the vindication of the dialectical school led by A. M. Deborin that the significance of dialectics for Soviet psychology was finally recognized. The incorporation of Leninist epistemology into Soviet psychology took place during the first half of the nineteen-thirties. It was motivated partly by the renewed effort to reconstruct psychological theory on the basis of Marxism-Leninism which was one of the outcomes of the defeat of mechanism, and partly by a new interest in Lenin's theory of reflection occasioned by the publication of the *Philosophical Notebooks* in 1929. These three elements, materialism, dialectics and the Leninist theory of knowledge remained the basic elements of Soviet psychological theory until 1950 when a new element was added in the form of an insistence on the theories of I. P. Pavlov.

The ideas and methods of I. P. Pavlov have only been part of the canon of Soviet psychology since 1950. The insistence that Soviet psychology must be firmly established on the foundation of Pavlovian psychology was a direct result of the six-day "Scientific Session on the Physiological Teaching of Academician I. P. Pavlov" held jointly by the Academy of Sciences of the USSR and the Academy of Medical Sciences of the USSR from June 28th to July 4th of that year.[10] The express purpose of the conference was to undertake "a critical and self-critical examination of how matters stand with regard to the development of Pavlov's legacy in the Soviet Union".[11] In the course of six days of discussion and debate the significance of Pavlov's ideas was stressed for all branches of the biological sciences, from physiology to spa-therapy. Though psychologists played a comparatively small rôle in the work of the conference, the decisions taken there had a profound effect on Soviet psychology. The resolutions adopted at the close of the conference clearly indicated that psychology must henceforward be guided by the teaching of Pavlov, and Soviet psychologists immediately set about evaluating the significance of Pavlov's ideas for their science. 'Re-evaluating' would perhaps be a better word, for the works of Pavlov were, of course, well known to Soviet psychologists and, as already pointed out, had exercized a profound influence on the development of psychology in the nineteen-twenties. However, in the wave of anti-mechanism which swept psychology in the first half of the nineteen-thirties, Pavlov's ideas fell into disrepute among the psychologists.

The part of Pavlov's work which is immediately relevant for psychology is his theories on higher nervous activity. Pavlov developed these theories in connection with his investigations into the phenomena of the conditioned reflex. The details of Pavlov's work on conditioned reflexes are well known and need only be briefly referred to here. In the course of his experiments on the physiology of digestion, Pavlov was struck by the fact that the laboratory dogs secreted saliva not only when food was placed in their mouths but also when some other stimulus associated with feeding was present, as for example, at the ringing of a bell. Having attempted, as he says, unsuccessfully, to explain this and similar phenomena in subjective or generally accepted psychological terms, Pavlov decided that the phenomena could only be scientifically investigated using the methods of physiology.[12] In the course of more that 30 years of research, Pavlov developed a complex theory of human and animal behavior based on the principles of reflexology.

It is impossible, within the limits of this article to set out Pavlov's theories at any length, but the most important points for psychology may be summarized as follows. Like Sečenov, Pavlov believed that the so-called psychic life of animals and men could be explained on the basis of the theory of reflexes. Pavlov distinguished two kinds of reflexes: *unconditioned reflexes* such as salivation when food is present in the mouth; and *conditioned reflexes,* as for example, salivation at the sound of a bell. The former, according to Pavlov, are relatively constant connections between the organism and its environment, while the latter are less stable and are acquired in the course of ontogenesis. The ability to build up conditioned reflexes is essential to the organism since this ability permits it to adapt itself to the changing conditions of its environment. Through the mechanism of the conditioned reflex an indifferent stimulus can signal those properties of an object which have a vital significance for the organism. The mechanism which controls the formation of conditioned reflexes, Pavlov called higher nervous activity.

109

Pavlov further distinguished between what he called the first and second signalling systems. The first system, which is common to man and the higher animals, is made up of stimuli which come immediately from the external world and which signal those objects which are necessary for survival. In man, however, there is a second line of signals which is constituted by words and which Pavlov refers to as the second signalling system. Words are signals of signals, and serve to generalize the multitude of signals of the first system. This second line of signals also allows a higher degree of analysis and synthesis. For Pavlov it is the possession of this second system which primarily distinguishes man from the brutes and is the principle of man's limitless power of adaptation.[13]

Since 1950 Pavlov has, for all practical purposes, been raised to the dignity of a 'classic' as far as Soviet psychology is concerned and his theories have been hailed as the natural-science corollary of the Marxist-Leninist teaching on the nature of mind and its relation to the material world. However, from the brief outline of Pavlov's ideas given above it appears that his views on the nature of psychic phenomena and even on the scientific status of psychology differ sharply from that found in the writings of Marx, Engels and Lenin. We must now consider at some length what standpoint on the two above-mentioned problems is implicit and explicit in Pavlov's works.

As already mentioned, Pavlov attempted to investigate the whole range of normal and pathological phenomena usually referred to as 'psychic' using the methods and terminology of physiology. This in itself suggests that Pavlov did not recognize any essential distinction between psychological and physiological events. Though this charge is vigorosly rejected by Soviet psychologists, there is considerable evidence to support it. Pavlov's innocence of any form of 'reductionism' was officially proclaimed at the Pavlov Conference of 1950, but it is significant that, according to I. P. Antonov[14], until the conference, many psychologists considered that Pavlov's ideas were mechanistic. It is true that Pavlov, in a much quoted text, seems to reject the charge of mechanism and speaks of the "absurdity of a reconciliation between the subjective and mechanical state".[15] However, read in its context, it is not certain that Pavlov there totally rejects the ideal of arriving at a mechanistic conception of man. In fact, his quarrel seems to be not with mechanism, but with the ability of science in its present state to arrive successfully at such an interpretation. In the same

110

place Pavlov goes on to say: "From my point of view, the point of view of a physiologist, I try to push our common problem a little further in the direction of a true general mechanics."[16] Commenting on the first quotation, W. Horsley Gannt, for many years a collaborator of Pavlov, remarks: "In spite of these denials, it must be admitted that Pavlov drew largely on the philosophy of Descartes who compared the animal organism to a machine."[17]

A form of reductionism is certainly implicit in Pavlov's theory of the relation between the first and second signalling systems. For Pavlov, the second system is that which primarily distinguishes man from the brutes. But, according to Pavlov, the second system of signals obeys the same laws as the first[18], which is the common possession of man and the animals. In certain texts Pavlov refers to the conditioned reflex as "an elementary psychic phenomena"[19] while in others he calls it "a purely physiological phenomenon". Again he defines consciousness as a "nervous activity of a certain part of the cerebral hemispheres".[20]

In his 'Reply of a Physiologist to Psychologists', Pavlov expresses himself unequivocally on what he considers the true relationship of psychology to physiology. The most important present-day scientific undertaking is, in his opinion, that of "identifying the physiological with the psychological, the subjective with the objective".[21] Soviet writers usually try to explain away this and similar statements of Pavlov by saying that they are merely directed against "the idealist separation of the psychic from its material, physiological basis".[22]

Though the texts quoted above – and Pavlov's works abound with similar texts – seem to demonstrate conclusively that Pavlov's conception of the relationship between psychic and physiological events was mechanistic in the extreme, care should be taken when interpreting these and similar statements. It is clear, as Horsley Gannt remarks, that Pavlov "treated the subjective physiologically"[23] and that the philosophical implications of many of his statements are that he subscribed to an extreme form of reductionism. However, it must be remembered that Pavlov was above all a scientist committed to an objective standpoint and distrustful of anything that could not be subjected to mathematical analysis. Though he defined consciousness as "nervous activity" Pavlov made it quite clear that he did not wish to "discuss this question from a philosophical point of view, i.e. I shall not touch on the problem of how

111

the brain substance creates subjective phenomena".[24] Pavlov's attitude to psychic phenomena was fundamentally that of a naturalist and a scientist and we shall look in vain for clear philosophical statements in his works.

But the fact remains that Pavlov's ideas lend themselves easily to a mechanist interpretation which is incompatible with the doctrine of the 'Classics' on the nature of psychic events. Moreover, if there is reason to hesitate before labeling Pavlov a mechanist, there is even more reason for hesitating before calling him a materialist. Yet Soviet writers, particularly since 1950, have made extravagant claims for Pavlov's materialism. Not content with asserting that Pavlov's teaching on higher nervous activity provides a natural-science foundation for a materialist psychology and even that it provides a scientific confirmation for the Marxist-Leninist world view, some writers have gone so far as to claim that Pavlov was a "conscious" materialist.[25] But it is certainly nearer the truth to say that Pavlov was a mechanist but not a materialist than to say that he was a materialist but not a mechanist. If we understand materialism as a philosophical doctrine – and it is in this sense that Soviet authors use the word when speaking of Pavlov – then there is no evidence that Pavlov actually espoused materialism. As already noted, Pavlov explicitly refused to draw philosophical conclusions from his investigations. However, this is not to deny that Pavlov's works are open to a materialistic interpretation. But it is important to note that such an interpretation is only possible as an extension of Pavlov's implicit mechanism, i.e. it is a further interpretation thereof. Hence to deny that his thought was mechanistic is to destroy the possibility of claiming that it was materialist. When discussing Pavlov, Soviet writers seem to forget the unusual nature of dialectical materialism. As remarked above, it is the combination of dialectics with materialism that saves Marxism-Leninism from reductionism and there is no trace of dialectics in Pavlov's writings. Pavlov himself summed up his outlook in a speech delivered in 1941 in the following terms: "I am neither a materialist nor an idealist; I am a monist, or if one must commit oneself, a methodological materialist."[26]

The denials of official Soviet literature notwithstanding, one is forced to conclude that the theoretical model of human nature implicit in the theories of Pavlov is mechanistic. Consciousness, and subjective elements generally, have no place in his scheme of human behavior. The whole trend of Pavlov's thought is, in consequence, reductionist since he is forced by a refusal to take subjective factors into account in the study of human behavior to reduce man's so-called 'psychic' life to the status of higher neural phenomena. It is, moreover, behavioristic since it focuses attention exclusively on external human activity and refuses to admit the scientific validity of introspection. Pavlov's conception is radically monist but this monism is both categorial and substantial, that is to say, man is considered not only as one substance, but any essential distinction between psychological and physiological is denied.

CONCLUSION

We are now in a position to examine the claim that Pavlovian physiology and Marxist-Leninist philosophy form two complementary systems.

There is certainly a similarity between the Leninist theory of reflection and Pavlov's theory of higher nervous activity. Both present so-called psychic phenomena as a reaction of the organism to the stimuli of the outer world and both insist that this reflection is not a passive reception of impressions but an active response on the part of the organism.

Again, both systems are monist; they are united in excluding the possibility of having recourse to a non-material substance as the basis for psychic phenomena. But for Pavlov this exclusion is a scientific axiom while for Marxism-Leninism it is founded on philosophical materialism. However, the most important difference between Pavlov's theories and Marxism-Leninism on this point is that Pavlov's approach to the psychic is fundamentally mechanistic and reductionist whereas that of Marxism-Leninism is dialectical and consequently anti-reductionist and anti-mechanist. Soviet psychology is, in consequence, founded partly on a mechanist system which is not materialist in the full sense of the word, and partly on a materialist system which is definitely not mechanist. From this point of view there is a definite discrepancy between the two traditions on which Soviet psychology is founded, and this goes a long way towards explaining many of the inconsistencies in Soviet psychological theory.

University of Fribourg,
Inst. of East-European Studies

T. R. PAYNE

REFERENCES

* Originally published in *Studies in Soviet Thought* VI,2 (June 1966).
[1] 'Psixologija'. In M. Rosental', P. Judin (red.): *Filosofskij slovar'*. M. 1963, 374–375.
[2] F. Engels: *Anti-Dühring. MEW*, XX, 41.
[3] Engels: *Dialektik der Natur. MEW*, XX, 327.
[4] Engels: *Vorarbeiten zum 'Anti-Dühring'. MEW*, XX, 575.
[5] Engels: *Anti-Dühring. MEW*, XX, 33.
[6] Engels: *Dialektik der Natur. MEW*, 513.
[7] V. 1. Lenin: *Materializm i émpiriokriticizm (Materialism and Empirio-criticism). Polnoe sobranie sočinenie (Complete Collected Works)*. 5-oe izd., tom XVIII, 257.
[8] *Ibid.*, 149.
[9] *Ibid.*, 259.
[10] Cf. *Naučnaja sessija posvjaščennaja problemam fiziologičeskogo učenija akademika I. P. Pavlova. Stenografičeskij otčet*. M. 1950.
[11] *Ibid.*, 5.
[12] I. P. Pavlov: *Lectures on Conditioned Reflexes*. Transl. by W. Horsley Gannt. London, 1963, vol. 1, 39.
[13] *Ibid.*, vol. 2, 179.
[14] I. P. Antonov: 'Dialektičeskij materializm – teoretičeskaja osnova psixologii' (Dialectical Materialism is the Theoretical Foundation of Psychology). *VF* 1953, 1, 195.
[15] Pavlov: *op. cit.* vol. 2, 149.
[16] *Ibid.*
[17] *Ibid.*, 24.
[18] *Ibid.*, vol. 2, 179.
[19] *Ibid.*, 167–168.
[20] *Ibid.*, vol. 1, 221.
[21] *Ibid.*, vol. 2, 117.
[22] Antonov: *op. cit.*, 198.
[23] Pavlov: *Lectures on Conditioned Reflexes*, vol. 2, 28.
[24] *Ibid.*, vol. 1, 221.
[25] E. A. Asratjan: *Ivan Petrovič Pavlov. K desjatiletemiju so dnja smerti (1936–1946). (Ivan Petrovič Pavlov. For the Tenth Anniversary of his Death)*. M. 1964, 28.
[26] Statement made by Pavlov in 1931. Reported by F. P. Majorov: 'O mirovozzrenii I. P. Pavlova' (On the World-Outlook of I. P. Pavlov). *Vestnik Akademii Nauk*. 1963, 3, 14. Quoted by G. A. Wetter: *Dialectical Materialism*. London 1958, 30.

FRITZ RAPP

OPEN QUESTIONS IN CONTEMPORARY
SOVIET THEORY OF SOCIAL LAW*

The present paper gives an exposition of the Soviet discussion on the rôle of statistics in the knowledge of social phenomena and on the concept of social law as opposed to mere description by means of statistics. In the following critical evaluation of the Soviet arguments, the 'open questions' i.e. those treated by the Soviets in an unsatisfactory way, will be elaborated. Their philosophical discussion, which is still going on, began some years ago in connection with the application of statistical methods in investigating social affairs in the Soviet Union. This is of high interest, since empirical statements and their philosophical evaluation are directly confronted.

I. STATISTICS IN INORGANIC NATURE AND IN HUMAN SOCIETY

Surely there is nobody who will deny the obvious difference between a group of gas molecules and a group of human individuals. And yet in both cases the ensemble can be described by means of statistics. Thus it becomes necessary to investigate both cases and to show the difference between them as well as their common traits. The considerations presented by Soviet authors on this matter may be divided in the following way: (a) the difference between the phenomena of inorganic nature and those of human society, (b) the connection between nature and society, (c) the applicability of statistics.

(a) Soviet philosophers agree in acknowledging the fundamental *difference* which exists between events in inorganic nature and those within human society. The statistical set, which is formed by a human group, is marked by the fact that a number of persons live simultaneously within a certain district.[1] The connections within this statistical set are far more complicated than those of inorganic nature. If the fundamental differences between these two domains are neglected, one will arrive at a false mechanistic conception of human society.[2] The fundamental difference consists in the fact that in inorganic nature only unconscious and random

115

forces are acting, while the conduct of human individuals is marked by conscious and planned activities.[3]

(b) Notwithstanding all these differences, the *connections* between nature and society also have to be taken into account, for both of them belong to the very same world[4] and are to a large extent subject to the same laws. In a wider sense, society is also a part of nature, and furthermore man can secure his material existence only by acting on the surrounding nature.[5]

(c) In spite of basic differences, both the state of affairs in human society and events of inorganic nature can be described by means of *statistics*. This is possible, for those characteristics are found in both cases which permit the application of statistics.[6] Thus, in spite of the particular behavior of individual men, it is possible to state a general mode of behavior as the average comportment of the group in question.[7] But it has to be observed that statistical methods cannot be used with equal success in all fields.[8] They may be applied best to inorganic nature, with less success to organic nature, and they are least able to exhaust social phenomena.[9]

O. O. Jaxot mentions that two extreme positions are held in Soviet literature. (He rejects them both.) He reports that some authors claim that statistics are not at all applicable to social phenomena[10], while it is maintained by others that statistics can refer only to human society.[11] But, according to Jaxot, the correct solution is not a 'universalism', which applies statistics with equal justification to phenomena of inorganic nature and those of human society, for, by this approach statistics would be separated from the real events which it describes, and thus the specific traits of the objects investigated would be lost.[12] As Jaxot claims, there are several types of statistics which are adapted to the special nature of the phenomena under investigation.[13]

One can surely agree with Jaxot in his rejection of the above mentioned extreme positions. But his refusal of 'universalism' cannot be accepted. Of course, it is a reasonable demand to regard every phenomenon in its own specific particularity. But this does not mean that there are basically different kinds of statistics. For, in fact, phenomena in inorganic nature and in human society can be studied by means of statistics precisely because these phenomena possess certain traits which permit the statistical application. And, indeed, these traits which allow the use of statistics do not at all exhaust the studied phenomena. But it cannot be the task of statistics to take these peculiarities into account, since the use of statistics is made possible precisely by the neglect of specific traits.

This is clearly seen from the fact that, in contrast to the manifold applications of statistics, there exists only one mathematical statistics by which logical connections are studied without reference to any application. In general, it is characteristic for modern sciences, which apply mathematical methods, that the purely formal mathematical structure is distinguished from the concrete phenomena which are described by the mathematical apparatus. This distinction can never be abolished, whether one regrets its existence or not.

II. MATHEMATICAL DESCRIPTION AND PHILOSOPHICAL ESSENCE

The use of statistics in the investigation of social affairs raises serious questions for the foundations of Communist theory. For the main aim of Communist teaching, fixed in *historical materialism* by fundamental statements about human society and its development, consists in effecting a change in social conditions. But exactly formulated and directly testable statements about social conditions can only be made by means of statistics. Thus, the question arises as to what relations exist between such empirically investigated and mathematically formulated facts and the general statements of historical materialism. The situation is even more complicated by the fact that both statistical statements and general Communist doctrines on society and its development are held to be scientific.

In order to present a clear account, the arguments of Soviet philosophers referring to these questions will be divided into the following three points: (a) the usefulness of statistics, (b) the 'symptomatic' function of statistics, (c) the investigation of the 'essence' of social phenomena.

(a) Soviet authors think that the application of statistical methods is very *useful* for the investigation of social phenomena. Thus, for example, the *theory of games*[14] introduced by von Neumann and Morgenstern may be of great use for administrative and technical calculations.[15] The investigations recently carried out in the Soviet Union on the diminution of the difference between intellectual and physical work, on the increase of the cultural and technical level of the working class, as well as on the increase of the cultural level of the kolkhoz farmers are based on carefully selected and analyzed statistical data. O. O. Jaxot claims that, in general, the knowledge of statistics has become an absolute necessity for Soviet sociologists, and therefore the statistical education of young sociologists should be much more intensified.[16]

Only by statistics can social facts be stated in an unambiguous and reliable way. These facts correspond to experimental data which the investigators in other fields collect in the laboratory. And only by means of such scientifically confirmed facts is it possible to make general statements.[17] The combination of exact mathematical methods with the use of models for social phenomena makes it possible to transform social science, in the full sense of the word, into a science of engineering. In this way it will be possible to find quantitative statistical laws of social phenomena.[18]

But Soviet authors think that it is wrong to regard the relations revealed by statistics as the real laws of society.[19] For social events, like events on every other field, are produced by certain causes. But if the view is only limited to the connections which exist between the immediately grasped phenomena, the investigation remains superficial and the real essence, which consists in the causal relations, is not grasped.[20] Therefore the study of functional and correlative relations has to be deepened by the analysis of causal relations.[21] Factorial analysis also fails to take this situation into account when regarding the different factors as homogenous. But in fact there are always fundamental and decisive causes, which determine the process.[22]

(b) N. K. Družinin[23] and O. O. Jaxot[24] declare that in sociology the connections stated by means of statistics have above all a 'symptomatic' function. As the increased temperature of the human body indicates sickness, so are statistical relations the expression of real processes and internal connections in human society. Therefore, when statistical investigations show regularly appearing connections, it is necessary to look for the real causes which produce these connections.[25] But this does not mean that statistical connections have only a methodological function within the process of knowing. Rather, the connections stated by statistics hold whether or not they are known by men and whether or not the real causes of social phenomena are investigated.[26]

Both Družinin and Jaxot report that, in opposition to their view, two other extreme positions are held in the Soviet Union.[27] On the one hand, it is claimed that the connections stated by means of statistics are mere numerical expressions by which the range of social phenomena can be described and compared.[28] According to this opinion, which is held by some statisticians, these connections do not say anything about the real social conditions and their development.[29] This would mean that statistical investigations are of no relevance for the knowledge of the evolution of society. On the other hand, the very opposite position is also held according to which the connections stated by statistics coincide with the laws of society.[30] From this point of view the statistical connections are the exhaustive expression of social phenomena, so that a further analysis would not be necessary.[31]

(c) The *essence,* i.e. the real content of social phenomena, can only be recognized by an analysis of the internal connections which form the basis of visible appearances.[32] Therefore, the connections stated by means of statistics must always be investigated with respect to the class-relations which are their real causes.[33] Laws which really show the essence of social phenomena are, for example, the law of the conformity of the relations of production with the character of the productive forces, or the law of the accelerated increase of the means of production, according to which the means of production grow faster than the production itself.[34]

According to N. K. Družinin, the rôle of statistics in the knowledge of the essence of social conditions must be regarded in the light of the epistemology of dialectical materialism.[35] As the Marxist theory of knowledge teaches, every science starts with sense-experience and proceeds from it to abstract reasoning. In this process of abstraction concrete reality is reconstructed by means of concepts and general laws. And only this conceptual structure can show the essence of the phenomena investigated.[36] At the beginning of this procedure facts are always collected by means of a heuristic scheme, and these facts form the basis for further abstraction. The rôle of statistics for the investigation of society thus consists in the fact that it furnishes the systematically presented facts, which are later to be analyzed.[37]

The essence and the causes of social conditions become apparent only if the statistical collection of the facts, as well as the further analysis of this material, are based on the scientific outlook of Communism.[38] Because of this, even the questions to be studied must be chosen in accordance with the scientific Communist outlook.[39] The analysis of the collected material has to be made on the basis of the Marxist-Leninist theory of class-relations.[40] With this view, O. O. Jaxot rejects the position of a Polish author[41], who claims that the task of sociology consists in the theoretical elaboration of empirical data independently of any philosophical point of view.[42] According to Jaxot, statements about social conditions which are not based on a Marxist analysis are of no relevance, even if the statistical data on which they are based are consistent from a formal point of view.[43]

It is especially important to take the essence of social phenomena into account when statements are made about the situation in capitalist countries. This is so, because statistical data touch only on the surface of *bourgeois* conditions, while the contradictions of capitalist society remain unrevealed.[44] Therefore, the investigations of American sociologists in which the population of capitalist countries is grouped according to its income and not according to its relation to the means of production, do not give a competent view of the real conditions which are understood only in the context of class-relations.[45]

One can surely agree with the claim of Soviet writers that by means of statistics alone, one cannot exhaustively study social phenomena. The faithful adherence to the real events, which are the subject of statistics, is a good preventive against a merely functional approach. But the claim that any further analysis must always start from class-relations as the real causes of social phenomena is as doubtful as the thesis that only such an analysis can be called scientific.

Above all, the double meaning of the term 'scientific', clearly evident in the above-quoted literature, must be clarified. On the one hand such methods are called scientific which follow the procedure of the natural sciences and by which the phenomena under investigation are described by means of mathematical statistics. On the other, the 'scientific Communist outlook' allegedly gives the only possible guarantee for a really competent interpretation of social phenomena. But, the mathematical method of the natural sciences and a philosophic theory about human society are absolutely different things. This is also emphasized by the above quoted Soviet authors, who always insist on the fundamental difference between the description of empirically-gathered facts by means of statistics, and the speculative investigation of the real essence of these

120

facts. The common use of the term 'scientific' in both cases might, however, easily give rise to the impression that the Communist theory of society meets the strict criteria of the natural-scientific method. In order to avoid this false impression it becomes necessary to avoid the double meaning of the term 'scientific'. One could possibly make the following distinction, which would be in line with the Soviet position and would certainly clarify the situation. This would consist in calling the methods of natural science 'scientific', according to international usage, while the Communist theory of society would be labelled 'philosophical'.

Along with the unjustified use of the term 'scientific', the a priori and dogmatic character of Communist social theory is also untenable. Namely, if, according to the epistemology of dialectical materialism, the analysis of the essence of social phenomena has to begin with empirical facts, then the possibility must be allowed for that a change of facts will exert an influence on theory. But this very possibility is excluded if the collection of facts as well as their interpretation has to be made according to Marxist theory. This a priori claim to absolute validity is evidently intended to prevent a refutation of Communism by developments in Western countries. But then the Marxist scheme for interpreting society becomes simply a prejudice which can in no way claim objective validity.

It is only natural that friction arises when the Hegelian type of philosophical reasoning as adopted by Marx, and a statistical formulation of empirical facts, come into contact. Confronted with an empirically stated situation, it is not sufficient to demonstrate by means of general principles the internal evolution of opposites. Here the philosophical interpretation has to face reality, and it must run the risk of a possible falsification. Without the possibility of falsification there is no hope that a theory might be tested and thereby confirmed. This appeal to the actual state of affairs even fits in with the epistemology of dialectical materialism, where the decisive importance of practice, as the criterion of truth, is constantly emphasized.

III. INDIVIDUAL SPONTANEITY AND SOCIAL DETERMINATION

Historical materialism is based on the thesis that the evolution of society is a process determined with the very same inevitable necessity which characterizes the events of inorganic nature. But at the same time Soviet philosophers recognize the spontaneity of the acts of individuals. Thus the question arises how, (a) the spontaneity of individuals is compatible with (b) the strict law-bound determination of the society which is made up of these individuals. In connection with this, the freedom of will (c) must also be discussed.

(a) Although in a Socialist planned economy the 'capitalist anarchy of production' is removed, a planned economy is not a system which operates with computer-like necessity, for even in Socialist society events take place which were not intended in the planning.[46] Thus, for example, the demand for products, individual taste, and the personal needs as well as the purchasing power of the families (depending on the wages, state of health and personal character of its members) are *spontaneous* and not predictable quantities. Therefore, these factors, which are not strictly determined by law, must be investigated by means of statistics in order to avoid the unnecessary production of goods which cannot even be sold.[47] Statistics can be a valuable aid in ascertaining the general tendency of consumer-preference by taking random samples.[48]

(b) But the development of *society as a whole* is determined by objective laws which do not depend on the will and consciousness of men.[49] O. O. Jaxot and V. S. Nemčinov agree to this, as well as to the thesis that in a planned Socialist society objective historical laws are no longer acting 'blindly' as in capitalism, but are known and consciously applied.[50] Differences of opinion arise when it comes to characterizing the nature of social determination. While Nemčinov insists that the laws of society are the same as the laws of inorganic nature[51], Jaxot claims that in society necessity does not appear as strict and fixed inevitability (*odnosnačnaja žestkaja neizbeznost'*), there being also spontaneous deviations. Thus, for example, the phenomena mentioned in (a) cannot be fitted into a pre-determined scheme, but must be studied by statistics and the laws of probability.[52] It is precisely the task of statistics to uncover the necessity which runs through a mass of contingencies.[53]

S. F. Anisimov is even convinced that the laws responsible for the development of society cannot be influenced by the fate of an individual (which always has a fortuitous character), no matter how important a rôle he may play in history.[54] He thinks that the situation in society can be compared with the evolution of a new species of animals. The whole process of evolution is governed by the law that individuals will propagate and transmit those properties which are adapted to the surrounding conditions. But this statement, which concerns only the statistical average, does not take into consideration whether or not the individual meets favorable conditions and whether or not he propagates his species.[55] But in human society, as in the evolution of animals, the total results of individual destinies, which themselves have a purely chance character, are determined with strict necessity.[56]

(c) Anisimov declares that man will become aware of his *freedom of will* only if his behavior is not in accord with the *Weltanschauung* and habits of the majority. But as long as someone agrees with the accepted standards he will not perceive any constraint on his behavior.[57] Thus, a person who is self-employed in a *bourgeois* society feels that he is free, though in fact in the statistical average his way of life, including his wishes and needs, are determined by the interests of his class. Though it is possible that there are certain deviations from the class-standard, the general behavior of man is always determined by his class membership.[58]

O. O. Jaxot discusses the problem of free will in connection with the investigations of the French sociologist Quétlet, which were mentioned by Marx. Jaxot thinks that the number of crimes, suicides, and marriages which remains constant for years shows that human actions are determined by law.[59] Therefore, the behavior of men is not the result of absolutely free acts of mind. The statistical study of a large number of individuals shows that men are subject to certain laws in their behavior. Thus spontaneous acts of will are only of secondary importance. Because of this determined character of human conduct, some historians and statisticians even spoke of statistical materialism (*statističeskij materializm*).[60]

As the quoted texts show, an examination of the actual situation leads Soviet authors to admit a certain indeterminateness in the conduct of individual men. But this uncertainty will be overcome by the superior necessity of the whole, which is determined by class-conditions and can be taken as a statistical average.

Now, it is certainly a great service of Marxist social philosophy that it emphasizes the significance of social connections as opposed to the fiction of a collection of isolated individuals. It is furthermore clear that, in order to characterize the relations between individuals and society, one must take into account some sort of interaction between the individual and the whole which, evidently, is not possible without speculative

123

reasoning. But even when all these factors are considered, the arguments of the Soviet authors call for serious criticism.

First, it has to be said that, in spite of all the unconsciously accepted standards of conduct, the basic spontaneity and openness of the human mind cannot be ignored. This spontaneity manifests itself in the personal experience of having freedom of choice, and can be observed in all great personalities who have cast off the chains of their environment either through theoretical reasoning or practical action. And only by referring to this basic openness can the capacity of the human mind for detached objective judgments be explained. It is here that philosophical reflection – which is also practiced by Soviet authors – finds its genuine place.

Even more important is a second point, which concerns the basis for the determination by law of social processes. It is striking that the necessity claimed by Soviet authors is not rooted in the individuals who are acting, but appears rather as an autonomous and superior force which governs single events. It is exactly this conception which forms the fundamental philosophical error of historical materialism: in the Hegelian manner of hypostatizing ideas, the 'predicate is made into the subject'. Instead of taking man as the real subject and the partial social determination of his actions as predicate, historical materialism regards man as an inessential feature of the social whole. Thus this whole has its own autonomous status and is falsely taken as the 'subject'.[61]

That the idea of group-determination (regardless of whether or not social groups are analyzed in terms of the Marxist class-scheme) must always be reduced to individual agents can be clearly seen from the statistical examples cited by Soviet authors. For in fact a statistical average is only the sum total of the single cases which it includes, and apart from these cases there is no average at all. Thus the claim that social phenomena are determined with strict necessity appears to have little foundation.[62] In spite of the standard of behavior suggested by the group, there exists a certain spontaneity of individuals. If so, however, the total pattern of their behavior cannot be determined with strict necessity.

Bundesinstitut für Ostwissenschaft und
Internationale Studien, Cologne

BIBLIOGRAPHY

ANISIMOV, S. F.: 'Sootnošenie kategorij zakona, pričinnosti, neobxodimosti i slučaj-nosti'. *VF* 1955, 6, 45–56.
DRUŽININ, N. K.: 'Nekotorye filosofskie voprosy statistiki'. *VF* 1966, 1, 22–31.
JAXOT, O. O.:
[1] 'Ob ob"ektivnoj prirode statističeskich zakonomernostcj'. *VF* 1956, 4, 33–44.
[2] 'Determinizm i statistika'. *VF* 1958, 10, 56–65.
[3] 'Sociologičeskie issledovanija i nekotorye teoretičeskie voprosy statistiki'. *VF* 1963, 5, 54–66.
[4] 'Zakon bol'šich čisel i social'naja statistika'. *VF* 1965, 12, 80–90.
MASLOV, P. P.: 'Statistika i sociologičeskie issledovanija'. *FN* 1965, 3, 60–70.
NEMČINOV, V. S.: 'Sociologia i statistika'. *VF* 1955, 6, 19–30.

REFERENCES

* Originally published in *Studies in Soviet Thought* VI,3 (September 1966).
[1] Nemčinov, p. 23.
[2] Jaxot, [3], p. 65.
[3] Maslov, p. 61; Nemčinov, p. 22.
[4] Maslov, p. 62; Jaxot [3], p. 65.
[5] Jaxot [3], p. 65.
[6] Jaxot [4], p. 82; Maslov, p. 62.
[7] Maslov, p. 62.
[8] Jaxot [4], p. 82.
[9] Nemčinov, p. 28.
[10] Jaxot [3], p. 64.
[11] Jaxot [3], p. 64; [4], p. 82.
[12] Jaxot [3], p. 64–5; [4], p. 81–2.
[13] Jaxot [3], p. 64–5; [4], p. 82.
[14] The basic work on this subject is: von Neumann, J., Morgenstern, O.: *Theory of Games and Economic Behavior*. Princeton, Oxford, 1944.
[15] Maslov, p. 60.
[16] Jaxot [3], p. 66.
[17] Jaxot [3], p. 56.
[18] Jaxot [3], p. 65.
[19] Maslov, p. 60.
[20] Jaxot [2], p. 63; [1], p. 43; Maslov, p. 61.
[21] Jaxot [2], p. 65; [4], p. 90.
[22] Jaxot [2], p. 65.
[23] Družinin, p. 26.
[24] Jaxot [1], p. 38.
[25] Družinin, p. 26–7; Jaxot [1], p. 38.
[26] Jaxot [1], p. 38.
[27] Družinin, p. 23; Jaxot [1], p. 42.
[28] Družinin, p. 23.
[29] Jaxot [1], p. 42; [3], p. 56.
[30] Družinin, p. 23.

[31] Jaxot [1], p. 42.

[32] Jaxot [1], p. 44.

[33] Jaxot [1], p. 43–4.

[34] Jaxot [1], p. 43.

[35] Družinin, p. 25.

[36] Družinin, p. 25.

[37] Družinin, p. 25.

[38] Jaxot [3], p. 55–6, 62–3.

[39] Jaxot [3], p. 62.

[40] Jaxot [3], p. 63.

[41] According to Jaxot [3], p. 63 the Polish author is S. Ossowski, in his book: *Marksism i twórczość naukowa w spoéeczenstwie socjalistycznym,* Warszawa, 1957.

[42] Jaxot [3], p. 62–3.

[43] Jaxot [3], p. 63–4.

[44] Jaxot [1], p. 42.

[45] Jaxot [3], p. 57.

[46] Jaxot [3], p. 60–61.

[47] Jaxot [3], p. 61.

[48] Jaxot [3], p. 61–2; [4], p. 83.

[49] Jaxot [1], p. 40; Nemčinov, p. 22.

[50] Jaxot [4], p. 82–3; Nemčinov, p. 22.

[51] Nemčinov, p. 22.

[52] Jaxot [4], p. 83.

[53] Jaxot [1], p. 39.

[54] Anisimov, p. 50, 53.

[55] Anisimov, p. 53.

[56] Anisimov, p. 53.

[57] Anisimov, p. 52.

[58] Anisimov, p. 52.

[59] Jaxot [2], p. 57.

[60] Jaxot [2], p. 57–8.

[61] This is valid in spite of the fact that it was Marx who reproached Hegel for having exchanged the rôles of subject and predicate (K. Marx, *Kritik des Hegelschen Staatsrechts,* Frühe Schriften, I, ed. Lieber, H.-J., Furth, P., Stuttgart 1962, pp. 266, 275, 284). Thus, at least with respect to the orthodox doctrine of historical materialism, it is true that Marx fought all his life against Hegel and always lost.

[62] In the article 'Die Idee der historischen Notwendigkeit' *SST,* II,3 (1962), 181–203 H. Fleischer has analyzed in detail the idea of historical necessity in dialectical materialism. He especially emphasized the rôle of the individuals striving consciously for certain aims.

LASZLO REVESZ

OPEN QUESTIONS IN CONTEMPORARY SOVIET PHILOSOPHY OF LAW AND STATE*

I. THE STATE AND THE PREPARATION OF ITS OWN WITHERING-AWAY

The Marxist-Leninist Theory of State

The general Marxist-Leninist theory of state can be shortly summarized as follows:

The state, the political organization of society, is an especially important part of the superstructure which is built upon the economic base. It is a product and a direct consequence of the destruction of the original classless society, the result of which was a society with antagonistic classes. Parallel with the rise of private ownership of the means of production (originally of land, of domestic animals and even of men), there arose two basic classes: the propertied class and the non-propertied class. The propertied class then called the state into existence in order to guarantee its monopoly on private property and to be able to exploit the working-force of the propertyless class without any restriction.[1] Thus, the main internal functions of the state are 'suppression' and the organization of exploitation. The state is "a tool in the hands of the dominating class for suppressing the opposition of its class enemies".[2] In general, the state is the 'organ of power' of the ruling class.

A well-known Polish scholar of the older generation has given perhaps the most appropriate definition of the state in the Marxist-Leninist sense: "The state is an apparatus for coercion, hierarchically and territorially organized, which makes it possible for the class possessing the means of production to maintain its property and other interests as well as its leadership of the state over against its class enemy."[3] Thus, in Marxism-Leninism, the state is: (a) an element of the superstructure of the respective economic base, (b) a class product, and (c) a historical concept.

(a) As an element of the superstructure the state serves the economy, follows it in its development, and adapts to its needs. But the theory of state, 'enriched' by Lenin and Stalin and adapted to the needs of the twentieth century, emphasizes that the state must not only follow economic and social development but must influence and promote it. In the event that the state lags behind the development of its economic base and thus makes this development more difficult, the hitherto existing type of state must be replaced by a new, more expedient one. Likewise the relations of production (here property relations) hindering the development of the productive forces must be superseded by new ones.

(b) The state is bound to a class society. Marxist-Leninist theory distinguishes two basic forms of class society: in one type, the classes are hostile and antagonistic towards each other and carry on a bitter class-war; in the other, the classes are joined together by common tasks and goals (the building-up of Socialism or Communism).

Therefore the state is the instrument either of class-war or of social and economic construction in the interests of the whole people. In the society of antagonistic classes the state serves the suppression of the majority by the minority; on the other hand the state of the dictatorship of the proletariat serves the suppression of the minority (the remainder of the liquidated exploiting classes) by the majority (the working class and peasants). The state of the dictatorship of the proletariat is thus held to be the first class-state in which the public power is utilized and applied in the interests of the majority.

(c) Corresponding to economic and social development, one must distinguish in the development of the state several *types* of state which supersede one another (the state of the slave-holding society, the feudal state, the bourgeois state and the Socialist state). According to the original position of Marxism-Leninism, the transition from one type of state to another is supposed to be accomplished by a forceful revolution. Yet there is an essential difference in transitions, depending upon which class supersedes the other. If one exploiting-class supersedes another (as the bourgeoisie superseded the feudal lords) then there are no radical changes in the state. But after the Socialist revolution the working class must completely destroy the previous state apparatus, in order to secure the accomplishments of the revolution.

The dictatorship of the proletariat is the result of the objective laws of historical development; it cannot be skipped; its establishment is an objective law, which holds independently of the will of individuals and classes.

The question of how long the dictatorship of the proletariat is supposed to last is now being hotly discussed by the 'genuine Marxist-Leninists', the revisionists and the dogmatists.[4] Of course, each group claims that it has the only correct determination of the future development of Socialist society, or of the Socialist state. The official party theory of all three lines states that it is only the Communist Party which can foresee the future developments. But in spite of a common starting point and common methods the three Communist Parties reached diametrically opposed results. The Soviet theory asserts that the dictatorship of the proletariat is solely a transitional form between capitalism and Socialism. According to the Chinese position, the dictatorship of the proletariat must be maintained until the establishment of peoples' Communism. The Yugoslavian 'revisionists', on the other hand, represent the view that in Socialism not only the dictatorship, but also the state and party leadership must be diminished.[5]

There are, at present, also two diametrically opposed interpretations of the Marxist-Leninist theory in the basic question of the transition to the state of the dictatorship of the proletariat, although both positions proceed from a common point and apply the same methods of investigation. The Communist world conferences of 1957 and 1960, which were held in Moscow and dominated by the CPSU, supported the *possibility* of peaceful transition, whereby the dictatorship of the proletariat is to be established (in accordance with objective laws) after the victory of the peaceful Socialist revolution. The Chinese were reproached for categorically denying this thesis.

The 'Withering-Away' of the State

Since the state is a historical concept, it did not always exist and also will not always exist. With regard to its withering-away there are again various and mutually-exclusive interpretations. The withering-away does not take place by leaps but in the form of a gradual evolution of the Socialist state into communistic social self-government. The rise of all other state and social formations is preceded by a revolution[6]; but since Socialism and Communism are two phases of the same social and economic formation with numerous common laws, a transition brought about by revolution is not required.[7]

Soviet legal science has given particular attention, especially since the twenty-first Congress of the CPSU (January 27th to February 5th, 1959), to the development of the Soviet state in the period of fully established Communism. In 1959 and 1960 alone there were published forty books and brochures and thirty articles in scholarly journals which dealt with this problem; and a national conference was convened in July, 1960, to discuss the development of the Soviet state in the direction of Communist self-government.[8] The party program adopted on October 31st, 1961, took the following position on this problem: "The development of the social-istic state will gradually lead to the point where it transforms itself into social communistic self-government.... The historical development leads inevitably to the withering-away of the state. For complete withering-away certain internal preconditions are needed – as the construction of a developed Communist society, as well as certain external conditions – as the final elimination of the conflicts between Capitalism and Communism in the international arena." (Program of the CPSU, part 2, chapter III/2.)

The withering-away of the state, i.e., the transition to communistic self-government, is held to be an objective, law-bound necessity, which takes place independently of human volition and even in spite of all efforts against it. The withering-away takes place gradually and *by means of a constant strengthening of the state*. As Stalin declared, "the withering-away of the state does not occur by the weakening of state power but by its maximum strengthening"[9]; or as Khrushchev said at the twenty-first Party Congress, "One must not imagine the process of withering-away in such a simplified way, as the leaves of a tree wither and fall in au-tumn."[10] A weakening of the withering state would have a very harmful effect for all of Communism.[11] In the state which is withering away the function of suppression should be gradually eliminated; on the other hand, the external function (defense) will be complemented by the struggle for peace, i.e., for peaceful co-existence.[12]

A considerable discrepancy on this point arose between Soviet and Yugoslavian legal philosophers. The seventh congress of the Union of Communists of Yugoslavia took a position against the Soviets; this was worked out by Kardel' (on the ideological aspects) and Mirko Perovič (on the juridical side). Perovič demanded[13] the weakening of the state apparatus in the interests of extending democracy. This provoked sharp criticism in the Soviet Union: "Socialism without a state" is anti-marxist and false.[14]

130

Contemporary Soviet political theory looks for the strengthening of the state not in the consolidation of the state apparatus and in the extension of its organs of power, but in the transfer of state functions to society, to the social organizations. It is the production collectives, the labor unions, and the various commissions of the soviets which are (gradually) to take over the functions of the state; naturally, the party is a special case. This development must be conceived dialectically: as a consequence of the transfer of more and more functions, the state will not be weakened; on the contrary, through its increased contact with the masses it will continue to grow stronger.[15] In party decrees as well as in the writings of party philosophers, the transfer of state functions is considered as an extension of democracy. However, one must distinguish here between the transfer of functions from the central organs of the state and from other organs. The functions of the Union and Republic organs can be transferred only to those social organizations which are strongly centralized, e.g., the party, the unions, the Komsomol, the DOSAAF, etc. These functions are transferred directly to the social organs and in general not to society. The transference does not mean that the state relinquishes its rule and control. The soviets, as the future organs of communistic self-government, must change their methods in accordance with the new line of development in the state:

(a) The permanent commissions, whose jurisdictions are to be broadened, will take in several million workers.

(b) The administrative machinery will be made up of voluntary activists ("social instructors")[16]; there will be no professional administrators, and the category of professional officials will cease to exist.[17]

(c) The necessity of being elected by and accountable to the voters will gradually be extended to all leading functionaries (program of the CPSU, part 2, chapter III/1).

(d) The elected body, i.e., the soviet, and the executive organs will be combined.[18] And the administrative positions will lose their political character to the extent that full Communism is achieved.[19]

However, the following phenomenon must be mentioned. After the enactment of the new party program, the transfer of state functions and the replacement of the state's methods of coercion by social sanctions was brought about forcibly. This tendency was greatly overdone and led to the endangerment of state and social discipline. For this reason, recent

Soviet literature in legal theory warns against the premature elimination of state force, and against a conception of the comrades' courts and people's družinas (groups of citizens banded together to maintain law and order) which regards them as almost the main official organ of public protection. The expansion of Socialist democracy may not encroach upon Socialist legality.[20] The growing number of small crimes makes it questionable whether the present tendency is actually leading to the strengthening of the state.[21] But in the event that it results in a general loosening of discipline, this would mean that the objective laws are not completed correctly.

The fact that present-day society is a political society and is organized as a state does not mean, according to the Soviets, that this form is the only possible one for the organization of men. There are also other types of human organization which have no state character and no political forms. Among these the most numerous are those types in which men are organized as workers, i.e. the factory collectives. Thus in the course of the withering-away or transition (*pererastanie*) of the state, the organizational principle becomes more closely allied to production. The society which is based upon a union of the producers presents a new, higher type of social organization. The communistic social order will be based on the principle of work rather than on any political principle; not politics, but economics and work will underpin the new alliance of men. As is stated in the program of the CPSU, all productive units and all self-administered organizations will be brought together in one comprehensive, organized economy and society. "From that comes the distinctiveness of the communistic social order: in Communism the work- (or production-) collective ceases to be merely an economic unit – it becomes the basis of the whole society. One could also call these collectives 'unions of producers'. Since every member of society who is able to work will accomplish something, the members of society will be organized primarily as producers."[22]

Parallel to the withering-away of the state there will be a withering-away of law, since the two are inseparable. By promoting the development of the communistic base, law contributes to its own elimination, for the 'objective process' of the withering-away of law will occur together with the development of the socialistic into the communistic base.[23] The superstructure will continue to lose its political character[24] and the communistic superstructure will become qualitatively different from the socialistic one.[25] Law will yield its place to social norms which no longer have a political character. In theory this development is already in process: the production collectives and the social organizations operate not only on the basis of legal norms but also on social norms.[26] Social norms will gradually replace legal norms, and thus the socialistic and communistic superstructures (of which laws and social norms are a part) will gradually flow into one another.[27]

II. THE PEOPLE'S STATE AS THE TRANSITION
TO COMMUNISTIC SELF-GOVERNMENT

The Theory of the 'People's State'

At the twenty-second Party Congress, the Marxist-Leninist theory of state was 'enriched' by the concept of the state of the whole people: "One of the most important scientific discoveries of our epoch to enrich Marxism-Leninism is the idea of the Socialist state of the entire people. It was first clearly expressed in the program of the CPSU .... The state of the whole people characterizes a qualitatively new stage in the development of the socialistic *state*."[28]

The party program and all the philosophical and theoretical legal literature which followed its publication emphasized that in the Soviet Union the dictatorship of the proletariat has been replaced by a state of the whole people, and the class-democracy by a democracy for the entire people: "The state, which arose as a state of proletarian dictatorship, has become, in the new, modern period, the state of the whole people, an organ which lends expression to the interests and will of the entire people." (Party program, part 2, chapter III, introduction.) Thus the state is no longer the organ of a class, but that of the whole people; it is a 'regulator of classes'[29], whose leadership the working class continues to recognize. Therefore the people's state will not completely lose its class character (program of the CPSU, part 1, chapter II).[30] However, the means and methods of leadership in the people's state differ from those in the state of the dictatorship of the proletariat (of course, legal scholars are now reproached for not having taken up this question before). Among other things, the leading role of the working class is strengthened by the fact that its alliance with the peasantry is broadened and receives "qualitatively new characteristic features". Nevertheless, in spite of the alliance between the two classes, there are still considerable differences, which can be traced back to the two different forms of social property that serve as their respective social and economic bases. For this reason the people's state, as the political organization of the whole people, must take into consideration in its activity the class differences which still exist in society.[31]

Immediately after the introduction of this new concept, the question was raised in the literature of legal philosophy, whether or not one could still support the previous, widely accepted definition of the state as the "means of class domination", the "mechanism of the leading class for the suppression of the other classes". Legal literature came out against the preservation of this conception, since in the state of all the people there is an increase in institutions of "non-political social order" and thus an increase in social self-government. Yet a new, universally accepted definition was not given.[32] For a long time there was a dominant conception in the legal literature of the Soviet Union, according to which the Soviet Socialist state went through two stages in its development, and in both of these it appeared as a state of the dictatorship of the proletariat. The present-day view confirms those philosophers, who maintain that the development of the Soviet state went through three stages: the first two were stages of the dictatorship of the proletariat, and only in the third did the dictatorship of the proletariat change into a state of all the people.[33] As was stated in the Party Program (part 2, chapter III, Introduction) the dictatorship of the proletariat has its historical mission: the guarantee of the complete and final victory of Socialism, and thus of the transition to the full construction of Communism. And since this has been fulfilled, the dictatorship of the proletariat is "no longer necessary from the standpoint of the tasks of internal development in the USSR".

With regard to the appearance of the idea of a people's state, the following remarks must be made.

The conception of the people's state was worked out hastily without any thorough preliminary investigations (which was characteristic of the Khrushchev era); for that reason alone it could hardly lead to very great changes in practice. Rather than presenting a practical conception involving obvious changes, it is nothing more than a piece of sophistry. The twenty-first Party Congress of the CPSU (1959) was directly taken up with questions of law and the nature of the state, and yet it did not discover the concept of the 'all-people's state'. Even Soviet legal science based itself on the decisions of the twenty-first Party Congress until the publication of the draft of the party program in 1961: "The Socialist state, the dictatorship of the proletariat, is the highest form of democracy in a class society."[34] However, it came to light two years later that there exists still a higher form of democracy, that of the whole people, and that there is still a higher type of Socialist state, the state of the whole people. The National Congress of Jurists, held in the summer of 1960, which discussed precisely the questions of the transformation of the Soviet state in communistic social self-government, knew nothing about an intermediary stage between the Soviet state of that time and the final phase of Communism.[35] And this was exactly one year before the publication of the draft program of the CPSU! Only immediately before the appearance of the draft program did the juridical literature discuss the state of the whole people, which will develop 'at a later time'.[36]

Yet the draft program was hardly published, and journalists, philosophers and legal scholars immediately took up the new line, criticizing all those who were of the opinion that the dictatorship of the proletariat must be maintained until the realization of full Communism.[37] As usual, the official position was even surpassed: "The state and the law of the socialistic social order no longer represent a state and law in the old sense of the words", for both possessed *from the beginning* many features of the people's state and people's law.[38] There was an immediate recourse to the statement of Engels that already the Paris *commune* was no longer a state in the real sense of the word, and to Lenin's declaration, in the spring and summer of 1917, that the future Soviet state will be a *half-state*. (Nevertheless, after the October revolution he tried to strengthen the state apparatus and to erect a strong proletarian state which was hardly a "half-state".[39]) It was generally recognized after 1961 that the social, economic and political conditions for the transition to the people's state were present from the middle of the thirties on. And it was only Stalin who, by strengthening the organ of class struggle, stood in the way of development towards the people's state.[40]

The proclamation of the people's state is connected with the proclamation of the party of the whole people: "The Communist Party, the party of the working class, has today become the party of the whole people." (Statutes of the CPSU, Introduction.) Owing to the parallelism

135

between party and state (the latter being led and controlled by the former), if the party has already become a people's party, the state must also become a people's state. In this connection, it is clearly brought out in party literature that a people's party cannot arise in a bourgeois state, but only in a Socialist one.[41] Even the party of the working class cannot immediately be transformed into a people's party after the victory of the proletarian revolution; there are certain social, political and economic preconditions which must first develop.

By the fact that the party became a people's party, it did not thereby cease to be also a workers' party. It is only more comprehensive, being the party of the other social strata as well. In this context, the Chinese Communist Party is accused of not being able to understand correctly the class character of the party in a society without antagonistic classes. Thus, the Communist Party is a people's party, but in spite of that also a class party (as the people's state also remains a class state). In the discussion with the Chinese Communist Party, the Soviets brought out the following point: the development of the Communist Party into a people's party is an objective law[42], just as the path from the state of the dictatorship of the proletariat to Communist self-government unavoidably passes over the people's state.[43]

It is stated in party literature, that the leadership of the working class in the people's party is to be realized indirectly, by the fact that the CPSU represents the ideology of the working class and leads it to victory.[44] In Socialism the ideals of the working class, their politics, and their ideology were embraced by the whole people; for this reason, the transformation of the workers' party into a party of the whole people was a necessary, law-bound development. Yet it does not mean that the Communist Party ceases to fight for the class-aims of the workers.[45]

If the people's party remains a class party and is led by the working class, this must also hold for the state. Thus, even the people's state will continue to embody the politics of the working class; it will be led by this class both directly and indirectly (by the Communist Party under the leadership of the working class). It is the only class in the world, as the party literature says, that does not want to maintain its own dictatorship forever, but takes pains to bring about, after the victory of Socialism, the conditions for developing into the people's state. Thus the leading role of the working class is an objective necessity even in the people's state.[46]

136

If the leading rôle of the working class is an objective necessity in the people's state, then the leading rôle of the Communist Party must also be regarded as an objective necessity, just as in the state of the dictatorship of the proletariat.[47] It must even be constantly extended with the construction of Socialism and Communism: "It is a universal, historically-objective and well-founded claim, that parallel with the strengthening and development of Socialism there must also be a strengthening of the leading rôle of the Marxist-Leninist party in the life of each of the Socialist countries" (i.e., the USSR and the people's democracies).[48]

Functions of the People's State

The state of the dictatorship of the proletariat corresponds to the society of the transition from capitalism to Socialism; the people's state, the final form of the state, corresponds to the period of the Socialist social order, i.e., of the transition from Socialism to Communism.[49]

The functions of the people's state and those of the state of the dictatorship of the proletariat in its last stage of development cannot be sharply separated from each other. The people's state inherited from its predecessor its position in the international class struggle and its tasks in the sphere of foreign policy; its main duty is to carry on the class struggle in the international arena until Communism achieves a world-wide victory.[50] In addition to serving the function of defense, there is the struggle for peace and the strengthening of friendship and co-operation in the Socialist camp and with the developing nations.[51]

The internal political functions and tasks of the people's state are closely connected with the broadening of democracy, which receives a new content and a new meaning in the people's state. This extension of democracy is not limited to the broadening of the participation of the workers in the management of the state and economy; it includes a far-reaching decentralization in economic life, the extension of the rights of representative bodies over against the executive organs, the autonomy of the factory *vis-à-vis* the local and central authorities (above all in planning), and of the lower organs *vis-à-vis* the higher.[52] Thus, the people's state must work towards a general democratization[53] and promote 'Socialist autonomy'.[54]

In connection with the extension of Socialist democracy in the people's state, the unity of political action is maintained by (a) the strengthening of democratic centralism and (b) the extension of the leading rôle of the party. Both safety measures serve to maintain a centripetal tendency as a countermeasure to those centrifugal tendencies which can arise as a consequence of a false interpretation of the extension of Socialist democracy. The supremacy of the higher organs over the lower is guaranteed by the fact that they must invalidate those decisions which contradict a law or decree and can issue binding instructions, directives, orders, etc., to the lower organs. Although these are not legal norms, they are just as binding.[55]

The legislative (*pravotvorčestkij*) functions in the people's state take on special forms: (a) the activity of the state organs, in directly establishing norms, (b) the state's sanctioning of the legal documents worked out by the social organizations, (c) the special activity of the social organizations whereby they formulate new laws, a function transferred to them from the state, (d) the immediate creation of law by the people. As is emphasized in Communist theory, there appears in all of the above-mentioned forms a concrete form of participation by the people (which in the first category is only indirectly realized, since the Supreme Soviet and its presidium is elected by the people and thus are their representatives). As is foreseen in the party program, the right to take the initiative in legislation is given to the social organizations, but only through their Union and Republican organs.[56] Further, the Party Program comes out in favor of the possibility of a referendum (d), which will increase the rôle of the citizens' assemblies. Of course, it is nowhere set down in the Party Program whether this would be an advisory referendum or a referendum with the power of final decision. The legal literature supports the introduction of a referendum with decisive power in the matter of constitutional change.[57]

After the release of the new Party Program, in which the theory of the people's state was announced, there arose a demand in the legal literature to alter or complete the constitution in accordance with the concept of the state of the whole people. The decree of the twenty-first party congress mentioned only "certain changes and completions" in the constitution; however, the doctrine of the people's state had not yet been laid down at that time. Naturally, the new character of the state as a people's state demands a more thorough reworking of the constitution[58], at least if the theory is taken seriously.

The New Meaning of 'Democracy'

As was already mentioned, democracy also takes on a new meaning in the people's state, the very concept being changed. In Marxism-Leninism, democracy is an explicit class concept: there is no 'democracy in general' either in a Socialist or a bourgeois state."[59] With the concept of 'democracy' the question must always be asked – democracy for whom, for which class? Democracy is closely connected with dictatorship: bourgeois democracy means democracy for the minority and dictatorship for the majority, Socialist democracy just the opposite. Thereby democracy becomes, to a certain degree, a 'quantitative concept'; it becomes the more perfect, the more classes and individuals it includes.[60] Yet the basic difference between Socialist and bourgeois democracy consists in the recognition or denial of 'party-mindedness'. As Lenin emphasized, party-mindedness makes itself felt in the practical activity of bourgeois democracy just as in Socialist democracy, for the rejection of it is in itself a case of party-mindedness.[61]

In the new doctrine of the state and democracy of the whole people, the concept of democracy is just as radically changed as that of the state. According to the new version, democracy in the Soviet Union has nothing to do with dictatorship; it is not maintained by dictatorial means and is no longer concerned with suppressing the other classes.[62] But democracy still remains a political democracy; it keeps its political character, just as the people's state remains a class state whose activity is no longer directed at suppressing classes and social groups.[63] Democracy as a political concept will cease to exist only after the disappearance of all classes, parallel with the withering-away of the state. After it becomes perfect, it will be abolished[64] – however, this does not mean that the democratic methods of government will also be made to disappear.[65] The path to the perfection (and thereby the elimination) of democracy leads from a combination of representative democracy towards a full direct democracy. According to Soviet theory, this development can be observed in the Soviet Union. Strangely enough, the following thesis is put forward: in the development of the Soviet state, there were already present at the beginning, i.e. already in the period of the dictatorship of the proletariat, many characteristic features of the people's state. Thus it is also maintained that many characteristics of the 'all-people's democracy' already existed within the dictatorship of the proletariat, a fact which came to light only with time.[66]

The People's Law

If the state became a people's state then it is self-evident that the law must become a people's law, whereby the difference between the law of the dictatorship of the proletariat and that of the people's state corresponds to the difference between the two types of states.

"The will of the whole people becomes law under the leading rôle of the working class.... . This principle presents a very important qualitative feature of Soviet law."[67] While the old definition of law referred to the civil law of the early capitalist era and served the class struggle, several contemporary Soviet legal theoreticians maintain that the present Soviet law serves not the class struggle and class domination but the harmony of the working people. Thus law is no longer a form of expression of class domination, but it performs, in the Soviet Union, the function of a 'class regulator', as does the state. Therefore, it is only a half-law, which contributes to the transition from legal norms to social norms and brings the legal system closer to Communist morality. In this law, persuasion will gradually gain the upper hand over force.[68] The new people's law also contributes to the situation, that in Socialist democracy the leaders and those who are led do not present two separate groups, as in bourgeois democracy.[69] The idea itself, that Soviet law expresses the will of the whole people, is not new; one can find it in Soviet theory of law after the adoption of the current constitution (1936) and after the Second World War.[70] In spite of this, the idea of a 'people's law' is new, for earlier the same line of thought was used in reference to the dictatorship of the proletariat. It is precisely this fact which indicates the meager practical significance of this new 'discovery'.

The Concept 'People'

In conclusion, we must mention a special aspect of the theory of the people's state, namely, the concept of the 'people'.

The concept 'people' is, like that of the state, a dialectical, historical concept: not all citizens belong to the people; people and population are not identical.[71] According to one wide-spread conception, "the working masses of a country's population" form its people.[72] Both Lenin[73] and

140

Stalin[74] spoke about the people in this sense. There can even be found in Lenin a direct contraposition of the people and the citizens, with a categorial exclusion of the latter from the concept of the people.[75]

Moreover, the concept 'people' changes its contents constantly, in accordance with the rules of the dialectic. According to another more modern and more dialectical interpretation, 'people' includes those levels of society which advocate historical progress. "The objective demands of progressive development are the criteria on the basis of which one can determine which classes and population groups form the people."

Hence the concept 'popular masses' or 'people' refers to a historically changing community of social groups and levels. In certain periods, for example, during the struggle against foreign conquerors and exploiters, the people can include the overwhelming majority of the population. Also, the present national bourgeoisie of former colonial states belong to the people if they take a position against imperialism. Yet, here too, the change in the content of the concept is imminent, since at a later (higher) stage in the revolutionary transformations, the bourgeoisie leaves the revolution and thereby excludes itself from the people.[76]

The old position was revised in connection with the conception of the people's state: in the state of the whole people the people includes the whole population, for all levels of Socialist society have the same interests and goals [77], with the exception of those groups which pay homage to the remains of the past. The concept of the people thus becomes altered in the conception of the people's state, which divides the totality of citizens, *on an ideological and moral basis,* into two categories.

III. DIRECTIONS AND PERSPECTIVES

In the latter half of 1965 and the first half of 1966, the concepts of the people's state, the people's party and the democracy of the whole people were mentioned less and less often, and one was inclined to believe that Khrushchev's successors wanted to gradually drop his 'discovery'. At the twenty-third Party Congress every reference to the people's state was consistently avoided. Nevertheless, a leading editorial in the official organ for political and legal sciences supplies proof that these ideas are still alive and are to be regarded as a guideline for future development.

It is the task of present-day Soviet legal science to clarify the future paths of development of the people's state and people's law and to submit recommendations to the appropriate state organs. [78]

But neither the party nor the professional scholars are satisfied with the state of the juridical sciences, especially with the philosophy of law, and they urge the improvement of the level of literature on the history of law. The reproaches are most often laid at the doorstep of legal philosophy: "The development of Soviet legal science proceeds in a constant struggle against serious difficulties and deficiences which can be traced back to the past, during which the rôle and authority of the social sciences was down-graded. The struggle against dogmatism, against the practice of merely commenting, against quotationism [79] and against schematism is characteristic of the development of Soviet legal science during the past few years...." [80] According to the official position, the main task (since 1961) consists in working out the problems of the development of the people's state and the people's law, as well as that of Socialist democracy. [81] The theory of state and of law should clarify the objective necessities of the present-day development of the people's state. The basis for developing the theory of state and for the investigation of the above-mentioned group of problems is the following: above all, the decree of the Central Committee of the CPSU, of June, 1963, "on measures for the further development of legal science and for the improvement of juridical instruction in the country" [82], but also the decrees of the plenary sessions of the Central Committee in October, 1964, and March and September, 1965. Both the June plenary session and the Party Program of 1961 strongly urged further work on theoretical problems of the people's state and people's law. [83]

Some Soviet philosophers want to lead the philosophy of law out of the *impasse* it has reached, especially in connection with the theory of the people's state and people's law, by removing a considerable part of the theory of state (among other things, the theory of the people's state) from the philosophy of law and by making a special science of it: "political science". This new discipline would also absorb certain groups of problems concerning the basis of scientific Communism. Two respected philosophers of law, S. S. Alekseev and V. E. Čirkin, reproached other writers for the opinion that the philosophy of state and law is the only science which should treat the theoretical problems of these two phenomena. In their view this position is no longer tenable, since there is a conflict with the "political organization of society", whose importance was stressed by the Party Program of 1961. Thus the real, purely theoretical aspects of the theory of state should be left to this new branch of science.[84]

In January, 1965, *Pravda* published an article by F. M. Burlackij, entitled 'Politics and Science', in which he advocated the necessity of the new discipline. In February, 1965, at the general meeting of the 'Union for Political Sciences', a discussion was organized in connection with Burlackij's article. At this meeting the boundaries of the 'political sciences' were fixed in broad outline; from these one can clearly see that the investigation of the theoretical problems of the 'political and class relationships within a specific society as well as in the international sphere" are to be allocated to this new science.[85] One hundred and sixty leading philosophers and legal theoreticians took part in this meeting, and its decisions could possibly have the effect that, with time, the theory of the people's state will either be completely placed in the domain of this new science or be divided between it and the philosophy of law and state.

In line with the recommendation of a special discipline of 'political science', there is, in the framework of the Scientific Council of the Academy of Sciences "for the laws of the development of Socialism and of the transition to Communism", a special section for the "political organization of society", under the presidency of the well-known legal scholar P. S. Romaškin.[86] By virtue of the existence of this section, the organizational framework for promoting the theory of the people's state is already created to some extent.

Today there are but scattered attempts to put some life into an uncommendable, stagnating Soviet political and legal philosophy, and to bring it closer to practical life. The near future might decide whether or not the division of this discipline, advocated by numerous well-known theoreticians, will actually come about.

Schweiz. Ost-Institut, Berne

REFERENCES

* Originally published in *Studies in Soviet Thought* VI,3 (September 1966).
[1] F. Engels: *Der Ursprung der Familie, des Privateigentums und des Staates.* East Berlin, 1955.
[2] J. Stalin: 'Ob osnovach leninizma'. In: *Sočinenija*, vol. VI, 114.
[3] Stanislaw Ehrlich: *Teoria panstwa i prawa.* Warsaw, 1957, p. 55.
[4] *Izvestija*, Moscow, May 17, 1964. Further, *Sovetskaja Belorussija*, Minsk, May 19, 1964.
[5] Mirko Perovič: *Socijalizam i odumiranje države.* Belgrade, 1959.
[6] C. Stepanjan: 'O zakonomernostjach pererastanija socializma v kommunizm'. *Kommunist*, 1959, 14, 35.
[7] Ibid., 36–42.
[8] L. M. Karapetjan, V. I. Razin: 'Ob issledovanii razvitija socialističeskoj gosudarstvennosti'. *VF* 1961, 6, 154–161.
[9] J. Stalin: 'Die Ergebnisse des ersten Fünfjahresplanes. Bericht auf dem vereinigten Plenum des ZK der KPdSU (B) am 7. Januar 1933'. In: *Fragen des Leninismus.* M. 1948, 477.
[10] 'Über die Kontrollziffern für die Entwicklung der Volkswirtschaft der UdSSR in den Jahren 1959 bis 1965. Rede des Genossen N. S. Chruščev auf dem XXI. Parteitag der KPdSU am 27. Januar 1959'. *Neues Deutschland.* East Berlin, 29–30. 1. 1959, special supplement.
[11] P. Romaškin: '*Socialističeskoe gosudarstvo i kommunističeskoe samoupravlenie*'. *Partijnaja Žizn'*, M. 1961, 8, 9–16.
[12] P. Petrov, G. I. Petrov: 'Nekotorye voprosy razvitija sovetskoj gosudarstvennosti'. In: *Izvestija vysšich učebnych zavedenij.* Pravovedenie. M. 1959, 4, 3–14.
[13] See his work cited above.
[14] For the Soviet critique, see: B. S. Mankovskij: 'O povyšenii roli obščestvennych organizacii v stroitel'stve kommunizma'. In: *Ot socialističeskoj gosudarstvennosti k kommunističeskomu obščestvennomu samoupravleniju.* M. 1961, 125–129.
[15] See: A. D. Denisov: 'O sootnošenii gosudarstva i obščestva v perechodnyj ot kapitalizma k kommunizmu period'. *Sovetskoe gosudarstvo i pravo* (henceforth *SGiP*), 1960, 4, 39–40.
[16] J. Gončarov: 'O praktike vovlečenija obščestvennosti v rabotu leningradskogo rajonnogo soveta g. Moskvy'. In: *Ot socialističeskoj gosudarstvennosti*, 294.
[17] *Program of the CPSU*, part 2, chapter III/1. Also, Karapetjan-Razin, *loc. cit.*
[18] Fedoseev: 'Za dal'nejšij rascvet socialističeskoj demokratii'. In: *Ot socialističeskoj gosudarstvennosti*, 8.
[19] V. Ja. El'meev: 'Razvitie form organizacii obščestva v processe perechoda k kommunizmu'. *Vestnik LGU*, no 11. *Serija Ekonomiki, Filosofii i Prava.* 1964, 2, 48–56. Here p. 53. However, it might be mentioned that some theoreticians maintain that in full communism the governing of persons will continue, while others are of the opinion that it will be limited to things and production. See El'meev, *loc. cit.*
[20] 'XXIII. s'ezd KPSS i voprosy sovetskogo socialističeskogo gosudarstva i prava'. Leading article by the editors. *SGiP*, 1966, 5, 3–11.
[21] Especially the small thefts of social property and rowdyism. In 1963, twenty percent of all registered crimes against the state in the RSFSR were thefts of social property, not even counting the smaller ones which were handled by the social courts. See: V. I. Laputin: '*Aktual'nye voprosy ukreplenija socialističeskogo pravoporjadka*'. *SGiP*,

1964, 61, 3–11. Also in Czechoslovakia: *Rudé Právo*, Prague, Sept. 26, 1964, 2. Because of the fast spread of rowdyism it was declared as a "dangerous punishable action" in decree no. 17 of the plenary session of the highest court of the USSR on December 22, 1964. See: *Sovetskaja Justicija*. M. 1965, 3, 27–28. In 1961 in Poland, 30,8 percent of all convictions concerned alcoholism or rowdyism, which stand in a close relationship. See: *Glos pracy*. Warsaw, April 12, 1962, 1.

[22] El'meev, *op. cit.*, p. 52. The leading role of the party must be maintained, but it is realized without dictatorship. See: F. Burlackij: 'Voprosy gosudarstva v proekte Programmy KPSS'. *Kommunist*, 1961, 13, 37–48.

[23] Ju. F. Buchalov, I. H. Kulikov, M. F. Partolin: '*O razvitii nadstrojki sovetskogo obščestva v period razvernutogo stroitel'stva kommunizma*'. *FN*, 1961, 2, 171–173.

[24] According to Marxism-Leninism politics is the regulation of the relations of classes between each other and between them and the state. It is thus a tool of the class struggle. Internal politics takes in the class struggle within the state; foreign politics, on the other hand, deals with it in the international sphere. In the classless society politics cannot exist. See: Laszlo Revesz: *Ideologie und Praxis in der sowjetischen Innen- und Aussenpolitik*. Mainz, 1965, p. 44.

[25] P. E. Nedbajlo, R. V. Beršeda: 'Primenenie pravovych norm kollektivami i samo-dejatel'nymi organizacijami sovetskich graždan'. *SGiP*, 1961, 5, 30–38.

[26] Ibid. and V. V. Nikolaev: 'O putjach razvitija sovetskoj socialističkoj gosudarst-vennosti v kommunističeskoe obščestvennoe samoupravlenie'. In: *Ot socialističeskoj gosudarstvennosti*, p. 18. See especially: László Révész: 'Recht und Sozialnorm'. *SST*, V,1/2 (1965) 12–29.

[27] Nilokaev, *op cit.*, p. 14.

[28] I. P. Il'inskij: 'Razvitie gosudarstvennosti v evropejskich socialističeskich stranach'. *VF* 1964, 10, 3–14.

[29] Jerzy Kowalski: 'Pryzycnek do rozwažan' nad pojeciem prawa'. *Panstwo i prawo*, Warsaw, 1964, 1, 568ff.

[30] F. Burlackij, *op. cit.*

[31] 'XXIII. s'ezd KPSS', *op. cit.*

[32] N. O. Farberov: 'Obščenarodnoe gosudarstvo – zakonomernyj rezul'tat razvitija gosudarstva diktatury proletariata'. *SGiP*, 1962, 7, 14–24. "The state *loses the character of an instrument for class-suppression which had always belonged to it.* That means that precisely the function which constituted its essence in the whole course of its history now disappears...." Yet Socialist society cannot do without the state for several reasons. "First, because still long after the victory of socialism the state remains the most suitable and rational form of social management...." Further, the state is kept for reasons pertaining to foreign policy. In regard to the functions of the people's state see: *Osnovy marksizma-leninizma*. M. 1962.

[33] Cf. P. S. Čeremnych: 'Obščenarodnoe socialističeskoe gosudarstvo'. *VF* 1962, 4, 100. A. Kosicyn: 'Voprosy teorii obščenarodnogo gosudarstva'. *Kommunist*, 1963, 5, 118–124.

[34] A. Davlet'kelcev: 'Razvitie XXI s'ezdem KPSS učenija o socialističeskom gosu-darstve'. *Kommunist*, 1959, 14, 35.

[35] Karapetjan-Razin, *op. cit.* But especially the comprehensive book containing the congress papers, *Ot socialističeskoj gosudarstvennosti*, *op. cit.*

[36] G. I. Petrov, V. S. Petrov: 'Socialističeskaja gosudarstvennost' i obščestvennost'. *Izvestija vysšich učebnych zavedenij*. Pravovedenie. Leningrad, 1961, 2, 21ff.

[37] Burlackij, *op. cit.*

[38] Karel Bertelmann: '*Poznámký k sistému CS socialistickéh práva*'. Právnik, Prague, 1961, 8, 639–653.

[39] More extensively in: S. L. Fuks: 'K voprosu o "polygosudarstve." Izvestija vysšich učebnych zavedenij'. *Pravovedenie*, 1965, 3, 18–28. Here p. 26.

[40] Farberov, *loc. cit.*

[41] N. Lomakin: 'Partija vsego naroda'. *Kommunist*, 1963, 12, 12–22.

[42] 'Ot Partii rabočego klassa k partii vsego naroda'. *Kommunist Estonii*. Tallin, 1964. 5, 9–21.

[43] A. Butenko: 'Sovetskoe obščenarodnoe gosudarstro'. *Kommunist*, 1963, 13, 22–32.

[44] V. V. Petrenko: *KPSS v period razvernutogo stroitel'stva kommunizma*. M. 1963. Znanie Publishing House. p. 38.

[45] *Pravda*, December 6, 1964, 2–4. Article 1 by the editors: 'The State of the Whole People'.

[46] More extensively in: Il'inskij, *op. cit.*

[47] 'XXIII. S'ezd KPSS i voprosy sovetskogo socialističeskogo gosudarstva i prava', *op. cit.*

[48] B. Kozochin: 'Povysšehie rukovodjaščej roli kommunističeskich i rabočich partij evropejskich narodno-demokratičeskich gosudarstv v razvitia socialističeskoj demokratii'. *LGU*, no. 11. *Serija Ekonomiki, Filosofii i Prava*. 1965, 2, 87–95.

[49] A. I. Denisov: 'O prirode prevraščenija gosudarstva diktatury proletariata v obščenarodnoe gosudarstvo'. *Vestnik MGU*. Serija X. Pravo. 1965, 1, 3–11.

[50] Z. V. Šamarin: *Nekotorye osobennosti vneśnich funkcij sovetskogo gosudarstva v sovremennyj period*. Vestnik MGU. Serija X. Pravo. 1966, 1, 29–38.

[51] Ibid.

[52] There was a reversal on this matter after Khruschchev's fall in autumn, 1964. His successors began with a rapid re-centralization and with the limitation of the autonomous administrations of business in the union republics. In 1965 the number of absolutely centralized administrative areas was raised to 22, from 3 in 1962. *Pravda*, October 10, 1965, 1.

[53] Cf. some important sources: I. V. Pavlov: 'Nekotorye voprosy teorii obščenarodnogo socialističeskogo gosudarstva'. *SGiP*, 1962, 7, 3–13. G. S. Ostroumov: 'Pravosoznanie i obščestvennoe mnenie v obščenarodnom gosudarstve. *SGiP*, 1963, 11, 14–23. 'Pererastanie norm prava v pravila kommunističeskogo obščezitija'. *Sovetskaja Justicija,* 1964, 21, 1–3. A. O. Rafikov: 'Ispolkom gorodskogo soveta i privlečenie obščestvennosti k upravleniju'. *SGiP*, 1965, 8, 101–104. Zdenek Mlynár: *K nekterým teoretickým otažkam vselidové socialistické demokracie. Právnické študie.* Pressburg, 1963, 1, 5–28. C. A. Jampol'skaja: *Obščestvennye organizacii i razvitie sovetskoj socialističeskoj gosudarstvennosti*. M. 1965.

[54] The Polish scholar, Maurycy Jaroszynski, wrote, in his interesting article, 'Decentralizacja i samorzad w panstwie socjalistycznym': The expression "autonomy" returned in Soviet legal science after an interruption of more than forty years. But socialist autonomy is not to be confused with civil autonomy. While the latter is limited to local questions and is an explicit territorial autonomy, socialist autonomy is a "unified institution of the people in general". Every council as an organ of state power is an organ of the entire people, since the state power belongs to the whole people, is uniform and inseparable. Consequently, there are no boundaries between local matters and those which concern the entire state and people. In the latest developments in the Soviet Union, when they are speaking about autonomy, they are not thinking of autonomy in the juristic sense but as a kind of "social autonomy". *Panstwo i prawo*, 1961, 8–9, 292–332.

146

[55] Jaroszynski, ibid.

[56] N. Ja. Sokolov: 'Formy pravotvorčestva v uslovijach obščenarodnogo gosudarstva'. *SGiP*, 1965, 7, 126–130.

[57] Cf. the standpoint of the legal literature on the question of the referendum: R. Šafarov: 'Institut referenduma v uslovijach obščenarodnogo gosudarstva'. *SGiP*, 1963, 3, 19ff. Sokolov, ibid. Eugeniusz Zielinski: 'Instytucja referenduma w panstwie socjalistycznym'. *Panstwo i prawo*, 1965, 2, 232–240. But especially: V. Kotok: 'O razvitii form sočetanija narodnogo predstavitel'stva s neposredstrennoj demokratiej v SSSR'. *SGiP*, 1960, 12, p. 14ff. And also: V. Kotok: *Referendum v systeme socialističeskoj demokrati*. M. 1964.

[58] The Supreme Soviet decided, at its plenary session of April 25, 1962, to work out a new constitution, and it elected a commission under Khrushchev to write the draft. Yet after Khrushchev's fall there has hardly been anything said about the new constitution, although the necessity of a new constitution is emphasized again and again. Cf. *Prawo i zycie*. Warsaw, May 27, 1962, 2–3.

[59] N. G. Aleksandrov, F. I. Kalinycev, D. S. Karev, et al.: *Osnovy teorii gosudarstva i prava*. Moscow 1960, 104.

[60] Cf.: N. Chalepov: 'Marksistkaja dialektika i sovremennyj revizionizm'. *Kommunist Belorussii*. Minsk, 1960, 11, 4–15.

[61] *Sočinenija*, 6th ed., vol. X, 61. And Chalepov, ibid.

[62] B. V. Ščetinin: 'Nekotorye čerty obščenarodonogo socialističeskogo gosudarstva'. *Izvestija vysšich učebnych zavedenij*. Pravovedenie. Leningrad, 1962, 2, 12–21.

[63] Cf.: V. A. Vajčuk: 'Razvitie socialističeskoj gosudarstvennosti k kommunističeskomu samoupravleniju'. *FN*, 1962, 5, 160–164.

[64] Fedoseev, *op. cit.*, pp. 7–8.

[65] Nikolaev, *op. cit.*, pp. 44–45.

[66] Il'inskij, *op. cit.*, p. 8ff. V. I. Kozochin, *op. cit.*

[67] V. M. Semenov: 'Principy sovetskogo socialisticeskogo obščenaradnogo prava'. *Izvestija vysšich učebnych zavedenij*. Pravovedenie. Leningrad, 1964, 1, 16–26. In this article the principles of the people's law are listed in eight points.

[68] László Révész: 'Recht und Sozialnorm', *op cit.*, pp. 14–15.

[69] *Uj szo*. Pressburg, September 25, 1965, 5. Article by László Szántó, academician: 'Thoughts on Socialist Democracy'.

[70] Cf.: Hans-Jürg Bopp: *Marxismus und Rechtswissenschaft*. Zollikon, 1963, pp. 21–22.

[71] Cf.: Alexander Patrzalek: *Instytucje prawa wyboczego Polskiej Rzeczypospolitej Ludowej*. Warsaw, 1963, 6. Cf. also the review of the book and the position represented therein: *Panstwo i prawo*, 1964, 5–6, 902–904. Review by Zygmunt Izdebski.

[72] *Bol'šaja Sovetskaja Enciklopedija*, vol. 29, 131.

[73] *The people's proletariat and the peasantry*. *Sočinenija*, 4th ed., vol. 9, 40.

[74] "The revolution is led by the people; the people are the proletariat and the peasants". *Sočinenija*, vol. 1, 139.

[75] *Sočinenija*, vol. 10, 233, and vol. 9, 113.

[76] Cf.: G. Ašin: 'Kakovo soderžanie ponjatija "narod" v istoričeskom materializme'. *Političeskoe samoobrazovanie*. M. 1964, 7, 62–65.

[77] Ibid.

[78] 'XXIII. s'ezd KPSS', *op. cit.*

[79] A method of operation which restricts itself to quoting from the works and explanations of leading Communists, without commentating or taking a position on them, i.e. without expressing one's own thoughts.

[80] 'Juridičeskuju nauku – na uroven' zadač kommunističeskogo stroitel'stva'. Leading article by the editors. *SGiP*, 1966, 3, 3–14. Here p. 3.

[81] Ibid., pp. 5–6.

[82] 'Povyšat' rol' provovoj nauki v formirovanii kommunističeskogo mirovozrenija'. Leading article by the editors. *SGiP*, 1963, 8, pp. 3–14.

[83] *Kommunist*, 1964, 12, 70–74.

[84] Cf. *SGiP*, 1965, 5, 45–52.

[85] Cf. the report of E. V. Tadevosjan in *VF* 1965, 10, 164–166, with an enumeration of the individual problems of the new planned branch of science.

[86] Cf. the report in *SGiP*, 1963, 3, 120.

J. FIZER

THE THEORY OF OBJECTIVE BEAUTY
IN SOVIET AESTHETICS*

"What is involved here is a very complex question and
therefore should be solved in a friendly dispute, in sharp
polemics, which should facilitate the search for truth. Today there is hardly a daredevil who would say: 'I know
the answer to the question of what is beautiful, an answer
which is truly Marxian, infallible, exact, undisputable, and
on the level of science.'" (Jurij Borev, 'Četyre axillesovy
pjaty', *Oktjabr'*, 1961, V. II, p. 211)

I

Beauty, as an aesthetic category until roughly the 'thaw' period in Soviet
aesthetics, was seldom treated epistemologically. While reading the pre-
Stalinist works on beauty, one has a feeling that the nature and the
validity of knowing beauty has been proscribed from Soviet aesthetics.
One looks in vain for the psychological definition of beauty and for a
theory construed from the standpoint of awareness of those qualities or
relations of objects which impinge upon man's sensory processes, or from
the standpoint of ascription by an individual of his own experiences to
an outside external reality. Beauty was simply recognized as existent,
and no psychological probing or verification of man's knowledge of
beauty was attempted. Its objective existence was assumed to be confirmed by the classics of Marxist ideology and, therefore, all that Soviet
aestheticians were to do was to illustrate the correctness of such confirmation. It was also assumed that the objective existence of beauty in
reality was tantamount to the objective existence of physical reality, and
hence any inclination to doubt one meant doubting the other.

Yet, even with this unyielding dogmatism, Soviet aestheticians could
not sustain without some epistemology. But here, too, they were antici-
pated by the classics. Thus they parroted the childishly naive 'proofs' of
Černyševskij or Lenin's angry journalism. The vast knowledge amassed
by Western psychology, natural sciences and scholarship in general,
which has been so extensively utilized by Western aestheticians, was

passed by in silence in the Soviet Union. The complexity of the subject-object relation, primarily an epistemological problem, is one to which Western thinkers devote much attention and in fact makes the focal point of their concern. In Soviet aesthetics this problem was reduced to a secondary question.

Sensory apprehension for Černyševskij was a reliable way of proving that beauty is an integral part of material reality, and that only people with "artificial, corrupt to the point of deceit, fantastic demands, people who cannot be completely satisfied"[1], cannot conceive of beauty in nature. To prove that beauty is objective Černyševskij employs this illustration. "All that one needs to do is to take one of those people who complain that there are few beauties and let him walk on Nevskij during the time of outdoor fête. Soon he will start pulling your arm continuously and say: 'Look, what a beauty! . . . . Oh, and that one . . . . Oh, and there is another one, look, that one is truly a beauty.'"[2]

Beauty, for Černyševskij was immanent in reality, or, as he called it, in actuality. To be aware of it one has to be a normal and thinking man; one has to possess "an unspoilt aesthetic emotion".[3] But what these prerequisites are, i.e. what is a normal mind, what is normal perception in general and aesthetic perception in particular, Černyševskij did not say. For him there was beauty in reality and a normal person sees it, a normal creator reproduces it. "An object which is beautiful in reality remains such in our eyes retaining all its material aspects . . ."[4]

Thus Černyševskij equated 'normal' sense perception with reality and excluded the possibility of *tertium quid*.

Mutatis mutandis, Lenin shares in this concept. Briefly, his entire epistemology is reducible to two such postulates: (1) Things exist independently of our consciousness, independently of our sensations, outside of us. (2) There is not, and there cannot be, any difference in principle between the phenomenon and the thing itself. The difference amounts to what is known and what is yet unknown.[5] But while for Černyševskij it was enough to go to Nevskij Prospekt and eye the Petersburg beauties to attest the existence of beauty, Lenin construed a theory of knowledge which he thought was genuinely Marxist. To attest the objective existence of matter, transmitted to us by our sensual apparatus, he elevated activity to the level of an epistemological category. According to this theory, it is through engagement and practical activity that man recognizes matter as

150

real, as objective. "The point of view of life, of activity, must be the basic point of view in the theory of knowledge."[6] Man's sensory apparatus, properly conditioned through work, "photographs, reflects"[7], this objective reality. This photography, this reflection, however, only approximates the objective. Yet, the reflected exists independently of the reflecting.[8]

The level and the degree of conditioning of the sense apparatus predetermines the degree of approximation. Each perceptive act is relative. On the level of the perceiving individual there is a subjective relativism, on the level of society there is a historical relativism. Relativism, of both kinds in Lenin's thinking, is proof for and not against the existence of the objective world. Human cognition "though incapable of absolutely and finally mastering its object, approaches it in a constant and progressive evolution, and its unlimited improvement tends to make it more and more *like* reality; it imitates more and more faithfully all the time the properties and relations of the world, which are themselves independent of this effort, and exist in themselves outside human thought."[9]

To extend this kind of epistemology to the domain of aesthetics, and particularly to the problem of beauty, one cannot help but make the following conclusion: since human senses register natural beauty, they attest its objective being. Although the photography, the reflection of the beauty individually and socially, is relative, it is nevertheless proof of the "existing model".[10]

Yet Lenin, in spite of his manifold interests, did not make any direct statement on the question of beauty. It is through deduction and interpretation that Soviet aestheticians consider their views on beauty as Leninist. This is how such a deduction was reached: if man's perceptive apparatus reflects reality in its totality, then all the elements of the phenomenon must necessarily have their equivalents in actuality. If some of these elements appear to be beautiful, then they necessarily reflect beauty of the noumenal world.[11] Yet, by the same token, one can deduce that anything resulting from uninhibited creativity has a model in objectively existing reality. Here, however, the concept of practical activity checks and verifies whether a reflected, a photographed object does have a pre-existing model or whether it is falsehood or nonsense.[12] In turn, is practical activity the object of political manipulation? But what is this all-sanctifying "practical activity"? In his *Theses on Feuerbach*, Marx

151

attempts to define this activity as "human sensory activity". This definition, being as vague as it is, leaves the keepers and the practitioners of the official ideology free to engage in endless juggling with it. During the 'cult of personality' anything that the Communist Party did was a just activity and served as a verification of the Truth. Nowadays, that activity is considered arbitrary (*proizvol'nyj*) and beclouds the Truth. In brief, there is no stable Marxist interpretation of empiricism as a source of knowledge.

II

Since Stalin's death the problem of beauty has received a great deal of attention. A number of larger studies have been published, dozens of articles and symposia have appeared in various publications, and different points of view have been expressed. On the whole, post-Stalinist opinions on beauty can be classified into three distinct groups: (1) those which uphold the theory of reflection (*teorija otraženija*); (2) those which propagate the theory of acquisition (*teorija usvoenija*); and (3) those which support the theory of expression (*teorija vyraženija*). Yet, as is to be expected, all aestheticians who have engaged in the polemics on beauty and expressed different views claim to adhere to the Marxist-Leninist orthodoxy.[13] The three groups are also referred to as: (1) naturalists (*prirodniki*), (2) socials (*obščestvenniki*), (3) expressionists (*vyraziteli*).

To the group of naturalists adhere such aestheticians as: A. Egorov[14], Ja. E. El'sberg[15], U. Romanenko[16], N. Dmitrieva[17], S. Permjakov[18], K. Zelinski[19], A. Astaxov[20], P. L. Ivanov[21] and a few others.

These aestheticians assert that beauty is immanent in nature, that it is an element in the dialectical process of becoming and that it has an existence of its own independent of human consciousness. This, they assume, is the only possible view consistent with the materialistic philosophy. Beauty "exists objectively both in the world of nature as well as in social order. Consequently, the objectively aesthetical exists independently of human consciousness."[22] The objectively beautiful (object) affects the subjectively perceiving human being (subject), properly conditioned by practical activity, in such a way that the latter cannot but attest to the existence of the former. In the act of perception there is the '*ascendancy*'[23] of the perceived upon the perceiving and not *vice versa*. Although the aesthetical valuation of objects and natural phenomena is always done by people, these objects supply the criteria for such a valuation.[24]

When pressed to define objective beauty, this group of aestheticians is at a loss. All they say is that such beauty exists and that "aesthetics is to discover it, to explain it, and thereby to help the ideologically-creative growth of artists and masses which perceive art."[25] Is there a chemical, physiological, biological peculiarity to the structure of those objects which are beautiful? What is, in brief, essential to objective beauty? The aestheticians in question are mute on such a question.

In the history of aesthetics the position of these aestheticians is similar to those Western aestheticians who have also supported the imitation theory for reasons, of course, different. The Soviet criticism of their position, coming from those who profess the "theory of acquisition", also does not differ essentially from the criticism long entertained in Western aesthetics. Mr. H. Osborne sums up very well such criticism when he writes: "In order to know that anything is an imitation of something else you must be able to know independently both that thing itself and that which it imitates. If you cannot know that which is imitated except by knowing the imitation, you cannot know that the imitation is an imitation or how exact an imitation it is."[26] The aestheticians of the first group cannot define the thing imitated, reflected, and photographed.

III

The group of 'socials' includes these aestheticians: V. Tasalov[27], Ju. B. Borev[28], V. Vanslov[29], L. Stolovič[30], A. Burov.[31] In the same way as aestheticians of the first group, these listed here claim to uphold the fundamentalism of Marx-Lenin. Their views on beauty, however, are considerably different. A. Astaxov ascribes the difference to the fact that they "use the early philosophical-economical manuscripts of Marx"[32], and deliberately neglect the works of the mature Marx. Although Astaxov is correct in his statement, it seems to me that the reason for this difference lies somewhere else. This group of aestheticians is more acutely aware of the complexity of the subject-object relationship than the first one. Hence, its epistemology is more hypothetical and less dogmatic than the one considered above. Publicly they can ill afford the rejection of the Leninist theory of reflection, yet it is evident that this theory gives them little comfort. As a result, they attempt to reinterpret this theory, enlarge it and thereby encompass within it their views on beauty.

Beauty, according to these aestheticians, does not exist outside the emotional significance of the perceived object. In reality, in nature "in principle it is impossible to find the natural essence of beauty".[33] In fact "natural phenomena need not be beautiful".[34] If, however, objective reality is not a depository of beauty, where does it reside? According to Tasalov, "it exists only in the framework of the aesthetic perception of reality"[35], or, as he states on another occasion, it is "a relationship between man and object".[36] Beauty, therefore, can not be determined and defined "outside any dependence upon man".[37] It results from man's interference into nature and, therefore, it is a non-material phenomenon; it is a specific state of human consciousness. The question of whether it has existed before such interference is, in the opinion of these aestheticians, irrelevant. Any ascription of beauty to the structure of matter is metaphysical. Vanslov calls his opponents who defend the objective beauty "meditative materialist metaphysicians".[38]

Beauty, however, is not subjective. It is socially objective. The beautiful, the aesthetic, occurs only between the socially conscious man and a socially meaningful object. A rapport in any other type of juxtaposition cannot yield beauty. Hence both factors (the perceiving and the perceived), in order to produce beauty, must be socially predetermined. Therefore, not everybody can create and experience beauty and not everything can become an aesthetically productive object. "The object of the aesthetic perception and experience cannot be an isolated phenomenon but is instead a concrete-emotional phenomenon existing in the *objective* relationship with society."[39] Tasalov equates beauty with social importance. ". . . Beauty is an expression of such correspondence of form of the object and its internal sense which man achieves consciously and purposefully in the process of his creation and which serves as a confirmation of its social importance."[40]

What these aestheticians are actually saying is that it is only through socially and politically conditioned perception that man is capable of seeing reality aesthetically. Into this point of view it is rather easy, for these aestheticians, to inject the notions of class consciousness, party-mindedness, Communist ideology, and the like. And it is these factors which, they claim, make aesthetic qualities of the perceived object objective. Thus, beauty is only socially objective. Its existence or non-existence outside human consciousness has nothing to do with its objectivity. Stolovič wrote that recognition of the objective aesthetic qualities does not mean the recognition of their existence prior to the emergence of human society. To prove the objectivity of the aesthetic qualities simply means to prove that they emerge and exist together with man and human society.[41] Vanslov expresses similar ideas when he says that beauty exists "in the creation of human hands, in the products and the labors of humanity, in the recreation and the mastery of nature, in art – *it exists objectively as their social quality*."[42] According to Vanslov, the objectivity of beauty rests also in its historical universality, in its non-class character. "Each epoch in the development of society raises its own ideals of beauty incorporated in art. But along with this, being class ideals, . . . these ideals contain some universal human moments which are the more significant, the more progressive the class."[43]

It is only logical that for this group of aestheticians there are not the objective laws of beauty so vehemently propagated by the first group. Such laws, they state, deprive man of his creativity and turn him into an instrument or a criminal. Every time he dares to deviate from such laws he acts against the natural order of things. As a result all creativity either becomes a minute, faithful reproduction or a gross violation of nature. In face of such a dilemma Ju. Borev pathetically exclaims: "What kind of laws of beauty?"[44] The aestheticians in question, therefore, state that any laws related to beauty are socially created laws which have nothing to do with matter or its structure. Such laws are "closely connected with political and moral criteria".[45]

Finally, in what sense does the position of these aestheticians complement or contradict Marxist epistemology? To answer this question one would have to be sure what this epistemology is and this hardly anybody knows for certain. We are of the opinion that the position described above corresponds with some aspects of this 'epistemology' and contradicts others. It seems that it complements the Marxian notion of "humanization of nature"[46], according to which man, in accordance with his necessities, recreates the substance of nature on the basis of objective laws. In addition to making nature useful he makes it beautiful. Without objective reality, however, beauty would also be impossible. Marx coined an expression, "objectivization of man"[47], by which he meant that the objective world which surrounds man, his immediate environment and everything connected with it, more or less bears an imprint of his activity. In the process of 'humanization' and 'objectivization' man develops his perception and emotions; in brief, his cognitive and creative tools. Developing these, he begins to recreate nature. While creating and recreating he "contemplates himself in the world created by himself"[48], or, in terms of the above aestheticians, man contemplates beauty he himself created. A. Burov uses these expressions of Marx almost *verbatim* when he defines beauty: "the object becomes beautiful only to the point at which man recognizes himself in it, his creative possibilities, and the richness of his human essence."[49] Only humanized objects are beautiful and only objectivized man is capable of creating beauty. Lenin's emphatic stress upon practical activity, it seems, agrees with this position. Vanslov even speaks of beauty in terms of these two notions of Marx: "Beauty does not exist as an essential quality of nature but exists as a quality of 'humanized' nature, i.e. a nature involved in the system of social relations."[50]

On the other hand, no matter how hard one tries, it is impossible to reconcile this position with the theory of reflection if by reflection we mean what Lenin meant, "the image of the external world".[51] Seen from this point of view, the criticism directed against these aestheticians is to the point. As Permjakov states, the theory of "aesthetic appropriation leads one astray from the Leninist position of reflection of reality in the consciousness of man, replaces it with the notion of the appropriation of reality"[52], "puts to the forefront the subject and suggests the incursion of the subject into reality".[53]

IV

The third group of aestheticians, defending the theory of expression, is probably the most interesting and the most liberal in its interpretation of Marxist-Leninist ideology. It is hard to estimate how many people share in their theory, but, all considered, it appears to be popular with younger intellectuals and literati. B. Runin's article in *Novyj mir*[54] is the strongest defense of this theory. I. Vinogradov's study[55] tends also to uphold this theory. N. Koržavin[56], A. Men'šutin and A. Sinjavskij[57] adhere to it also.

These people are less concerned with the definition of beauty than the two groups described above. Their theory of expression, self-expression, and self-revelation suggests a totally different kind of definition of beauty. While the first group, both in the creative act and the aesthetic perception, gives preponderance to the object, this group gives such preponderance to the subject. The creative subject is all that matters. The subject does not reflect, photograph, objectify, acquire. It unfolds itself. "The objective picture of reality does not enter the contents of the creative act. Such contents are based upon the author's arbitrary idea."[58] Works of art do not need any outside justification. They need to be true only to themselves. "There is an old maxim", writes Runin, "which states that art does not need the recognition of its products as reality."[59] Any attempt to formalize or to summarize the relationship between the object and subject ends in failure. Such a relationship is beyond man's comprehension and should not be posited in a rigid, dogmatic manner. In fact, it should not be posited at all. It prevents man from a more encompassing understanding of the nature of art. This is what Runin says: "If we shall start with the harsh, categorical opposition of lyric and epic, of subjective and objective, of personal and social, then we shall never penetrate the nature of the artistic creation."[60] "Where the subjective starts and where it ends nobody knows for sure. How does the fusion of these two occur? There is no answer to this question."[61]

Such being the case, creative man should be "faithful to himself".[62] His creativity "is only the result of the inner tension which dominates him and occurs as a motif of all of his lyrical impetuosity".[63] To quote further, creativity is "the pathos of self-assertion".[64] Lyrical poetry, in particular, is a medium of self-revelation. "For the lyrical poet there should not be a division of life into his own and the one beyond. In his poems the poet can express only his own personal experience."[65] He himself is "the subject of cognition".[66]

The concept of beauty concomitant with this theory of self-expression is different both from the apriori concept of the first group and from the socially utilitarian concept of the second group. It is different from the first in that it does not dichotomize reality into subjective and objective. As far as the function of art is concerned, it does not expect art to create or recreate beauty. Beauty is accidental in the creative act and if it does occur it is neither objective nor subjective. It differs from the second group in that it believes that man can have his own view of beauty irrespective of whether such a view corresponds with the prevailing social or political *dicta*. With the second group it agrees that beauty is a relational property, a mental state, a form of awareness.

V

The Soviet discussion of beauty, presented in this article, is interesting from many points of view. From the standpoint of Soviet aesthetics it is interesting because this is the first time that Soviet aestheticians have publicly disagreed on an issue which was considered to be solved and beyond dispute. From the standpoint of aesthetics in general it is interesting because Soviet aestheticians have found it possible to discuss beauty in a way that their Western colleagues have done for a long time. It is also interesting for the over-all status of Soviet ideology. That ideology claimed to be universally sufficient, claimed to have ready answers for all problems and eventualities. But here it failed to be even a sufficient framework for discussion, let alone a directive force. This discussion conceded that there is no Marxian answer to this question and that what has been suggested in the past as Marxian was only an arrogance of those who control thought. Behind this discussion one senses the presence of a mind intoxicated with the desire for freedom. That mind does not want 'canned' answers. All it pleads for is freedom to search for itself without official guarantee of finding what it hopes to find. N. Koržavin expressed this desire very well when he said: "But if it is known in advance what one has to search for, how to search for, what to find, what is then the role of an artist?"[67]

Rutgers, The State University

REFERENCES

* Originally published in *Studies in Soviet Thought* IV,2 (June 1964).
[1] Černyševskij, N. G.: *Estetika*. Moskva. 1958. p. 147.
[2] *Ibid.* p. 99.
[3] *Ibid.* p. 128.
[4] *Polnoe sobranie sočinenij* II. p. 157.
[5] Lenin, V. I.: *O literature i iskusstve*. Moskva. 1957. p. 11.
[6] *Ibid.* p. 15.
[7] *Ibid.* p. 12.
[8] Lenin, V. I.: *Sočinenija*. 4th ed. Vol. 14. p. 57.

[9] Kołakowski, Leszek: 'Karl Marx and the Classic Definition of Truth' in *Revisionism*. New York. 1962. p. 180.

[10] Lenin, V. I.: *Sočinenija*. Vol. 14. p. 123.

[11] *Idem*.

[12] On the basis of what was said the reader might interpret Lenin's views as analogous with the pragmatist epistemology. L. Kołakowski differenciates the two systems in this way: in Marxist theory of knowledge man's practical activity does not create truth but only determines its realization while in the pragmatist theory utility is treated as an instrument to create rather than to establish truth. (See his *Studia Filozoficzne*, 1952, p. 2).

[13] Astraxov, I.: 'Éstetičeskij sub"ektivizm i problema prekrasnogo'. *Oktjabr'* 1961, 3, p. 198.

[14] Egorov, A.: 'Protiv sub"ektivnogo istolkovanija prekrasnogo'. *Kommunist* 1957, 9.

[15] El'sberg, Ja. E.: 'Skolastičeskie koncepcii'. *VF* 1961, 1.

[16] Romanenko, V.: 'Real'nost' krasoty v prirode'. *Voprosy literatury* 1962, 1.

[17] Dmitrieva, N.: *O prekrasnom*. Moskva. 1960.

[18] Permjakov, S.: 'O sub"ektivistskix tendencijax v éstetike'. *VF* 1961, 5.

[19] Zelinski, K.: 'O krasote'. *Voprosy literatury* 2 (1960).

[20] Astaxov, I.: 'Éstetičeskij sub"ektivizm i problema prekrasnogo', *Oktjabr'* 1961, 3.

[21] Ivanov, P. L.: 'Éstetika v ob"ektivnoj dejstvitel'nosti'. *VF* 1962, 12.

[22] Ivanov, P. L.: *op. cit.* p. 51.

[23] Permjakov, S.: *op. cit.* p. 113.

[24] Ivanov, P. L.: *op. cit.* p. 52.

[25] Egorov, A.: *op. cit.* p. 114.

[26] Osborne, H.: *Theory of Beauty*. New York. 1953. p. 60.

[27] Tasalov, V.: 'Ob éstetičeskom osvoenii dejstvitel'nosti'. *Voprosy éstetiki* 1958, 1.

[28] Borev, Ju.: *Osnovnye éstetičeskie kategorii*. Moskva. 1960; *Éstetika texnicizma*. 1960.

[29] Vanslov, V.: *Problema prekrasnogo*. Moskva. 1957.

[30] Stolovič, L.: *Éstetičeskoe v dejsvitel'nosti i v iskusstve*. Moskva. 1959. 256 str.

[31] Burov, A.: *Éstetičeskaja suščnost' iskusstva*. Moskva. 1956. 292 str.

[32] Astaxov, A.: *op. cit.* p. 195.

[33] Vanslov, V.: *op. cit.* p. 60.

[34] *Ibid.* p. 64.

[35] *Voprosy marksistsko-leninskoj éstetiki*. Moskva, Gospolitizdat. 1956.

[36] Tasalov, V.: *op. cit.* p. 87.

[37] *Ibid.* p. 83.

[38] Vanslov, V.: *op. cit.* p. 64.

[39] Stolovič, L.: *op. cit.* p. 114.

[40] Tasalov, V.: *op. cit.* p. 83.

[41] Stolovič, L.: *op. cit.* p. 60.

[42] Vanslov, V.: *op. cit.* p. 64. (Italics supplied.)

[43] *Ibid.* p. 65.

[44] Borev, Ju.: 'Metod i sistema éstetiki'. *Voprosy literatury* 1961, 2, 104.

[45] Vanslov, V.: *op. cit.* p. 75.

[46] Marks, K.: *Iz rannix proizvedenii*. Moskva. 1956. pp. 592–594.

[47] *Ibid.* p. 563–567.

[48] *Ibid.* p. 566.

[49] Burov, A.: *op. cit.* p. 222.

[50] Vanslov, V.: *Problema prekrasnogo*. p. 80.

[51] Lenin, V. I.: *O literature i iskusstve*. p. 57.
[52] Permjakov, S.: *op. cit.* p. 113.
[53] *Idem.*
[54] Runin, B.: 'Spor neobxodimo prodolžit''. *Novyj mir* 1960, 11.
[55] Vinogradov, I.: *Problemy soderžanija i formy literaturnogo proizvedenija*. Moskva. 1958.
[56] Koržavin, N.: 'V zaščitu banal'nyx istin'. *Novyj mir* 1961, 3.
[57] Men'šutin, A., Sinjavskij, A.: 'Za Peotičeskuju aktivnost'. *Novyj mir* 1961, 1.
[58] Vinogradov, I.: *op. cit.* p. 26.
[59] Runin, B.: *op. cit.*
[60] *Ibid.* p. 199.
[61] *Ibid.* p. 197.
[62] Men'šutin, A., Sinjavskij, A.: *op. cit.* p. 228.
[63] *Ibid.* p. 226.
[64] *Ibid.* p. 225.
[65] Runin, B.: *op. cit.* p. 197.
[66] *Ibid.* p. 202.
[67] Koržavin, N.: 'V zaščitu banal'nyx istin'. *Novyj mir.* 1961, 3, 238.

PART TWO

STUDIES ON THE RELATION OF
WESTERN AND SOVIET THOUGHT

GUSTAV A. WETTER

FREEDOM OF THOUGHT
AND IDEOLOGICAL COEXISTENCE*

In recent years one could observe a number of occurrences within the Communist world-movement which aroused the impression that attempts were being made, if not to sever the bond between Marxism and *Weltanschauung*, then at least to loosen it considerably.[1] Previously the Communists had not only declared that Marxism represents a complete *Weltanschauung*, but they also made the claim, at least within the sphere of Soviet Communism, of leading the whole population, and not only the party members, to this *Weltanschauung*!

But this is no longer the case. For example, the Communist party of Italy declared at its last party meeting that it is opposed to "the state granting privileges to any one ideology, philosophy or religion or to any one cultural or artistic tendency to the disadvantage of others".[2] Soon after, the Communist party of France made a similar declaration and officially professed the principle of freedom of art and religion. Even within the CPSU such tendencies have allegedly been observed, although to a much lesser extent. For example, it is maintained that after the fall of Khrushchev, the new Soviet leadership showed a tendency towards pragmatism. And one points to the fact that Soviet ideology opened up several new sciences, such as empirical sociology, social psychology, information theory, etc. However, in the West, one is inclined to hope for similar tendencies in connection with the principle of peaceful coexistence. That is, whoever has only a superficial knowledge of this doctrine of Soviet ideology is inclined to interpret it in the same way for all areas of its relevance, as a readiness to live together peaceably with the non-Marxist world.

However, anyone who is more closely acquainted with the Soviet interpretation of this principle is well aware that its validity is restricted to the political and economic sphere, while the realm of ideology and thus of *Weltanschauung* is expressly excluded. This raises the question: is thereby all freedom of thought basically denied? Is freedom of thought limited solely to the inner sphere of the person? Is the principle of the impossi-

163

bility of peaceful coexistence in the province of ideology to be understood in the following way: you may think whatever you want but woe to you if you think too loudly or even seek to win from others recognition for your thoughts?

It is this question on which we want to concentrate in the present paper. It is not our intention to present a comprehensive study of the problem of freedom of *Weltanschauung* in Communism. We are limiting ourselves to the special point we have mentioned, namely the question as to whether the principle of the impossibility of peaceful coexistence in ideology restricts freedom of thought to the inner sphere of the person, in Marxist terminology to the sphere of individual consciousness, or whether, in spite of the rejection of ideological coexistence, freedom of thought is also possible in the realm of social consciousness. Since the question of ideological coexistence did not immediately become acute with the initiation of the politics of coexistence but began to come forward only at a later date, it would be appropriate to make some prefatory remarks about the genesis of the doctrine of coexistence.

In spite of its relatively young life, the Soviet doctrine of coexistence already has its history. When shortly after Stalin's death the new Soviet leadership instituted a policy of *détente* in the name of coexistence, Soviet ideology, in establishing the theoretical basis of the doctrine, placed the accent in a simple, undifferentiated way on the avoidability of war.[3] It was maintained that the principle of peaceful coexistence is a direct consequence of Marxist-Leninist teaching, the reasoning being as follows: It follows from Lenin's theory of imperialism that in the age of imperialism the chain of capitalistic countries exhibits stronger and weaker links. From this results the possibility for the militant working class to break the chain at its weakest link, and, from this as its base, to assault the entire front of capitalism. This means that Socialism will not be realized simultaneously in the whole world but only gradually, as one country after another 'falls away' from capitalism. Thus Socialist and capitalist countries will exist side-by-side during the course of an entire historical epoch, which means – to coexist.

With this we already have coexistence, but not yet *peaceful* coexistence. That this existence side-by-side of Socialist and non-Socialist countries will have a peaceful character supposedly follows from another basic thesis of Marxism. According to this thesis the transition to Socialism can only be carried out if the necessary subjective and objective preconditions for its realization have fully developed within the particular country. The insinuation that Socialist countries could harbor the intention to bring about Socialism in non-Socialist countries by the use of military force is rejected with indignation. Socialism cannot be exported like a commodity from one country to another. This appeal to Marxist-Leninist ideology is supposed to render especially credible the sincerity of the Soviet offer of coexistence.

A new note in the Soviet strain of coexistence was heard at the twentieth Party Congress of the CPSU in 1956. Khrushchev, in his report, expressed opposition to those comrades who wanted to extend the principle of peaceful coexistence to the area of ideology.[4] He emphasized that peaceful coexistence applies only to the political and economic relations with the West, but not to the ideological relations. In the realm of ideology all that is possible is a constant struggle between Communist and bourgeois ideology.

It is well known that the Chinese very soon started to accuse Khrushchev of revisionism because of his doctrine of coexistence. In order to meet them half-way, he made an effort, beginning about 1959, to give this doctrine a more aggressive appearance. The thesis of the avoidability of war, which had formerly received the main accent, was now to some extent pushed into the background. Peaceful coexistence signifies only the renunciation of military means in the conflict with the capitalist world, and not the renunciation of the struggle altogether. On the contrary, peaceful coexistence is nothing else than a form of class struggle, more precisely, class struggle "in the international arena".[5] Since the October revolution in Russia, the working class has had at its disposal in its battle against capitalism a weapon which it had never possessed before – the state. Since that time the class struggle has extended beyond the mutual relations between classes within individual countries to include the area of international relations. But this international class struggle should not be conducted with military means but exclusively with the weapons of political, economic, and ideological warfare.[6] And just as the struggle between the working class and the bourgeoisie within the individual countries must necessarily end in victory for the working class, so also, on the basis of the same historical necessity, the global conflict between Socialist and non-Socialist states will end in a victory for Socialism on a world scale.

From this sketch of the genesis of the Soviet doctrine of coexistence it is apparent that the question of ideological coexistence arose only at a rather late date. Originally coexistence meant nothing more than the avoidability of a new world war. Only subsequently did Khrushchev expressly limit the doctrine of coexistence to the political and economic sphere and exclude from it the realm of ideology. And then, at a still later date, the principle of class struggle was transferred back from the ideological sector to cover the political and economic sector as well, and coexistence was defined as class struggle in the international arena.

For the purposes of our discussion, we must first of all examine the more specific and detailed statements of Soviet ideology on the ideological class struggle. When in 1959 the doctrine of coexistence began to be propagated as a form of class struggle, *Kommunist* (the theoretical organ of the CPSU's Central Committee), published a leading article entitled 'Peaceful Coexistence and the Ideological Struggle', in which this tenet of Soviet ideology was more thoroughly substantiated.

The ideas presented in that article can also be found in subsequent Soviet publications on this subject; its contents can be shortly summarized as follows:

(1) The necessity of an ideological battle in spite of all peaceful coexistence results from the fact that the principle of coexistence concerns not the relations of states to each other but only the reciprocal relations of states with different social orders. Now, the state in the Marxist sense is a form of the political superstructure. It is a tool in the hands of the dominating class for the suppression of the other class. The states in the capitalist camp embody the domination of the capitalist class, the states in the Socialist camp that of the working class. The reciprocal relations of states with different social orders cannot be limited to diplomatic relations, important as these might be. Since there is an inexorable struggle going on between the working class and the class of capitalists, this struggle is necessarily expressed also in international relations, and, like every class struggle, in the form of an economic, political and ideological battle.

(2) This struggle is an objective, social, law-bound necessity. It cannot be avoided by any kind of settlement, even if one wishes to do so. And it will end, following the same inexorable necessity, with the victory of the more progressive class, i.e. the working class. Even the strongest party

and the strongest government cannot put an end to this international class struggle. All that can be done, and this is the goal of the policy of peaceful coexistence, is to see to it that this struggle does not lead to a military conflict, but is replaced by a competition among the various systems to win the support of the popular masses. Not weapons, but the will of the people should decide which social order is better, i.e. which produces a higher standard of living for the workers, more freedom and greater cultural development. But such a struggle necessarily presupposes the continuation of the battle of ideas, since the capitalist and Socialist systems are wrestling with one another for the recognition of the people.

(3) For this reason, the only view which does justice to the real state of affairs is that which links peaceful coexistence with ideological struggle. To claim to put an end to the ideological struggle would necessarily be either an act of deception or a betrayal by the Communists of their own *Weltanschauung*. But it cannot be demanded of Communists that they make ideological concessions and thereby demonstrate their good will, and that they show tolerance towards bourgeois ideas. Communists themselves do not demand, by the principle of peaceful coexistence, that the bourgeoisie surrender any of their ideological principles. Compromises can be made on some political questions, but not on basic, theoretical issues.

(4) An alternative to the ideological struggle accompanied by peaceful coexistence could be found only in ideological uniformity or at least in a kind of ideological truce. But both are equally impossible. Ideological uniformity would entail that all countries have to accept either the capitalist or the Socialist ideology. But since neither of the two sides is ready to surrender its ideology, such a plan would not be a program for peace and international friendship but a program for a crusade for the 'true faith', that is, a program for war.

It would be equally impossible to have an 'ideological truce', which would require that both sides, while retaining their own social orders and ideologies, would in the future refrain from any ideological warfare. In a time when millions of men are involved in social upheaval and the eyes of the world are focused upon them and ready to draw comparisons between the Socialist and capitalist systems, words have less ideological significance than do achievements, i.e., the level of the workers' standard of living in the various countries, economic and social accomplishments

167

in the sphere of democracy, science and technology, etc. It is impossible to set up any insurmountable barriers between individual countries in such a way that what happens on one side remains unknown on the other.

(5) Of course, not everything which goes by the name of ideological struggle is compatible with the principle of peaceful coexistence. Ideological struggle is not synonymous with cold war or psychological warfare. It is one thing to carry on a struggle of ideas, a fight over the evaluation of this or that phenomenon or process in reality, over the ways and means of realizing the ideals which are recognized by the larger part of humanity, over the advantages and disadvantages of this or that social system; such a battle of ideas can present no obstacle to the betterment of mutual relations between capitalist and Socialist countries. But it is quite another thing to support slanderous propaganda, provocation, war-mongering, incitement to sabotage and the spreading of rumors which could cause confusion and sow discord among the population. Such propaganda is not a struggle of ideas, even if it touches ideological questions, but subversive activity and interference in the internal affairs of other countries. This is nothing else than 'cold war', understood as the employment of all means to prepare for and then to kindle a 'hot' war; and the same applies to constant meddling in the internal affairs of the opposing side, in order to promote the downfall of the prevailing social order.[7]

In view of this development of the doctrine of ideological struggle, one will certainly have to agree to the view that the principle of peaceful coexistence, originally proposed for the political realm, cannot be carried over, without more ado, to the realm of ideology. In the problem of 'ideological coexistence' two levels must be distinguished – the level of theory and the level of practice. On the level of theory it is impossible to have peaceful coexistence between two theses which formally contradict one another. The principle that truth and falsity do not have equal rights applies here. But the matter takes on a different appearance if we pose the problem in the practical order, i.e. with regard to the practical intercourse of men having contrary convictions. Here we need a few clarifications, which should be made with the aid of the basic law of materialist dialectics: the law of the unity and struggle of opposites.

As is well known, this law regards contradiction as the driving force of all development, not only in the realm of thought, but also in the realm of being, i.e. in nature and society. Of course, to speak precisely, one would have to say that contradiction as such should not be regarded as the driving force; rather, as recent discussions by Soviet philosophers have also established, the contradiction is only the element which mobilizes and triggers the real, positive forces that push the development further. Nevertheless, it is very important to keep in mind that contradiction becomes a motive force only under the condition that one seeks to resolve it.

With regard to the actual conduct of two persons engaged in a discussion and faced with a contradiction, the following types of behavior are conceivable:

(a) The contradiction is simply allowed to remain; one does not try to solve it, but the mutually contradictory opinions are left unreconciled, standing in a vacuum.

(b) One regards his own position as the only valid one, not even considering the possibility that he himself might be at least partially wrong; instead, he tries in some way to silence his opponent.

(c) An attempt is made to resolve the contradiction by allowing the arguments of the opponent to confront those which one brings forth in support of one's own position, being ready to correct that position if necessary.

Only this last attitude is worthy of man and only with it can there be an advance in the discovery of truth. The first of these three positions, i.e. that which simply allows the contradiction to stand, would imply that one had despaired of the possibility of settling the question of truth; but if the question of truth is insoluble, then, in the end, human activity is robbed of its meaning, and this position would unavoidably lead to nihilism.

To consider one's own position as exclusively valid and to try to get rid of the troublesome contradiction by silencing the opponent or, even worse, by physically annihilating him would indicate that one is not concerned about the truth but only about the effectiveness of his theory. Such a theory would become ideology in the bad sense of the word – one whose only purpose is to justify its own interests and be able to make more effective propaganda.

Only the third attitude is worthy of man, who alone can let himself be guided by knowledge and the search for truth. And only this attitude can be designated progressive, since an advance in the knowledge of truth can only be attained by the resolution of a contradiction – which itself will prove beneficial to human practice.

169

Let us try, now, to apply these findings to the problem of ideological coexistence, particularly on the level of practice, the level of actual intercourse of men with opposing convictions.

The first attitude, which we designated as erroneous, was that which permits the contradiction to remain and does not strive for its resolution. This is an attitude which is frequently encountered in the West. The pluralism of world-views tolerated in the West, which is often regarded today as its spiritual foundation, is frequently misunderstood as meaning that differences in this area are irreconcilable. Thus, according to this view, to discuss the differences would be senseless; all that one can do is leave aside all areas of conflict in ideology and try to come to terms on practical problems. This is an attitude which I would like to designate 'lazy pluralism' – in Hegelian terms, one which avoids the 'strain of the concept'. It is in the Soviets' rejection of such a 'lazy pluralism' that one finds the core of truth in their view, i.e. that the principle of coexistence is inapplicable in the realm of ideology, since there can be no compromise between truth and falsity. But that does not rule out a correctly understood pluralism. Nevertheless, there must be at its basis an inner attitude which does not avoid the question of truth.

The second erroneous attitude which we mentioned is that which considers only one's own view as valid, without even entertaining the possibility of being partially or wholly in error, and thus attempts to keep the opponent from speaking (or even physically annihilating him). The error in this position lies in the fact that one passes by inference from the impossibility of peaceful coexistence between mutually contradicting *doctrines* to the impossibility of peaceful coexistence between mutually opposed *men*; also, theoretical differences are here settled by non-theoretical means. In the above-mentioned article in *Kommunist*, it is stated that no one can demand of Communists, in the name of ideological coexistence, that they renounce their principles and give up their *Weltanschauung*. No one can require them to embrace a different theoretical point of view, as long as they are not convinced of it. But dissenters can demand with the same right that Communists allow them their opinion as long as they have not become convinced of the contrary, and that the struggle against their convictions be carried out exclusively with intellectual weapons. Where dissenters have no access to publication media, where certain occupations, such as teaching, are inaccessible to them, and where students who profess

170

a religion are forbidden entrance to the university, it is undeniable that non-intellectual means are being used to wipe out intellectual differences.

The attitude which, in our analysis, proved to be the only one worthy of man and at the same time the only progressive one is that which attempts to solve the contradiction. By an examination of two contrary positions it can turn out that one's own position was right while the other side was wrong. But it can also happen that one's own view was wrong while the other side was right. Yet in the majority of cases it will turn out that both parties were in one respect correct and in another respect wrong, and that each of the two could learn something from the other. But, in any case, a resolution of the contradiction can only be attained through dialogue. If, in dialogue, one of the parties realizes that his opponent is advancing a genuine truth which previously remained hidden from him, then in this realization he is carried forward in his knowledge of the truth and in its actual embodiment in life. Consequently, it is just the person who holds highest the banner of progress that must also be the most ardently in favor of having dialogues with representatives of other positions. It does not befit him to silence or eliminate his opponent.

What was just said leads us back to the problem of pluralism. We just saw that contradiction brings about a progression only under the condition that one strives for its resolution. But this does not oblige us to go so far as to maintain that *only* contradiction and its resolution can be the source of progress. There could perhaps be still other such sources. Thus, the possibility of progress even in non-pluralistic societies cannot be denied *a priori*.

But, on the other hand, it is a fact that there were always differences of opinion among men, and there is no reason to be seen why this should be any different in the future. In view of this factual situation, it follows from our previous considerations that it is not only unworthy of man but contrary to the interests of progress not to make use of contradiction as a forward-driving force. This ought to be noted by those who feel the inclination to reduce everything to an undifferentiated uniformity.

Also contained in these remarks is a very important consequence for the adherents of pluralism, namely that contradiction brings about progress only when one strives for its resolution and does not attempt to preserve forever the particular contradiction with which one is presently faced. Perhaps there is a fear that resolving the contradiction could

171

put an end to any further development. But this worry would betray a very low opinion of the truth, as if at any stage in the development of our limited human knowledge the truth could ever be totally exhausted, as if after the resolution of the particular contradiction tormenting us today there would not arise new ones, which would force us to search again for new solutions. To despair of ever solving the particular contradiction which faces us today and to let it stand unresolved is to assume that attitude which we designated above as 'lazy pluralism'. To this attitude we must oppose a 'dynamic pluralism', which does everything in its power to resolve the contradiction disturbing us today, knowing well that after its resolution new contradictions will again arise, but knowing also that precisely because of and through this continual resolving and reappearing of contradictions a higher stage of development will be achieved.

As a result of our previous considerations we can set down the following statements: The impossibility of ideological coexistence holds on the level of theory, since peaceful coexistence between two mutually contradictory *doctrines* is impossible; but between the *men* who adhere to different doctrines peaceful coexistence is not only possible but is absolutely required. Of course, it necessitates a struggle between the two parties, but a struggle that is carried on only with intellectual means. The goal of this struggle can only be progress in the knowledge of truth, and not the elimination or physical liquidation of the opponent.

Perhaps one will object that all of this holds for the reciprocal behavior of individual men but not for the relations of classes and states. The principle of peaceful coexistence pertains to the relationship of states with different types of social orders. Just as there is an economic, political and ideological battle going on between the individual classes, so there is also a battle between the states which are governed and controlled by different classes.

There is much to be said against this theory; however, here we can only make a few brief remarks. First, it has to be noted that the theory rests upon the very problematic concept of class consciousness. As the different classes create for themselves their own political institutions, in the form of political parties and states, so in like manner the various classes also bring forth various and opposing types of social consciousness, in the form of art, morals, social-philosophical doctrines, etc. All these different forms of social consciousness have a class character; that is, they express the interests and aspirations, of a particular social group at any given time. For this reason there is an opposition between the bourgeoisie and the working class, which is just as irreconcilable in the ideological sphere as it is in economics and politics.

Again, much could be brought forward in criticism of the concept of class consciousness. Nevertheless, even setting aside this very controversial concept, one must challenge the substantiation of the impossibility of ideological coexistence which bases itself on the ideological class struggle. It must be asked who it is that carries on this ideological class struggle. If the individual class members are considered the only and exclusive bearers of this ideological struggle, then no further difficulty arises. But in this case everything that was said above retains its validity, i.e. what was said about the mutual behavior of individual men faced with a contradiction, especially the demand that contradictions in the realm of theory be resolved only by intellectual means.

But since the principle of coexistence is applied to the conduct of states towards one another, the fear readily appears that the authors of the doctrine of coexistence regard the state as the bearer of the ideological class struggle. The state as the political organization of a class is without doubt the bearer of the political struggle; it is also the bearer of the economic class struggle in those countries where it has a monopoly on foreign trade. Now if the state is also considered as the bearer of the ideological class struggle, this means that even ideology, i.e. philosophy, art, literature, and to some extent the sciences (especially the humanistic sciences), would be subject to the control of the state, and that there must exist a state art, state philosophy, state science, etc.

However, we have here the view which we rejected above as an incorrect position, namely, that differences of opinion and contradictions in theoretical questions are not solved through dialogue but are removed by administrative means. It cannot be a concern of the state to settle scientific, philosophical, artistic and literary controversies. Also, one may not object that it is nevertheless an affair of the state to protect from unsettling disturbances the particular trends which 'prevail' in a certain nation. One of the leading Soviet philosophers once remarked that it could occur that one person was right while all of the rest were wrong; and in these areas it is usually just those trends which initially experience almost universal opposition that become the wave of the future. If, in this case, the state wanted to support the 'prevailing' trends, it would thereby become reactionary. The state can only assume a neutral attitude in all of these areas.

This ideological neutrality of the state is called for first of all in its attitude in matters of internal policy. In many countries religion is allowed only freedom of practice; the right to propagandize is reserved for atheism, while it is forbidden to religion under the principle of the impossibility of ideological coexistence. Such an arrangement does not satisfy the demand for ideological neutrality on the part of the state. This means already that atheism is not carrying on its struggle against religion with purely theoretical weapons but with the help of the state's apparatus of force. What kind of a battle of ideas is it where one side can propagate its convictions freely and with the help of all types of modern mass media, while the other side finds itself in trouble with the police at the first attempt to do the same?

Now, the ideological neutrality of the state must logically also hold for the sphere of international relations. Truth is indivisible. If it cannot be a concern of the state to settle scientific controversies and other such disputes within a single country, then its competence in this area is not in the least increased by the fact that such questions are brought to it from outside.

In this connection the concept of 'ideological diversion' needs clarification. One must certainly reject the use of such methods as slander and provocation in the ideological dispute; and surely the states have the right to put up resistance when subversive activity is carried on under the pretence of ideological confrontation. However, if one understands by ideological class struggle the attempt to clarify for the people the advantages or disadvantages of this or that social system and to gain their acceptance, then the same right must hold here for everyone. And then Communists may not on the one hand call it 'ideological class struggle' to make propaganda in another country for their social system, and on the other label as 'subversive activity', as 'interference in the internal affairs of other countries with the intention of overthrowing their social order' the propaganda effort of the other side in the Socialist countries for its own social order and cultural values.

In conclusion I would like to formulate the results of our considerations in the following theses:

174

(1) The Soviet doctrine of coexistence strictly excludes the possibility of applying the principle of coexistence to the realm of ideology. But upon closer examination it turns out, paradoxically, that this does not necessarily rule out real freedom of thought.

(2) Marxism rightly emphasizes the impossibility of peaceful coexistence in the sphere of ideology, if by that it means the reciprocal relationship between mutually contradictory theories. There can be no peaceful co-existence between truth and falsity.

(3) However, if we are speaking about men with different, mutually contradictory convictions, then it must be unconditionally demanded that their mutual relations take the form of peaceful coexistence.

(4) From these theses there follows a further demand, that the ideological contradictions between men with different convictions be resolved by purely intellectual means, and not by force. What is especially demanded is the strictest neutrality on the part of the state's apparatus of coercion; it is better not to entrust the solution of theoretical controversies to the police.

(5) It follows from what was said above that there is a certain parallelism between the application of the principle of peaceful coexistence in the political and ideological realms: just as in the realm of politics the principle of peaceful coexistence does not exclude all political struggle between states having different social orders, but only one carried on with military force, so also the very same principle of peaceful coexistence does not exclude all ideological struggle between men of different convictions; it must only be demanded that this struggle be carried on exclusively with weapons of a spiritual nature and not – as Georg Lukács once put it – with weapons borrowed from the Red Army.

Pontifical Oriental Inst., Rome

REFERENCES

* Originally published in *Studies in Soviet Thought* VI,4 (December 1966).
[1] As, for example in the new party program adopted at the twenty-second Party Congress. Cf. B. Meissner, *Das Parteiprogramm der KPdSU 1903 bis 1961*, Cologne 1962, p. 226.
[2] *L'Unità*, Rome, 26. 1. 1966.
[3] Cf. A. Leont'ev, 'O mirnom sosuščestvovanii dvux sistem', *Kommunist* 1954, 13, 43–58.

[4] N. S. Khrushchev, 'Otčetnyj doklad Central'nogo Komiteta Kommunističeskoj Partii Sovetskogo Sojuza XX s"ezdu partii', in *XX s"ezd Kommunističeskoj Partii Sovetskogo Sojuza*, Moskow 1956, p. 116.

[5] L. Iliciov, 'La pacifica coesistenza e la lotta di due ideologie', *Problemi della pace e del socialismo*, 1959, no. 11, p. 8.

[6] 'Mirnoe sosuščestvovanie i ideologičeskaja bor'ba', *Kommunist*, 1959, 16, 7f.

[7] *Ibid.*, pp. 7–12.

J. M. BOCHEŃSKI

ON PHILOSOPHICAL DIALOGUE*

I

Studies in Soviet Thought is an organ of a group of men who claim to be exclusively devoted to philosophy, i.e. to theory. Of course, each of them is also a citizen and might, as such, take part in practical activities. The author of the present article has done so many times in the past and is still prepared to act similarly if he considers it his duty. But – and this is a second characteristic of the group – they do believe that specialization is not only possible – it is necessary. They believe that a man devoted to a particular important activity should, in the course of it, abstract from points of view and aims which are not proper to the given field. In particular, they assume that a philosopher acting as such should forget about everything else except his proper task, which is the solving of philosophical problems. To be more precise, it is assumed here that the philosopher acting as such is exclusively interested in *theoretical* problems and that he tries to solve them, not for the sake of anyone else but in order to increase his own knowledge. The attitude of a philosopher as understood here is first, theoretical and secondly, egotistical.

This assumption being made, it appears that the following aims are completely alien to the philosopher as such:

(1) The persuasion of other people. If a philosopher engages in a discussion, as he often does, this will not be in order to convince his adversary. The only thing he desires to achieve is *his own* conviction. He hopes either that he might learn from his opponent that his views are wrong and so gain a new and better grasp of reality, or that the arguments of his adversary may help him to formulate better, improve and strengthen his views. Of course, as a man, he may feel some charity towards the poor fellow who does not understand or just talks nonsense. But charity is conspicuously wanting in a purely philosophical attitude. As long as one engages in a philosophical discussion, he is not even allowed to use it in any way.

(2) The philosopher will feel even less the need for victory in a contest. He is always prepared to abandon his own views if he finds that the other person's ideas are more correct. Of course, we are all men, and just as we may fall under the influence of charity, so also – and easier still – we may become victims of the fighting spirit. But it is possible to avoid it and many instances are known of men who were and are completely devoid of such desires when acting as philosophers. Once again, the philosopher wants one thing only: better understanding for himself, not any 'victory'.

(3) Far less still will he be interested in any directly political or similar aim. To quote just one instance, the celebrated need for a better mutual understanding and possibly for love between East and West leaves him completely cold. That is, he might consider such aims as desirable, but on the condition that they are necessary or useful for his main goal, namely for learning. For instance, he might believe that a better understanding between Moscow and Washington would facilitate his entering into talks with Soviet philosophers from whom he hopes to learn something. But even in that case the philosopher will consider the efforts in that direction to be the concern mainly of other men, e.g. politicians, but not his concern.

And that means that the philosopher does not wish any sort of dialogue which has this or any similar aim. He does appreciate the efforts of men of good will who try to bring about some progress in human relations. But he is not directly interested. He does not work either for peace or for mutual understanding, does not seek any kind of victory, and does not wish to teach anybody; he only wants to increase his knowledge.

II

The above analysis needs to be completed from another point of view, i.e. by considering the social nature of scientific and consequently also of philosophical research. It is a well known fact that we cannot be successful in research work without a human context, i.e. without the possibility of consulting other workers and testing our ideas by submitting them to their examination. It is to be noted that this social aspect of the activity of a philosopher does not diminish in any way his theoretical and egotistical character. He tends exclusively toward one end only, namely his own knowledge. But in order to achieve that aim, some circumstances must be present, without which success is not possible. One such condition is the possibility of consulting other specialists.

Now this being so, the philosopher as such, because of his own interests, will naturally try to bring about this possibility. And that means that he will occasionally cooperate in helping other men to reach a level they must necessarily attain in order that they might be able to help him. The same rules of dialogue apply which are stated below with regard to this intermediate goal. The partners must have something to say pertaining to the field in which the philosopher works, and they must move in that field with sufficient knowledge and competence.

It follows that the philosopher can and even should behave in such a way that the level of thought in general be improved. That is probably what moves philosophers to communicate their thoughts and, generally, to teach. As a matter of fact, it is known that all philosophers did teach in one way or another. Some will perhaps say that they had to do so, because teaching is the only service they can render to society, which, after all, pays them. But, while this might have often been the case, it seems that the philosophers did not teach for that reason only. For one thing, many among them did not obtain much from their respective societies. Socrates got only poison, and many a philosopher was living from other activities – as Kant the Librarian and Marcel the Novelist. The deeper reason why the philosopher teaches is that he wants the level of thought to be improved, in order to help himself.

But if that be true, then the philosopher might also engage in dialogue with other philosophers for *that* sake. It will be not alien to his vocation to desire to meet and discuss with such men even if he cannot learn much from them, but on the assumption that his meeting them will help them to improve their level of thought and consequently enlarge the social groups he himself needs in order to develop his thought.

Yet, that sort of dialogue will not only be considered by the philosopher as having a secondary importance, subordinated to his main aim, but it will also take place rather rarely. He cannot forget that his main aim is the acquisition of knowledge and that *any* sort of other activities might divert him from it. Also to assume that sort of attitude towards a colleague supposes a feeling of superiority, which, as such, does not seem to befit a true philosopher. It must be admitted that, as a class, philosophers are not very conspicuous models of modesty. Still, at least the ideal of a philosopher is that of a man full of wisdom, i.e. of a thinker who knows better than the others just how little he does know, to use the famous statement ascribed to Socrates. There may be cases in which the inferiority of the level of someone's thought might be evident: but it is suggested that such cases will be rare and that a philosopher true to his ideal will seldom harbor feelings of superiority.

III

This having been said, let us ask the question: "What are the conditions on which a philosophical dialogue will be possible?"

Before attempting to answer this question, it will be useful to deal with the following preliminary problem which contemporary philosophers learned to consider from Moore: "What sort of question is it?" The answer will be that it is a purely *analytical* one. In order to know the conditions on which a philosophical dialogue will be possible, we cannot use any method other than the analysis of both nouns occurring in the question itself, namely of 'philosopher' and of 'dialogue'.

One aspect of the meaning of the term 'philosopher' has been described above: it has been said that a philosopher is a man who pursues only one aim, namely his own *understanding*; at least this is the way we do use the term 'philosopher' here. It should be added that the philosopher seeks this understanding *in his own field*, not, e.g. in biology or political science. He seeks the solution only of philosophical problems.

By the term 'dialogue' is meant an exchange of thoughts by means of writing or speech. It follows that at least two parties are needed for a dialogue, meaning not only two physically different persons or groups of persons, but also two different views, in our case, two different philosophical views. This needs to be stressed, because some people seem to consider their rôle in a dialogue as consisting in a simple acceptance of the views of their adversaries. That is, of course, completely wrong: a dialogue – or at least a philosophical dialogue – is not possible without opposing views. Moreover, a dialogue between philosophers will necessarily take the form of a discussion. It will be not only an exchange of thoughts, but also a clash of opposing views, i.e. an exchange of arguments by which the engaged parties will try to justify their own views and attempt to weaken or falsify those of their adversaries. Briefly, a philosophical dialogue will be an exchange of arguments between at least two persons or groups of persons, representing different and opposing philosophical views.

IV

It is now possible to obtain, by deduction, several statements concerning the conditions on which a philosophical dialogue will be possible, i.e. the necessary conditions of such a dialogue. They fall into two classes: some conditions are required in the philosopher himself, others in his partner or opponent. We shall first consider the former.

The philosopher engaged in dialogue must, if he is acting as a philosopher, enter into the dialogue with the sole aim of acquiring more understanding; the only possible social aim which makes an exception to that rule has been stated above. Otherwise, the dialogue may be interesting, useful and fruitful for other purposes, but it will not be a philosophical dialogue.

But a philosopher who seeks to increase his knowledge by the dialogue, does it by taking into consideration the views and arguments of his opponent. Therefore, two further conditions will be required of him: he must try to understand those views and be capable of doing so. The first – the will to understand – is obviously required by the very meaning of the term 'dialogue' as explained above. As to the capacity to reach that understanding of the opponent's views, the philosopher is obliged to know the general frame of reference within which his adversary moves. Consequently, if he wishes to do his job in a proper way, he will have to know his opponent's language, historical background, basic assumptions and other similar things without which a thorough understanding of another man's thoughts is impossible (especially the thought of a philosopher belonging to another school). In order to anticipate what we shall have to say about the dialogue between Communists and non-Communists, we must note the deplorable fact that so many persons in both of these groups believe that they can engage in a dialogue fruitfully without knowing a word of their opponents' language and without the slightest understanding of their background and frame of reference.

Moreover, it seems that the main effort of a philosopher participating in a dialogue will be directed toward understanding what his partner really means. The dialogue will therefore not be a simple opposition of

181

divergent views. To a large extent it will consist of questions asked by the philosopher in order to make clear what his adversary means. Consequently, immanent criticism, mostly in the positive meaning of that expression, will be a further essential part of the dialogue.

Finally, it is well known that a deeper understanding of certain doctrines is impossible if the philosopher who studies them is unable to feel toward them at least a degree of sympathy. That does not mean that he should accept them at their face value and become uncritical. But the criticism should always follow understanding and the latter is not possible without a successful attempt to forget, for the moment, the negative criticism, and just follow the doctrine under examination with the greatest possible sympathy.

The necessary conditions of a philosophical dialogue on the side of the philosopher are in brief: the will to know, the knowledge of the opponent's language and frame of reference, an effort to understand what he means and what is entailed by the latter, and a sort of sympathy for the doctrine in question.

V

If we turn now to the opponent, we find that several conditions must be present in him too, in order that the dialogue be possible.

First, the philosopher will discuss only with someone who is supposed to have something to say about the problems he is interested in himself. He may listen to or question biologists, politicians or engineers, but he will not discuss with them, if they do not happen to have something to say about philosophical problems. For as a philosopher he could not possibly gain anything from such a discussion.

Second, he will require in his opponent not only an interest in his own problems, but also a certain capacity for dealing with them, because what the philosopher expects from a dialogue is either to be convinced that his views are wrong, or to see their truth more clearly in the light of the objections. He usually hopes to clarify and strengthen his position by the dialogue. But a man who does not understand the problem or who is not able to think on a scientific level cannot possibly help the philosopher to achieve this. Consequently, he may be the object of a 'maieutic' conversation or of fun, but not a partner in a dialogue.

It seems that those conditions are not only necessary but also largely sufficient and that no other qualities are required in the opponent. However, it has been asserted that two further qualities are necessary: first that he should be a rational philosopher, or (this expression being redundant) a man who, like the philosopher himself, seeks only understanding and nothing else; and second, that he should comply with the Platonic rules of dialogue, i.e. refrain from insults and arguments *ad personam*.

Now, both of these requirements are to a certain degree justified. It is clear that a complete irrationalist cannot possibly be a partner in a philosophical dialogue, for he cannot supply rational arguments, which alone interest the philosopher. But assuming that he supplies at least some such arguments, a philosopher may discuss with him, even if his basic attitude is not that which the philosopher assumes himself. For even in that case the latter can learn something and consequently can engage in the dialogue profitably. This point has often been misunderstood under the influence of a position which is itself not philosophical, but rather mystical, namely that of illuminism ("les philosophes", said Whitehead, "were not philosophers").

The following instance may make this point more clear. Suppose the philosopher meets a partisan of the Advaita Vedanta, for whom monism is a religious dogma, i.e. a dogma accepted on non-rational grounds. Will it be possible to discuss philosophically with such a man? Of course it will, but only under the following condition – that the Vedantist be able to supply some rational arguments in favor of the monism and to do so on a sufficiently high level of insight and sophistication. Such a discussion may be very fruitful indeed. Only someone who has never had any contact with, say, Çankara, can deny that the profit may even be enormous.

The second condition mentioned above, namely that the opponent should keep to the Platonic rules of dialogue, also has some justification. It is a fact that a man who insults his adversary renders the dialogue more difficult. The philosopher may get angry, and that is not a very suitable mood for speculative thought. So if there is too much abuse and *ad personam* argument, it may appear that the dialogue is useless or of little value. But this is an extreme case. Normally, as long as the opponent keeps within certain limits, and is able to come forth with interesting, rational arguments, the philosopher will be ready to suffer for the sake of knowledge some discomfort caused by his partner's barbaric attitude. So it seems that the second condition suggested above is not essential, at least within certain limits.

In order to avoid misunderstanding, it will be good to mention that this kind of behavior may legitimately lead the philosopher to refuse personal relations with a man who behaves badly. The knowledge he is seeking can usually also be found elsewhere, and no one is condemned to discuss only with Mr. X or Mr. Y. If that is the case, it seems to be the right of the philosopher to refuse such a man personal relations and even discussion.

That is what many people seem not to realize. There are quite a number of writers who first grossly insult someone and then write him kind letters asking for books, personal help, etc. If they were forced to behave like that, one could perhaps consider their request. But usually they are not, as is shown by the fact that many of their colleagues, i.e. those of the same country and school, behave decently. It is suggested here that philosophers should show more character in refusing to talk to such uncivilized boors. They could by doing so help improve the general atmosphere of discussion and so contribute to making it more profitable.

However, a certain amount of this boorishness is not fatal to philosophical discussion if the ill-mannered participant at the same time offers some rational arguments which are worth considering.

To sum up: the philosopher will be willing to enter into a philosophical dialogue with every man who says something competently on problems the philosopher is interested in. These seem to be the main and fundamental conditions for a philosophical dialogue.

VI

It is possible to think of a type of a dialogue which we could call 'philosophical' in the fullest meaning of the word. This is a discussion between two philosophers who, while sustaining different and opposed views, are both pursuing the same aim. This would be the case when both are philosophers and both desire only to learn something by the dialogue. In order that such a dialogue be successful all conditions enumerated above will be required in both opponents. Each of them will consequently be obliged to know his opponent's language, frame of reference and basic assumptions. Each will try, above all, to understand the other and, while doing so, will try to engender the greatest possible sympathy for the adversary's views. Each will have to be interested in the same problems and be able to deal with them in a competent way.

A dialogue of that sort is surely a most desirable thing for every philosopher. For it not only gives him the possibility to test his opinions against the arguments of another philosopher but the partner also helps him considerably in working out those opinions by asking him questions and trying to understand them for his own sake. Such a dialogue, however great the opposition between the views in question, may become a true collaboration in a common effort toward the solution of problems in which both philosophers help each other to reach a higher level of understanding.

Unfortunately, this ideal is very seldom achieved. Most of the instances known to the present writer are dialogues between members of the same philosophical school, where the discussion is concerned not with basic problems, but with questions of detail. There might exist other more deep-reaching discussions between representatives of radically divergent views, but they are rare and very difficult to obtain.

Yet the dialogue of a philosopher does not need to achieve this perfect form. Even if it is carried on with a man who does not aim solely at understanding, with an opponent who does not care to understand well what is said, the mere fact that it offers an opportunity to test our views in a clash renders the dialogue useful and sometimes even very fruitful. Of course, the adversary who does not carry on a dialogue in the ideal manner just described will gain less than the philosopher who does; but it must be recalled that the final aim of the philosophical dialogue is always egotistic: increasing the philosopher's own insight, not that of someone else.

VII

Let us apply our results to the problems of philosophical dialogue between Communists and non-Communists. This problem is of central importance for Sovietologists working in the area of philosophy. It is true that they might continue their research without any sort of dialogue with the Communists. They do, of course, desire personal contacts with their Communist colleagues, but this does not need to be a philosophical dialogue. Up to now, such contacts consisted mainly in the Sovietologists asking questions, the aim of which was simply to learn about the views of the Soviet philosophers. In other words, the Sovietologists in philosophy usually functioned as historians of philosophy, not as philosophers.

However, a historian of philosophy is normally interested in theoretical, systematic questions. Therefore most students of Soviet philosophy would probably wish to enter into a dialogue with Communist thinkers, if only such a dialogue – namely a philosophical one – were possible.

But is it? In order that it be possible, a number of conditions must be present both in the philosopher himself and in his opponent. Let us begin with the former and ask if there are, among non-Communist philosophers, thinkers who satisfy the conditions formulated above.

One among these conditions is certainly present: there are many men in the free world who may be called 'true philosophers', i.e. men who desire nothing else than better understanding of philosophical problems. This may be asserted in spite of its denial by the Communists and also in spite of the existence of a minority of philosophers who preach the so-called *'philosophie engagée'*, i.e. the necessity of pursuing some practical aims. It is simply a fact, that the vast majority of our philosophers are philosophers in the true sense of the term.

There is also often no lack of will to understand the Communist doctrines and to enter a dialogue with them. Far more serious is the nearly universal lack of the special knowledge necessary for such a dialogue. The great majority of non-Communist philosophers do not know Russian, are not very informed about the historical background of their partners and often have little knowledge of their explicit ideological assumptions. Under such conditions the dialogue cannot be fruitful.

However, there exists a small group of philosophers who possess said knowledge. They are, indeed, very few – perhaps no more than two dozen. Those men could and, it is believed, should try to enter into a philosophical dialogue with the Communists – on the condition that the qualities required for it are present in their partners.

VIII

But are they? One might first think that this is not the case. Let us begin with the first condition. The partner in a philosophical dialogue should be interested in the same type of problems as the philosopher with whom he is discussing, i.e. he should be interested in philosophical problems. Now when we consider what is often published in the official Soviet academic journals devoted to philosophy, we see that this condition is often absent. We find first, that the leading authors, the *peredovye*, treat mostly political and not philosophical questions. Here are a few examples from recent [1966] issues of the most important Soviet philosophical journal, the *Voprosy Filosofii*: Nr. 1 on the penetration of the Cosmos, by two cosmonauts[1]; Nr. 2 a dissertation on the 'Leninist Course'[2]; Nr. 5 an article by I. G. Kurakov on the efficiency of industry[3]; Nr. 7 another by G. O. Zimanas on the relations between socialist countries.[4]

Moreover, even if we leave aside the *peredovye* and consider the subject matter of the normal articles appearing in the academic journals, as well as that of many books, we find that many of them do not have anything to do with philosophy as it is understood outside the Communist world. Let us take another volume of the *Voprosy Filosofii*, that of 1965. We find there, among other articles, the following: H. V. Adfel, on the organization of the economy[5]; I. L. Andreev, on social processes in the liberated African countries[6]; G. S. Deborin, on the international impact of the construction of Communism in the S.U.[7]; V. N. Jagodkin, on the function of the material interests of the worker in the development of industry.[8]

Those few instances were quoted in order to show that the situation as represented, e.g. in the Fribourg Bibliography of Soviet Philosophy, did not change much in that respect during the last few years.

That is probably the reason why so many non-Communist philosophers feel that a dialogue with Communists is useless. They believe that Communists are not interested in their problems. However, those who share this view are simply wrong. Alongside of political, sociological and economic speculation, one finds in the Communist literature in general, and in the Soviet writings in particular, many items which are explicitly concerned with classical philosophical subjects.

But even when Soviet philosophers are considering subjects which, as such, are clearly philosophical, the type of problem they discuss is often very peculiar. They dedicate much time and effort to solving questions which would never arise if they did not presuppose the sayings of the 'classics' as established once and for all. One typical case is the truly enormous amount of work and writing in the Soviet Union which has been devoted to the famous problem of *sovpadenie*, i.e. of the coincidence between dialectics, theory of knowledge and logic. This is a question which I believe would never bother any philosopher who is not a Leninist, not even an adherent of dialectics, not even a pure Marxian. Another similar problem is that which arises from Engels' statement that the unity of the world consists in its materiality. Or let us just mention the chapter titles of the recent report by Dr. H. Fleischer on Soviet philosophy in 1964–1965[9]: 'Opposition between matter and consciousness'[10]; 'Universal and social dialectics'[11]; 'One or more dialectics?'[12]; 'On the 'Basic Contradiction' in Socialism'[13]; 'The contradictory character of movement'.[14] Very few non-Communist philosophers would consider such questions as philosophically interesting.

All that being true, one can understand the position of many non-Communist philosophers who after meeting such problems, decided that a dialogue with their Communist colleagues would not be useful since the latter do not seem to study the same kind of problems as they do.

IX

But that is not the whole story. Not all Soviet writings are about political or other non-philosophical questions; and not everything they are debating is so closely linked with their peculiar assumptions that it can be studied only by them. On the contrary, it is easy to show that Soviet and other Communist philosophers often discuss those very questions which are being debated by non-Communist philosophers. Here are a few instances: In ontology, much work has been done in the Soviet Union on the categorial problem.[15] In theory of knowledge, the Communists always defend a strictly realist doctrine[16], which one may not accept but which certainly is one among the possible solutions of a generally recognized philosophical problem. They often study the problem of universals and of abstraction.[17] In logic, there exist now in the Soviet Union two mutually opposed schools, one which might be called more formal, the other more dialectical[18]; and whatever one may think about the solutions proposed by them, the problems of the foundations of logic, of general methodology, etc., which they discuss are again classical philosophical problems. In psychology, the problem of the relation between mind and body has repeatedly been the subject of considerable work.[19] The foundations of morality are perhaps examined in an unsatisfactory way, but

188

they still are examined.[20] The same is true about the foundations of art and the theory of aesthetic experience. All these topics may be treated differently than they are by other philosophers, but the problems – and that is the point here – are very often the same.

If this is the case, it satisfies the first condition required of a Communist philosopher, in order that he might become a partner in a philosophical dialogue.

X

Now, is the second condition also met? Do Communist philosophers work on these problems with sufficient knowledge? Is their level of information, insight and method sufficiently high, that a serious non-Communist philosopher might profit by carrying on a dialogue with them?

To this question also most non-Communist philosophers have given, and still give, a negative answer. Indeed, it looks as if the vast majority of them up to now considered the level reached by Communist philosophers as quite insufficient. The latter often seem not to realize this because their own press presents some unimportant writers, who do not have any noticeable influence in the philosophical world outside the Communist bloc, as the great thinkers of the West. But that is surely a mistake. The sore fact is that Sovietologists who try to persuade their non-Communist colleagues that there *is* something valuable in Communist philosophy have had as yet very little success. Most non-Communist philosophers of any importance refuse the dialogue because they are convinced that there is no one with whom to discuss.

It must be said in their favor that they could hardly be expected to have a more correct picture of the real situation. What is presented to them by the Communist side – mostly through local, insignificant and belligerent Western Communists – is usually below any acceptable level. Moreover, even when sympathetic and informed authors, like Fr. Wetter, report competently on the philosophical life in the Soviet Union, those reports are published late and are read – if they are, because mostly they are not – a number of years after they have been drafted, i.e. still later after the appearance of the writings on which the reports are based. On the whole, non-Communist philosophers have at their disposal only an image of Communist philosophy which belongs to past years. But during those years an incredible amount of primitivism and nonsense was pruned out of Communist philosophical books and journals.

But even now there are serious reasons for disbelieving that among the Communist philosophers there are a number of men who move on an intellectually decent level. The Communist countries, and especially the Soviet Union, usually send abroad men who very often astonish their foreign colleagues by their lack of information and insight. This is a painful subject and the present writer would like to avoid mentioning names. But he might say that quite recently, at a large international meeting, there was a young man who was talking about Heidegger, Kant, the analytic school and various other things without the slightest knowledge of them, and when some people present told him that what he said was simply untrue, he could not even answer. Unfortunately that was no exception. The Communist countries seem to insist on preventing real philosophers from going abroad and on presenting to the non-Communist philosophers only a strictly limited group, which by no means represents the best in Communist thought.

The result is, as has been said, that the great majority of non-Communist philosophers disbelieve the possibility of a philosophical dialogue. Some of them will probably be ready to carry on a dialogue for other aims – political, religious, humanistic, etc. –, but this is not a philosophical dialogue, for that is regarded as impossible.

XI

The truth is that while many Communist philosophers still work on a low level, there are among the thinkers of the Soviet Union and the other Communist countries, many men who do not deserve to be judged as inferior to their colleagues in other countries. This is a contention which has constantly been made in *Studies in Soviet Thought*, and an effort has been made to substantiate it by monographic studies. We are not going to repeat here what has been stated in those studies; a few examples will suffice.

Whoever read N. Lobkowicz's *Das Widerspruchsprinzip* [21] will know that some Soviet philosophers deal with the Zenonian paradoxes in a competent and relevant way. The book by A. A. Zinov'ev on philosophical problems of many valued logic [22] might have displeased some reviewers, yet it seems to be one of the most significant books in the field. The studies of Birjukov on Frege[23] are certainly pieces of decent work. What K. Ballestrem brought out in his bibliography of Soviet translations of Western classical philosophers[24] shows that the level of information is perhaps not quite satisfactory, but still respectable. Ingarden's highly speculative and difficult essays have been edited in Russian with a truly excellent preface.[25] This only covers the Soviet Union. In Czechoslovakia, the name of Kosik alone will suffice to show that there *is* serious philosophy in that country. In Poland, even if we disregard those philosophers who are not Communists, Schaff stands out as worthy of respect, whatever one's views might be. One might perhaps list as a further example the Yugoslavian *Praxis*, which is a very interesting philosophical journal, even if it is claimed – not without reason – that the general status of philosophical thought in Yugoslavia is far from clear.

Moreover, it is a fact known to every Sovietologist interested in philosophy, that the level of information of method and of insight into problems is steadily rising in all Communist countries, above all in the Soviet Union. One phenomenon must be mentioned in this context, namely, the wide gap which separates the technical publications like the *Filosofskaja Enciklopedia* and the more official popular writings. While the former often attain an excellent level, the latter usually lag far behind them. And yet a clear improvement is visible even in those official and popular writings. To quote just one instance, the new *Philosophical Dictionary* is quite different from the (really scandalous and ignorant) old one.[26]

There is some competent philosophical thinking in the Communist countries and its level is improving.

XII

The conclusion is that also the second condition required of the partner in a philosophical dialogue is often found in Communist philosophers. And so, both conditions being satisfied, the dialogue appears to be possible.

Of course, the ideal type of truly philosophical dialogue will be far more difficult to achieve, because of the Communists' *partijnost'*. Yet it is perhaps not an over-optimistic estimation to say that even that type of dialogue is not completely excluded at the present moment and the prospects for the future seem to be still better.

It is believed that philosophical dialogues with Communist philosophers could serve a special purpose for non-Communists. The fact is that Communist thinkers assume principles and methods which are often radically different from those used by their non-Communist colleagues. For one, they are as a group by far the most important representatives of metaphysics (of course in the non-Communist, not in the Engelsian meaning of the word). They belong also to the rather small group of present day philosophers who hold strongly to the doctrine of real essences. While there are also Hegelians elsewhere, it seems that the Soviet Union is the country where the influence of the German thinker is by far the most alive – with unexpected results, e.g. in methodology. Even in ethics, a part of philosophy which appears to be lagging behind other disciplines in the Communist countries, there is an unmistakable attitude which differs radically from that assumed by most non-Communist philosophers. Last, but not least, one is impressed by a completely new approach to the history of philosophy, one which overcomes our own deplorable Eurocentric attitude.

It might therefore be expected that non-Communist philosophers, whatever their own standpoint might be, could greatly profit from a philosophical dialogue with their Communist colleagues.

University of Fribourg,
Inst. of East-European Studies

REFERENCES

* Originally published in *Studies in Soviet Thought* VI,4 (December 1966).
[1] *VF* 1966, 1.
[2] *VF* 1966, 2.
[3] *VF* 1966, 5.
[4] *VF* 1966, 7.
[5] *VF* 1965, 3, 10ss.
[6] *VF* 1965, 8, 564ss.
[7] *VF* 1965, 10, 119ss.
[8] *VF* 1965, 6, 38ss.
[9] Helmut Fleischer, *Philosophie in der Sowjetunion 1964–1965* (Berichte des Osteuropa-Instituts an der Freien Universität Berlin, Heft 74). Berlin 1966.
[10] *Op. cit.*, p. 54.
[11] *Op. cit.*, p. 56.
[12] *Op. cit.*, p. 59.
[13] *Op. cit.*, p. 61.

[14] *Op. cit.*, p. 64.

[15] Cf. G. Planty-Bonjour, *Les catégories du matérialisme dialectique* (Sovietica). Dordrecht 1965.

[16] Cf. Th. J. Blakeley, *Soviet Theory of Knowledge* (Sovietica). Dordrecht 1964.

[17] Cf. the items 'Abstraktion' (p. 48a) and 'Allgemeine' (*ibid.*) in: *Bibliographie der Sowjetischen Philosophie* (Sovietica). Dordrecht 1964.

[18] Cf. W. F. Boeselager, 'Soviet Dialectical Methodology', *SST* 1966,2, 135–144 (reprinted above, pp. 94–103).

[19] Cf. T. R. Payne, 'On the Theoretical Foundations of Soviet Psychology', *SST* 1966,2 (reprinted above, pp. 104–114); and the bibliography of S. L. Rubinštejn by the same author, *SST*, 1964,4, 78–80.

[20] R. T. De George, 'The Soviet Concept of Man', *SST*, 1964,4, 261–276; 'Soviet Ethics and Soviet Society', *ibid.*, 1964,3, 206–217.

[21] N. Lobkowicz, *Das Widerspruchsprinzip in der neueren sowjetischen Philosophie* (Sovietica). Dordrecht 1959.

[22] A. A. Zinov'ev, *Filosofskie problemy mnogoznačnoj logiki*. Moskva 1960. Cf. *SST*, 1962, 1, 37–48.

[23] B. V. Birjukov, *Two Soviet Studies on Frege*. Translated and edited by I. Angelelli (Sovietica). Dordrecht 1964.

[24] K. G. Ballestrem, 'Bibliography of Soviet Historiography of Philosophy: Editions in Russian Translation', *SST*, 1963,2, 170–175. Cf. 'Soviet Historiography of Philosophy', *SST*, 1963,2, 107–120 by the same author.

[25] R. Ingarden, *Issledovanija po estetike*, IIL. Moskva, 1962, 572 pp. Preface by W. Razumnyj, translation by A. Ermilova and B. Fedorov.

[26] Cf. *SST*, 1964,1, 71–74.

ERVIN LASZLO

THE SECOND SOVIETOLOGY*

In his paper 'Why Studies in Soviet Philosophy'[1], Professor Bocheński advanced two premises to substantiate the theoretical as well as practical import of philosophical Sovietology: "(i) not all Soviet philosophy is nonsense; on the contrary, much of it is philosophically interesting; (ii) Soviet philosophy is not irrelevant; it is an important factor in the phenomenon of Communism which, as everybody will agree, is important both theoretically and practically."[2] Among the additional reasons for engaging in Sovietology Bocheński gives overcoming that kind of philosophical sectarianism which makes Western thinkers unwilling to give serious consideration to the work of their Soviet colleagues.[3]

These are good and valid reasons for studying contemporary Soviet and other Marxist-Leninist philosophies[4], for they explicate why an up-to-date knowledge of their results may be valuable to the cause of contemporary thought. Sovietology, they imply, has the important task of obtaining and passing on information about current Soviet philosophy in Western philosophic circles.

I wish to suggest here that, if Sovietology is truly to advance the cause of contemporary thought, it has another and equally important task: that of obtaining and passing on information about contemporary *non*-Communist philosophy in *Soviet* philosophic circles. I shall call this type of endeavor 'second Sovietology' in distinction to the standard kind delineated by Bocheński, to which I shall refer as 'first Sovietology'. This paper is devoted to exposing the theoretical justification and the practical feasibility of *second* Sovietology.

I. THE JUSTIFICATION OF SECOND SOVIETOLOGY

A number of questions need to be considered. I shall formulate and try to answer each in turn.

(i) *Is information about Western philosophy of potential benefit to the philosophical concerns of Soviet thinkers?* Let us consider where Soviet

194

philosophy stands at present in relation to the ensemble of schools and theories which make up the great complex of contemporary non-Communist thought.

The relative accomplishment of current Soviet work in philosophy has been emphasized by Bocheński in justifying his affirmation of its philosophical interest; but he had to admit that, aside from the classification of ontological categories, where the Soviets are ahead of the United States, even accomplished Soviet work (as in logic) is at best no more than comparable to that of Westerners. Other specialists make clear that practically all major fields of endeavor in Soviet philosophy are plagued by still unresolved problems. (Bocheński himself concedes cosmology, psychology, social philosophy, axiology, and the history of philosophy.[5]) The 'special issue' of *SST*, on 'Open Questions in Contemporary Soviet Philosophy' (VI,3) pinpointed and discussed open questions in Soviet ontology, epistemology, theory of social law, and philosophy of law and state. Specialists writing in this same journal have made the presence of such open questions clear as regards Soviet ethics[6], the doctrine of *'partijnost'*[7], the philosophy of physics[8], aesthetics[9], and even such special but basic concepts and problems as the notion of practice[10] and the problem of materialism.[11] In addition to difficulties on these fields, there are areas of investigation in Soviet philosophy which are, to use Buchholz's term, 'empty domains'. Buchholz listed these in 1961 as: the question of the meaning of life; the problem of death; intuitive knowledge; and all questions of the individual and his particular problems.[12] While since then some have been discussed and hence are no longer 'empty' (e.g. the questions of the individual, by Kołakowski and those Polish, Hungarian and Yugoslav thinkers who go back to the concerns of the young Marx), other fields, such as meta-ethics (in which S. Stojanovič is still something of a rarity), meta-philosophy in general, descriptive metaphysics and linguistic analysis are still underdeveloped, if at all cultivated. This is not to deprecate current Soviet philosophy. It is incomparably more accomplished than it was even in the 'fifties, and criticisms advanced of it in those days by such authorities as Bocheński and Wetter no longer fully apply – as these thinkers readily admit. It may be safely said, however, that, on the whole, Western philosophy is more accomplished than Soviet philosophy. Hence it stands to reason that information on accomplished Western work would be of benefit to Soviet thinkers. This would be true *if* we could affirm that at least *some* of contemporary Western philosophy is directly relevant to current Soviet concerns.

(ii) *Is contemporary Western philosophy relevant to the philosophic concerns of Soviet thinkers?* To discuss this question I shall refer to what I called the "tentative list of the root-axioms of contemporary Marxist-Leninist philosophy in Eastern Europe".[13] This list seeks to include the basic (and axiomatically accepted) propositions upon which contemporary Soviet philosophy is constructed, and goes something like this: "*Realism*: 'the world exists independently of its perception and is objectively knowable.' *Materialism*: 'Reality reduces ultimately to an ontic stratum or substratum which can be denoted «matter».' *Dialectics*: 'The laws of thought as well as of objective reality may be analyzed into contradictory elements which do not mutually exclude each other, but which make up the true nature of the analyzed thing or process.' (Synthesis, and new opposition on a higher level, is no longer a universally accepted notion.) *Historicism*: 'The knowledge of the history of any natural or social thing or event is at least the sufficient (and perhaps also the necessary) condition of its true knowledge.' *Evolutionism*: 'Each thing evolves according to objective (and knowable) laws or principles, from lower to higher, from less perfected to more perfected forms.' *Sociologism*: 'History is the interaction («struggle») of groups («classes») rather than of individuals; the latter are comprehensible mainly in the context of the group.' *Historical subjectivism*: 'True knowledge is dependent on historically determined cognitive processes.'"

The list (I have said) could be extended at will. Yet, many further propositions could be analyzed into the acceptance of the above (e.g. optimistic social evolutionism into a combination of realism, historicism, evolutionism and sociologism; Marxist ethics into optimistic social evolutionism; Marxist-Leninist revolutionism into Marxist ethical value-judgements, and so on). Each of these axiomatic propositions is capable of a wide variety of interpretations, and if only one of them were to be analyzed in the work of diverse East-European philosophers, little agreement would be evident. But, the *combination* of these propositions, much as their specific interpretations differ, still gives something like an identifiable philosophic position, and that position, in Marxist-Leninist terminology, is known as 'dialectical materialism'. If this is true, then dialectical materialism could also be characterized as a 'realist-materialist-dialectical-historicist-evolutionist-sociologistic-historically-subjectivist, ontological, ethical, social, economic and aesthetic doctrine'. It is evident that such a vast edifice, built almost entirely from elements shared with one or another of the Western schools of thought, is relevant in its entirety to *some* of the work done currently by Western thinkers.

This point was emphasized by Bocheński as well. "We say that Soviet philosophy is relevant to philosophy *tout court*. Whoever is interested in philosophical problems has an interest in what is being done on such problems in the Soviet Union." [14] Now, this relevance of Soviet philosophy to contemporary philosophy in general, entails, *mutatis mutandis*, the relevance of contemporary philosophy to Soviet philosophy. Hence we may paraphrase Bocheński in saying that "whoever is interested in the problems of Soviet philosophy has an interest in what is being done on such problems in the West". And we may add that, since what is done on such problems in the West tends to be more accomplished than what is done on them in Communist countries, whoever is interested in the problems of Soviet philosophy would most probably *benefit* from an acquaintance with work done on these problems in the West.

(iii) *Is the relevance of contemporary Western philosophy correctly assessed by Soviet philosophers?* Soviet philosophers, especially of the younger generation, show a pronounced and apparently still increasing interest in Western philosophy. This is not a guarantee, however, that their interest can be satisfied in a way conducive to the correct assessment of the relevance of that philosophy to their own problems. For one thing, Soviet philosophers cannot pick and choose the school about which they would like to be informed, but must restrict themselves to those which are made accessible in virtue of being deemed important to refute or to make some partial use of. For another, even within these selected schools the choice of source materials is restricted, with preference often given to those authors whose work is the most readily refutable. (This has resulted in Soviet authors playing up some rather lesser lights of Western philosophy as 'well-known' authorities. [15]) There are even official incentives to study Western philosophy these days, the refutation of the philosophical expression of the 'bourgeois ideology' being included in the philosophic planification at least of one, and very likely of all, Communist countries. [16] But while the outcome of all this is undoubtedly an awakening of interest in Western philosophy, the possibilities for satisfying it do not seem to be

197

conducive to the *objective* knowledge of Western work – a precondition of the correct assessment of its relevance to Soviet concerns.

(iv) *Are Sovietologists qualified to bring about the correct assessment of the relevance of contemporary Western philosophy to the philosophic concerns of Soviet thinkers?* In order to introduce into Soviet philosophic circles information on the relevance of contemporary Western theories, the following qualifications appear to be required: (a) a thorough knowledge of current Soviet work, (b) an equally thorough knowledge of at least the relevant portions of contemporary Western thought, and (c) an appreciation of the conditions under which information concerning the relevance of Western to Soviet philosophy would be given earnest consideration by Soviet scholars. The first two requirements are evident already because 'relevance' is a relational term, the use of which presupposes that one knows *what* is relevant and *to* what it is relevant, while the third has been made clear to all people who have attempted to put propositions to Soviet theoreticians: the latter appear to be willing to consider propositions if they are formulated from their own (Marxist-Leninist) point of view and not necessarily otherwise.[17]

Now, there are almost 3000 active philosophers in the USSR, perhaps as many again in the other Communist countries put together, and over 12000 in the Western world. But of all these a thorough familiarity with both Western *and* Soviet philosophy, as well as an appreciation of the conditions for acceptance of propositions on the Soviet side, can be said to be possessed only by the Sovietologists: Western philosophers who have a good academic knowledge of Soviet thought and had prolonged experience in communication with Soviet theoreticians. These scholars are few in number (perhaps no more than two dozen[18]), but they appear to be qualified to bring about the correct assessment of the relevance of contemporary Western philosophy to the philosophic concerns of Soviet thinkers.

(v) *Is it incumbent upon Sovietologists to bring about the correct assessment of the relevance of contemporary Western to contemporary Soviet philosophy?* I conceive of this as an ethical question, and not (or not necessarily) as a political one. Two things have to be clarified in answering it: (a) what, if anything, is incumbent upon a Sovietologist; and (b) is bringing about the correct assessment of the relevance of Western to Soviet philosophy among the things that may be incumbent upon him?

198

(a) Let us try to sketch out an answer to the first question without entering too deeply into the problems of axiological ethics. We may assume that 'right' has not only an emotive meaning (as for Ayer), but that it may be defined as the meaning of the act which is conducive to the welfare of some individual or group. 'Welfare' can further be made dependent on 'value', so that right will be defined as the act which realizes values for some individual or group. If we assume that the Sovietologist is morally obliged to do the right thing, much as anybody else, we assume that he has to realize values for some person or persons. Inasmuch as he is a Sovietologist, the values he should realize are of those persons who read or listen to what he has to say. Lecturing and publishing is a matter of personal decision which is morally justifiable only in reference to the realization of value for the student and reader. It would follow then that realizing values for whomever attends their lectures and reads their publications is incumbent upon Sovietologists (as it is incumbent upon *any* scholar).

(b) Just what can be expected to result from the clarification of the relevance of Western to Soviet philosophy? As I said above, the improvement of that philosophy may result from this, as regards its still problematic questions to which relatively accomplished answers have already been proposed by Western thinkers. But this is not all. Since Soviet and Western philosophies are mutually relevant, if Soviet philosophy becomes more expert, the work of Soviet thinkers becomes of greater interest for Western philosophers. While one's sense of proportion must be kept, he may say that an eventual betterment of Soviet philosophy would open possibilities of improvement for certain branches and theories of Western philosophy (e.g. philosophy of physics). This comes down to affirming that whoever contributes to the technical level of Soviet philosophy *ipso facto* contributes to contemporary philosophy itself.

And this is still not all. A further, although more indirect, result of the clarification of the relevance of Western to Soviet philosophy may be the realization on the part of Soviet thinkers, that there is nothing fundamentally wrong with Western philosophy, and that it cannot therefore be merely the outcome of the efforts of bourgeois thinkers to hypostatize their crumbling social order. The realization of facing similar or analogous problems and of the validity of similar or analogous solutions to them could make for an improved understanding, and perhaps eventually lead to the approval of important elements of Western thought by the Soviet intellectuals. Since Marxism-Leninism claims to be first and foremost a philosophy, this would pave the way for the positive Soviet attitude necessary for a potentially fruitful East-West dialogue on a high theoretical level. Hence, in the last analysis, the result of the clarification of the relevance of Western to Soviet philosophy may well turn out to be a contribution to East-West understanding.

We may now relate the above points. First, we said that it is incumbent upon the Sovietologist to realize value for whomever hears or reads what he has to say. Second, we claimed that the clarification of the relevance of Western to Soviet philosophy may be of benefit to the cause both of contemporary philosophy and of East-West understanding. Therefore, if we assume that the progress of contemporary philosophy as well as of East-West understanding is of value to serious students and readers of Sovietology (and this is an entirely reasonable assumption), then we must affirm that it is incumbent upon Sovietologists to bring about a more correct assessment of the relevance of Western to Soviet philosophy.

II. THE PRACTICE OF SECOND SOVIETOLOGY

(vi) *Are there practicable ways and means by which relevant information about Western philosophy could be communicated by Sovietologists to Soviet philosophers?* This raises the problem of whether second Sovietology is a practicable discipline or merely a theoretical postulate. Before entering on its consideration one more point needs to be clarified: would engaging in second Sovietological work – assuming that one *could* do so – conflict with the important tasks of first Sovietology?

I believe that there need not be conflict between providing objective and relevant information about each other's work to philosophers East and West. Such endeavor merely demands the realization that the basic task of first Sovietology is not to criticize its subject-matter, but to point out how and why it is important for one to learn to know it. As in all fields, here too, overemphasis on negative elements is barren. Errors, while permitting one to learn from them, do not contribute more to his understanding if repeated. Objectivity demands reference both to failures and accomplishments, but does not determine relative emphasis. Reporting on failure is necessary if failure is the case, but reporting on successive failures of the same kind is of limited value. If first Sovietology would consist primarily in such reports, it would not provide information of much value to Western scholars. It would merely reconfirm their suspicion that they are wasting their time with Soviet philosophy, and would thus be self-annihilating.

But, if the overwhelming majority of recent Sovietological work in philosophy is a good indication of the assessment of the real tasks of first Sovietology, providing objective and relevant information, and not mere criticism, is the aim of this discipline. Because of this, Sovietologists need not go back on any of their principles if engaging in second Sovietology. And, because their true aim is apparent, they can engage in it with chances of success: they are beginning to be taken seriously by the Soviet philosophers themselves, notwithstanding the persistent attempts of dogmatists to make them out as plain falsificators of Marxist-Leninist philosophy.[19]

Consequently there need not be either conflict in theory or incompatibility in practice between first and second Sovietology. But the question remains, whether the tasks of second Sovietology can be fulfilled at all.

A number of communication media are at the disposal of Sovietologists, including lectures and publications. Most of these, however, are designed for the attention of Western students and scholars. They are eminently suited to working in first, but not in second Sovietology. Very likely other media will have to be sought for the latter. What may these be?

First of all, there are the many international conferences, seminars and symposia attended by Soviet philosophers. These might provide occasions for fruitful discussions on the mutual relevance of the respective philosophical concerns. Unfortunately, their value is diminished by the fact that dogmatists and party-hacks may be sent to such meetings, and these are ideologically insulated against novel ideas.

Sovietologists cannot make sure of reaching genuine and sincere thinkers merely by attending meetings. They *can* make sure of this, however, if they themselves go to the academic centers of Soviet philosophy. There, a whole range of possibilities for intellectual contact opens up. Despite occasional fluctuations of ideological pressure as regards the 'struggle with bourgeois philosophy', there are more opportunities today than ever before for Western thinkers to visit the institutions of the countries of the Soviet bloc and even to lecture and publish there. Some

201

non-Sovietologist philosophers have made use of this opportunity[20], but it is evident that Sovietologists are the most interested in doing so. In fact, many of them make regular study trips to the USSR and elsewhere in Eastern Europe.[21] The primary purpose of such trips is to be better informed on Soviet and related philosophy through personal contacts and first-hand information. This aids in the first-Sovietological task of objectively reporting to the Western public on current Soviet philosophy. But fulfilling it does not exclude engaging in second Sovietology: one may at the same time as obtaining information, also provide it.

Providing information to Soviet philosophers is no longer a purely Quixotic adventure – if the information is formulated from the viewpoint of relevance to current Soviet concerns, it tends to be received with attention. Taking an active part in the philosophic activity of an East-European Communist country is becoming entirely possible for Western scholars: increasingly numerous and extensive cultural and academic exchange programs are currently operating and additional contacts readily open up upon personal acquaintance.

My own experience in Hungary over the past three years gives concrete support to this claim. My endeavors, although unexceptional, intermittent and modest, did succeed in catalyzing a long-term *Auseinandersetzung* of Hungarian philosophers with phenomenology, meta-philosophy and Whiteheadian metaphysics. They appear to have resulted in a better appreciation of contemporary Western philosophy by Hungarian thinkers.[22] Similar second-Sovietological work could be performed today in the Soviet Union and most other countries of Communist Eastern Europe.

Engaging in a systematic pursuit of second Sovietology is practicable. If practiced, it may result in a signal contribution both to the cause of contemporary philosophy and to the progress of East–West understanding.

The University of Akron

REFERENCES

* Part of a study originally published in *Studies in Soviet Thought* VI,4 (December 1966).
1 Above, pp. 1–10.
2 *Ibid.*, p. 2.

[3] *Ibid.*, p. 7.

[4] Although in the above study Bocheński seems to refer exclusively to philosophy in the Soviet Union, he suggested in an earlier paper ('On Soviet Studies', *SST* I) that the term 'Soviet' in 'Sovietology' does not stand for the USSR alone but refers to any country from the point of view of Soviet influence (p. 1). Inasmuch as what I shall have to say about Soviet philosophy applies to the other Marxist-Leninist philosophies as well, I shall use 'Soviet' in the inclusive sense it has in 'Sovietology' and avoid the cumbersome suffix '... and other Marxist-Leninist philosophies'.

[5] *Ibid.*, p. 3–4.

[6] R. T. De George, 'The Foundations of Marxist-Leninist Ethics', *SST* 1963, 2 (reprinted above, pp. 49–60) and, by the same author, 'Marxist-Leninist Ethics: A Rejoinder', *SST* 1964, 4, 305–307.

[7] J. M. Bocheński, 'On Partijnost' in Philosophy I' *SST* 1965, 1–2.

[8] S. Müller-Markus, 'Soviet Discussion on General Relativity Theory', *SST* 1965, 3, and by the same author, 'Die Komplementarität in der Sowjetphilosophie', *SST* 1964, 1.

[9] E. Laszlo, 'Recent Trends in Marxist-Leninist Aesthetics', *SST* 1964, 3, and J. Fizer, 'The Theory of Objective Beauty in Soviet Aesthetics', *SST* 1964, 2 (the latter reprinted above, pp. 149–160).

[10] N. Lobkowicz, 'Is the Soviet Notion of Practice Marxian?', *SST* 1966, 1.

[11] R. Thomas, 'Bemerkungen zum Materialismusproblem', *SST* 1965, 4.

[12] A. Buchholz, 'Problems of the Ideological East-West Conflict', *SST* I, 130.

[13] E. Laszlo, 'Philosophy in Eastern Europe: An Introduction', *Inquiry*, 1966, 1. Abstract reprinted in *SST* 1966, 3.

[14] *Op. cit.*, p. 4. Bocheński makes the very point I am making in 'On Philosophical Dialogue', pp. 177–193, esp. p. 189.

[15] In reviewing current Soviet criticism of the 'bourgeois falsificators of Marxist-Leninist philosophy' P. Beemans asked in some perplexity, "where do the Soviets dig up these 'well-known American philosophers' whom they are perennially quoting in so many of their books?" *SST* 1965, 4, 331. Also see Bocheński, p. 189 above.

[16] This writer found that nine out of a total of 38 official research projects assigned to Hungarian philosophers are expressly devoted to the criticism of contemporary Western philosophy. Cf. E. Laszlo, 'The Planification of Hungarian Marxism-Leninism,' *SST* 1965, 4, 284–286.

[17] Cf. A. Buchholz, *op. cit.*, p. 130.

[18] Estimate by Bocheński in 'On Philosophical Dialogue', p. 186 above.

[19] Despite individual criticism directed at some specific Sovietological papers (e.g. De George's 'The Foundations of Marxist-Leninist Ethics', *op. cit.*) and wholesale criticism directed at the first-Sovietological endeavor as a whole (the latest one being *Protiv sovremennyx buržuaznyx fal'sifikatorov marksistsko-leniniskoj filosofii*, Moscow 1965) most Sovietologists visiting in Communist countries (cf. note 21) find their opinions being taken seriously there.

[20] The most acute interest generated by such a visit was accorded A. J. Ayer in March, 1962. For an account of the contacts and controversies between Ayer and the Soviets, see D. D. Comey, 'A Positivist Among the Dialecticians', *SST* 1962, 3.

[21] E.g. G. L. Kline, R. T. De George, H. Fleischer, D. D. Comey, J. P. Scanlan, the undersigned, etc.

[22] For a full account see *SST* VI,4 (1966) 282–290.

ABBREVIATIONS

AN Akademija nauk (Academy of Sciences: of the SSSR unless otherwise specified)

AON Akademija obščestvennyx nauk pri CK KPSS (Academy of Social Sciences of the CK KPSS)

CK KPSS Central'nyj komitet kommunističeskoj partii sovetskogo sojuza (Central Committee of the Communist Party of the Soviet Union)

FN Naučnye doklady vysšej školy. Filosofskie nauki (Scientific Reports of the Higher Schools. Philosophy)

IF Institut filosofii (Institute of Philosophy: of the AN SSSR unless otherwise specified)

IIL Izdatel'stvo inostrannoj literatury (Foreign Languages Publishing House)

Izd. Izdatel'stvo (Publishing House)

LGU Leningradskij gosudarstvennyj universitet (University of Leningrad)

M Moskva

MGU Moskovskij gosudarstvennyj universitet (University of Moscow)

SSSR Sojuz sovetskix socialističeskix respublik (USS)

SST Studies in Soviet Thought

UFN Uspexi fizičeskix nauk (Progress of Physics)

VF Voprosy filosofii (Questions of Philosophy)

VP Voprosy psixologii (Questions of Psychology)

VPŠ Vysšaja partijnaja škola (Upper Party School)

ŽTEF Žurnal eksperimental'noj i teoretičeskoj fiziki (Journal of Experimental and Theoretical Physics)

Further abbreviations are given under the various 'References'.

204

INDEX OF NAMES

INDEX OF SUBJECTS

SOVIETICA

Publications and Monographs of the Institute
of East-European Studies, University of Fribourg, Switzerland

edited by J. M. Bocheński

PUBLICATIONS

BALLESTREM, KARL G.: *Russian Philosophical Terminology* [in Russian, English, German, and French]. 1964, VIII + 116 pp.   *f* 20.—

BIRJUKOV, B. V.: *Two Soviet Studies on Frege.* Translated from the Russian and edited by Ignacio Angelelli. 1964, XXII + 101 pp.   *f* 18.—

BLAKELEY, THOMAS J.: *Soviet Philosophy. A General Introduction to Contemporary Soviet Thought.* 1964, VI + 81 pp.   *f* 16.—

BOCHEŃSKI, J. M.: *Die dogmatischen Grundlagen der sowjetischen Philosophie (Stand 1958). Zusammenfassung der 'Osnovy Marksistskoj Filosofii' mit Register.* 1959, XII + 84 pp.   *f* 12.50

BOCHEŃSKI, J. M.: *The Dogmatic Principles of Soviet Philosophy (as of 1958). Synopsis of the 'Osnovy Marksistskoj Filosofii' with complete index.* 1963, XII + 78 pp. *f* 15.—

BOCHEŃSKI, J. M. and BLAKELEY, TH. J. (eds.): *Bibliographie der Sowjetischen Philosophie*
I: *Die 'Voprosy filosofii' 1947–1956.* 1959, VIII + 75 pp.   *f* 12.25
II: *Bücher 1947–1956; Bücher und Aufsätze 1957–1958; Namenverzeichnis 1947–1958.* 1959, VIII + 109 pp.   *f* 15.75
III: *Bücher und Aufsätze 1959–1960.* 1962, X + 73 pp.   *f* 18.50
IV: *Ergänzungen 1947–1960.* 1963, XII + 158 pp.   *f* 28.75
V: *Register 1947–1960.* 1964, VI + 143 pp.   *f* 26.50

BOCHEŃSKI, J. M. and BLAKELEY, TH. J. (eds.): *Studies in Soviet Thought,* I. 1961, X + 141 pp.   *f* 17.50

FLEISCHER, HELMUT: *Kleines Textbuch der kommunistischen Ideologie. Auszüge aus dem Lehrbuch 'Osnovy marksizma-leninizma' mit Register.* 1963, XIV + 116 pp. *f* 17.50

FLEISCHER, HELMUT: *Short Handbook of Communist Ideology. Synopsis of the 'Osnovy marksizma-leninizma' with complete index.* 1965, XIV + 97 pp.   *f* 19.75

*LASZLO, ERVIN: *Philosophy in the Soviet Union. A Survey of the Mid-Sixties.* 1967, VIII + 208 pp.   *f* 24.—

LOBKOWICZ, NICOLAS (ed.): *Das Widerspruchsprinzip in der neueren sowjetischen Philosophie. Die Moskauer Tagung zur Frage der dialektischen Widersprüche 21–26 April 1958.* 1960, VI + 89 pp.   ƒ 14.35

VRTAČIČ, LUDVIK: *Einführung in den jugoslawischen Marxismus-Leninismus. Organisation. Bibliographie.* 1963, X + 208 pp.   ƒ 29.50

MONOGRAPHS

BLAKELEY, TH. J.: *Soviet Scholasticism.* 1961, XIV + 176 pp.   ƒ 19.75

BLAKELEY, TH. J.: *Soviet Theory of Knowledge.* 1964, VIII + 203 pp.   ƒ 24.—

JORDAN, ZBIGNIEW A.: *Philosophy and Ideology. The Development of Philosophy and Marxism-Leninism in Poland since the Second World War.* 1963, XII + 600 pp. ƒ 58.—

LASZLO, ERVIN: *The Communist Ideology in Hungary. Handbook for Basic Research.* 1966, VIII + 351 pp.   ƒ 68.—

LOBKOWICZ, NICOLAS: *Marxismus-Leninismus in der ČSR. Die tschechoslowakische Philosophie seit 1945.* 1962, XVI + 268 pp.   ƒ 35.50

MÜLLER-MARKUS, SIEGFRIED: *Einstein und die Sowjetphilosophie. Krisis einer Lehre:*
I: *Die Grundlagen. Die spezielle Relativitätstheorie.* 1960, XVI + 481 pp.   ƒ 64.—
II: *Die allgemeine Relativitätstheorie.* 1966, X + 509 pp.   ƒ 84.—

PLANTY-BONJOUR, G.: *Les catégories du matérialisme dialectique. L'ontologie soviétique contemporaine.* 1965, VI + 206 pp.   ƒ 27.—

*PLANTY-BONJOUR, G.: *The Categories of Dialectical Materialism. Contemporary Soviet Ontology.* 1967, VI + 182 pp.   ƒ 30.—

* Sole-Distributors for the U.S.A. and Canada

FREDERICK A. PRAEGER INC., PUBLISHERS
NEW YORK · WASHINGTON